The Revised
Vault of Walt

Praise for the
Revised Vault of Walt

Jim's vast knowledge of Disney has constantly amazed me, and he understands how the Disney Studios, Theme Parks, and Disneyana all tie together. Jim is an excellent Disney Heritage writer and speaker, and it's about time he put together this collection of stories he has gathered over the years.

– Tom Nabbe
Disney Legend (2005) and Disneyland's original Tom Sawyer

Jim's storytelling has always mesmerized me. Now some of his Disney tidbits are in a book! Let me put it this way. Chatting with Jim is a delicious nine-course meal. Hours with his book will be a mouth-watering feast.

– Margaret Kerry
Actress, author, and original reference model for
Tinker Bell in Disney's *Peter Pan*

No one knows more hidden nooks and crannies in the vast history of Disney animation than Jim Korkis. I'm delighted that he's gathered his fact-filled columns in this book.

– Leonard Maltin
Author of *The Disney Films*,
Host and consultant of *Disney Treasures DVDs*

Disney history is full of unexplored byways, and no one has done a better job of mapping many of them than Jim Korkis. Even the most knowledgeable Disney buffs will be surprised and delighted by what they find in this book.

– Michael Barrier
Disney history expert, and author of
The Animated Man: A Life of Walt Disney

Disney stories are insightful as well as fun, and no one tells them better than Jim Korkis. Jim truly loves his material, and so will you. I heartily recommend his new book and I guarantee you'll love every page.

– Floyd Norman
Disney Legend (2007), artist, and writer whose career at
Disney spanned from Walt's era through Eisner's reign

THE REVISED
VAULT OF WALT

Unofficial, Unauthorized, Uncensored
Disney Stories Never Told

Jim Korkis

Foreword by
Diane Disney Miller

Theme Park Press
Orlando, Florida

Editor: Bob McLain

Original Cover Concept and Design:
Jennifer Solt, 24 Communications [www.24c.co]

Revised Cover Design:
Glendon Haddix, Streetlight Graphics [www.StreetlightGraphics.com]

Layout/Typesetting: Bob McLain, Theme Park Press [www.ThemeParkPress.com]

Printed in the United States of America

First Printing (Revised Edition) 2012

ISBN 978-0-9843415-4-2

Theme Park Press
www.ThemeParkPress.com

Address queries about this book to queries@themeparkpress.com

If you have a Disney story to tell, Theme Park Press can help you tell it.

We offer generous compensation and the most author-friendly terms in the business.

To learn more: www.ThemeParkPress.com/writeforus. Or email bob@themeparkpress.com.

This book, as always, is dedicated to my father and my mother, John and Barbara Korkis, who passed away less than a decade ago but whose unconditional love, constant support, common sense, and good humor continue to inspire me to this day.

Contents

Welcome to the Revised Edition

How did we get here? What is a "revised" edition? Why are some stories missing from the original publication?

As always, it is an interesting story.

For over three decades, I have researched and written about Disney history for a variety of magazines and special projects. Two years ago, the opportunity presented itself for me to select some of my favorite stories and have them published in a book.

The Vault of Walt was released in fall 2010. I was overjoyed that the book was so warmly received by both reviewers and fans, and has continued to sell well ever since. In the last two years, I have had the opportunity to attend many events across the United States, where people shared their love of the book, and I have received many e-mails filled with praise.

In all that time, there have been no factual corrections identified in the text; it is very pleasing to be assured that I did the best I could with my original research. However, as I noted in the original introduction to the book, there is always more to be told about any story.

It has always been my intention to do an updated version of the book, especially since I keep uncovering new information. For instance, last year I was a guest speaker at the wonderful Disney Family Museum in San Francisco. During my time there, I examined even more closely part of Walt Disney's fabled miniature collection. The chapter in this book about Walt's hobby remains accurate; however, on my visit, I discovered new things and a new perspective which enriches that tale.

I thought about pulling the book from distribution for a period of time so I could work on an updated edition. Sadly, even in this age of electronics, books do go out of print for a period of time. I have been disappointed when books that I delayed purchasing went out of print within the first six months of being issued.

While I was contemplating how to handle this situation, I partnered with a new publisher, Theme Park Press, for a book just recently released: *Who's Afraid of the Song of the South? And Other Forbidden Disney Stories.*

That book is the first extensive look at the history of the making of Disney's most controversial film from its very beginning in 1938 through 2012. The rest of the book is filled with stories the Disney Company never wanted told, such as how it produced television commercials in the 1950s, why working at the Disney Studios depressed director Tim Burton, why Walt Disney became a Republican, the secrets about Jessica Rabbit, and much more.

Theme Park Press also purchased all the publishing rights to *The Vault of Walt*, with my full approval. As I discussed the proposal for updating the book with them, we decided for a number of reasons that it would be wiser to keep some form of the book in print until the fully updated version is ready.

The compromise is what you now hold in your hands. Since the publication of *The Vault of Walt* there have been significant changes in the publication of Disney-related books. I wanted a more streamlined, travel-size version available at a more affordable price. It was agreed that doing so might attract new readers who were intimidated by the size and the price of the original edition, despite all the good reviews.

So, to make a more compact package, some stories that appeared in the original book are missing from this book. However, just like Walt himself, I always want to give my readers something extra. There are five new chapters in this book:

- "Eating Like Walt" answers the question that if we are indeed what we eat, then what recipes created and sustained Walt's unique genius?

- "And the Oscar Goes to ... Walt Disney" shares the stories-behind-the-stories of some of the many Academy Awards Walt won during his lifetime.

- "The Carousel of Progress" discusses how the park attraction has changed over the decades but still remains an homage to the vision of Walt Disney.

- "The Man Who Shot Walt Disney" reveals the photographer behind the iconic pictures of Walt Disney, and how they were created.

- Finally, as a preview of what to expect in *Who's Afraid of the Song of the South*, there is a chapter devoted to some of the most commonly asked questions about the film.

Who's Afraid of the Song of the South answers these questions in much more detail in its dozens of pages as well as provides never-before-told information about the screenplay, the actors, the animation, the filming and, of course, the misunderstandings that surround the film.

If this is your first experience with *The Vault of Walt*, there are many treasures to uncover about the worlds of Disney. If you are an owner of the original edition (perhaps soon to become a collectible curiosity), this book provides five brand new stories to maintain your interest until the updated edition is released. If you are upset that some stories are missing, the publisher has made them available as a Kindle book entitled *The Vault of Walt Sampler*.

So, to summarize, there is the original edition of *The Vault of Walt*, which is going into hibernation; the revised version that you hold in your hand right now with some new stories; and a Kindle "sampler" with the missing stories from the original edition.

That's *my* story, and I am sticking to it.

Jim Korkis
Disney Historian
November 2012

Foreword

Some years ago, our son Walt brought to my attention an article on the MousePlanet website. It was that rare thing; an honest, well written piece that was so authentic, so true to my dad's spirit, so unprejudiced and non-judgmental, that as I read it I could see the twinkle in dad's eye, hear his laugh.

I immediately wrote the author, Wade Sampson, a letter of appreciation. Some weeks later I received a reply, and learned that Wade Sampson was actually the pseudonym of Jim Korkis, who worked for the Walt Disney World Company as a Coordinator at the Learning Center and was well-known and respected as a Disney historian. Since that time I looked forward eagerly to "Wade's" ongoing output, learning some things I didn't know, but always delighted with what he chose to write about and his obvious understanding and even affection for his subject.

Jim does not put my father on a pedestal, but he does like him, and I do not think that disqualifies him from having objectivity in his opinion of him. I find myself in the same position.

I am so pleased that many of his writings are now bound together in this book. Dad's personality, character, and values are displayed in the selections Jim has offered here.

I have not hesitated to correspond with Jim whenever I think of something that might interest him, or to add some insights into something he has written about. Dad did not hide anything about his life. He loved to talk about it. But he never really talked about religion, and his feelings about prayer, and I learned from Jim's article how deeply these feelings went.

I look forward to his continued exploration of dad's life and times. Something interesting and illuminating always seems to turn up, some little event and angle that adds to the story of his very good life.

Diane Disney Miller
July 2010

Diane is the eldest daughter of Walt and Lillian Disney and a noted philanthropist. Among many other achievements, she was instrumental in the creation of The Walt Disney Family Museum in San Francisco that opened in 2009.

Introduction

What's all this? Unauthorized, unofficial, uncensored Disney Stories? Is all that really true?

Yes, that's true but don't expect to find scandals, rumors, urban legends, and fanciful assumptions in these pages. The history of Disney is so rich that, despite all the books written about the subject, many great stories were never told. These are just a few of those fascinating "lost" stories and the facts behind them.

Sometimes, these stories are missing simply because there was no more space in a book to explore these interesting little tangents. Often, they were missing because the author had no clue that these stories even existed or had no access to the necessary research to tell the story.

Think of this book as a Disney history companion filling in some of those nooks and crannies that may only be mentioned in a brief sentence or two, if at all, in other Disney history books. These chapters truly are the forgotten but fascinating Disney stories.

Each individual chapter is a self-contained story, so feel free to open the book to any page and begin reading. These chapters were originally written to be read one at a time and savored, so don't feel the need to gorge on the new information all at once. Think of the book as a box of chocolates with different delights and maybe some tasty hidden surprises to enjoy during a pleasant afternoon.

Some of these stories appeared in preliminary draft form under my writing pseudonym of "Wade Sampson" on MousePlanet.com every Wednesday for several years. However, all of these chapters have been rewritten extensively, with new information and quotes added, and all corrections made.

My affection, respect, and fascination for Walt Disney led me to choose mostly stories that occurred during Walt's life.

As you read these fact-filled stories, please do not be fooled into believing that they are the definitive versions. There is always more to tell about any story. I have discovered that, the moment I commit a story to print, suddenly a previously unknown anecdote or insight will magically appear to taunt me, despite decades of research. Fortunately, some of those unexpected gems were found at the last moment before this manuscript was sent to the publisher, and so could be included here.

You won't find these stories anywhere else, and certainly not with the wonderful quotes from people who actually lived through them.

To make it easier for you to find what you want to read, the book is divided into four sections:

- Walt Disney Stories
- Disney Film Stories
- Disney Park Stories
- The Other Worlds of Disney Stories

If you have half as much fun reading these stories as I had writing them, then I had twice as much fun. I hope you enjoy and share these stories with others.

Jim Korkis
a/k/a Wade Samspon
July 2010

Part One

The Walt Stories

On my book shelves, I have over three dozen different biographies of Walt Disney. Some are scholarly tomes. Some are barely a hundred pages in length because they were meant for children. Some are done in a comic book format. Some are in a foreign language. In addition, I have dozens of different biographies of Walt that have appeared over the decades in magazines and newspapers.

None of the stories in this section appear in those other sources except, on rare occasion, in a brief sentence or two.

Having interviewed animators, Imagineers, and associates of Walt for over thirty years, I am continually surprised at how much more there is to discover about this amazing man.

Everyone seems to have different perspectives and different stories about Walt. It is like the classic story of the blind men and the elephant. Each blind man is led to experience an elephant for the first time. One feels the trunk and assumes the elephant is like a tree branch. Another feels a leg and immediately believes that an elephant is like a pillar. Yet another feels the ear and feels the elephant must be like a big leaf fan. They each experience just a small part, never the whole picture, and as a result make some odd assumptions.

Even over four decades after his death, new information and insights about Walt Disney are unearthed nearly every day. I wanted to write about some of the stories not covered elsewhere and to share that "lost" information with others to help keep the stories alive.

Besides the many interviews I have done, and the decades of locating crumbling, yellowing documents from letters to newspapers to magazines to unpublished material, I have been fortunate to have had my own personal experiences that allowed me to do things like examine part of Walt's famed miniature collection up close, and in particular, the Granny Kincaid Cabin for which he personally crafted many of the miniatures.

I have also been fortunate to have established a friendly relationship with Diane Disney Miller, Walt's sole surviving daughter. She has been gracious and generous to pre-read some of my articles and to supply her own personal insights and memories, and where necessary, make gentle corrections. Surprisingly, even Diane didn't know some of the material I uncovered about her father.

In these articles, I have tried as much as possible to let people speak for themselves. I apologize if some of the quotes seem too lengthy or frequent, but for some of these people, especially those who have passed away, this is their only chance to tell their own stories. In particular, I have made every effort to allow Walt to share his own thoughts in his own words through interviews, speeches, publicity material, and letters.

I hope these stories will give you a richer understanding of Walt Disney as a son, a brother, a husband, and a father. He was an amazingly complex and an amazingly simple man. Walt was once asked how he would like to be remembered. He replied, "I'm a storyteller. Of all the things I've ever done, I'd like to be remembered as a storyteller."

Here are some stories about that memorable storyteller.

The Miniature Worlds of Walt

Strangely, for a man who always had big dreams, Walt Disney took some of his greatest delight in the world of miniatures. For decades, he both constructed and collected a huge variety of intricate tiny objects. Sometimes, those small objects inspired much bigger things, including attractions at Disney theme parks.

It is believed that Walt first seriously worked with miniatures when he helped build a Lionel train layout for his nephew, Roy E. Disney, in the early 1930s, working intently on the surrounding landscape and the structures for the train track.

However, Walt's fascination with the magical power of tiny worlds was really launched in 1939, when he saw the famous Thorne exhibit at the Golden Gate International Exposition in San Francisco. Using miniature furnishings and accessories gathered by her uncle during his world travels, Mrs. James Ward Thorne had created exquisite rooms decorated to represent European and American interiors of different eras. The rooms were so perfectly crafted that some said viewing them was like becoming miniaturized and entering another time. They captured Walt's imagination.

In the late 1940s, Walt merged his love of trains with his love of miniatures to build a small-scale railroad, the "Carolwood Pacific", that steamed around the backyard of his home on Carolwood Drive. He was especially proud of the bright yellow caboose, with its diminutive oil lamps, brass doorknobs, and actual working spring latches.

Walt painstakingly crafted a pint-sized potbellied stove for the caboose as well. He wrote:

> I had a pattern made up, and it turned out so cute with the grate, shaker and door, and all the little working parts, I became intrigued with the idea. I had a few made up: one was bronze, another black, and I even made a gold one! Then we made more and started painting them in motifs that fitted the period at the turn of the century.

Each of these five-and-a-half-inch tall stoves had a different design, and eventually about one hundred were made. Walt gave some to friends, and even sent some to an antique gift shop in New York where, to Walt's delight, Mrs. Thorne herself purchased two to add to her renowned collection, the same collection that had inspired Walt's hobby. They sold for twenty-five dollars each, and Walt made no special effort to market them or turn a profit. He just was curious to see if there was any interest and, by 1957, the supply was depleted.

Walt said:

> It has been fun making them and others appreciate them, too, so all in all, I feel well repaid.

Actor Richard Todd, who performed in several of Walt's British live-action films, recalled visiting Walt's home, where he saw:

> ... cabinets full of the objects he loved: tiny things, miniatures of all sorts in china, wood or metal. He gave me a tiny potbellied stove that he had made himself, a beautiful little thing about six inches high, painted in white, green and gold.

Walt began seriously collecting miniatures during his European travels, bringing home countless tiny objects of glass, wood, china, and metal. In a letter to a friend in 1951, he wrote:

> My hobby is a life saver. When I work with these small objects, I become so absorbed that the cares of the studio fade away ... at least for a time.

When Walt's collection was inventoried in the mid-1960s, the tally was over a thousand items, including paintings and books like the Holy Bible, *Tennyson's Poetical Works*, *A Miniature History of England*, and eighteen volumes of the plays of William Shakespeare. There were musical instruments like three banjos, a mandolin, a guitar, and an organ crafted by conductor Frederick Stark. A set of dueling pistols was near a leather case inscribed "The Colt Story in Miniature" that had fourteen six-shooters. There were eleven classic cars, including a 1915 Model T Ford, a 1903 Cadillac, a 1904 Rambler, and a 1911 Rolls Royce. Walt also displayed a model battleship and a steamboat.

Collecting these tiny treasures was not enough for Walt. He wanted to create an entire miniature world. In the early 1950s, he asked animator Ken Anderson to draw twenty-four scenes of life in an old Western town. Walt planned to carve tiny figures and build the scenes in miniature. When he had made enough, he would send them out as a traveling exhibit.

Walt told Anderson:

> I'm tired of having everybody else around here do the drawing and the painting. I'm going to do something creative myself. I'm going to put you on my personal payroll, and I want you to draw twenty-four scenes of life in an old Western town. Then I'll carve the figures and make the scenes in miniature. When we get enough of them made, we'll send them out as a traveling exhibit. We'll get an office here at the studio and you and I will be the only ones who'll have keys.

Walt immediately put advertisements in newspapers and hobby magazines seeking vintage miniatures of all kinds for his tableaus. Fearing prices would soar, Walt asked his two secretaries at the time, Kathryn Gordon and Dolores Voght, to use their names in the advertisements rather than announce that Disney himself was looking for these items.

Several newspapers and hobby magazines carried the ad:

WANTED
Anything in miniatures to a scale of 1½" to the foot or under. Up to and including early 1900's. Give full description and price. Private collector. K. Gordon (and her address).

Besides pixie-sized furniture, Walt collected miniscule tableware, including delicate Limoges and Havilland tea services, small Toby jugs, sky-blue Wedgewood pitchers, Willow Ware washing bowls, and Bennington crocks and jars. Sparkling wine and perfume bottles, drinking glasses smaller than thimbles, several sets of silverware fit for fairy queens, silver tea services, and a candelabra as delicate as a cobweb completed the collection.

Walt spent countless hours carefully constructing the first of his tiny tableaus. The first scene, "Granny Kincaid's Cabin", was based on a set from his live-action feature, *So Dear to My Heart* (1949). To build the chimney, Walt picked up pebbles at his Palm Springs vacation home, the Smoke Tree Ranch.

Inside the cabin, a hand-braided rag rug warmed a floor of planks not much larger than matchsticks. A china washbowl and pitcher, guitar with strings thin as cat whiskers, and a small family Bible sat on the table. A tiny flintlock rifle hung on the wall and a spinning wheel with flax sat in the corner. The scene looked as if Granny herself had just briefly stepped outside. Granny, however, was never constructed. Instead, viewers would hear a recording of her voice describing the cozy scene. Walt had recorded a narration by actress Beulah Bondi, the famous character actress who played the part of Granny in *So Dear to My Heart*.

Imagineer Wathel Rogers revealed Walt's original plan for a cabin that would have featured Granny herself:

> The interior of Granny's cabin was completely dressed up with miniatures. Walt made the rocking chairs and the rest himself. He then said, "Let's make up a cross section. Let's have Grandmother rocking, Bible in hand, with a diorama behind her depicting the outdoors. Granny would say, 'Oh hello there, I'm just reading my Bible.' She'd chat for a while, then return to her reading."

The cabin was exhibited at the Festival of California Living at the Pan-Pacific Auditorium in Los Angeles from November 28 to December 7, 1952. A press release announced that it represented the beginning of Walt's new miniature Americana exhibit called "Disneylandia".

In a letter dated December 4, 1952, to his younger sister, Ruth, Walt wrote:

> I'm enclosing a newspaper clipping which gives you some idea about my newest project. I am hoping it will become a reality but at this point it's very much in the thinking and planning stage. This cabin (which I built myself) is a replica of Granny Kincaid's cabin from our picture *So Dear To My Heart*. I also made a spinning wheel, bed, tables, kitchen

sink, rocker, chairs, and a number of other items that you are unable to see in these pictures, which are not particularly good anyway.

I've been collecting all sorts of miniature pieces for the past three or four years, with this project in mind. It's been a wonderful hobby for me and I find it is something very relaxing to turn to when studio problems become too hectic.

In a 1953 interview, Walt explained:

This little cabin is part of a project I am working on, and it was exhibited as a test to obtain the public's reaction to my plans for a complete village.

With the public's positive reaction as encouragement, Walt once again returned to his workbench and the miniscule hammers, screwdrivers, clamps, and magnifying glasses that were part of a miniature-maker's craft.

Gradually, two more small tableaus took shape. One was a frontier music hall stage, complete with a one-eighth scale, three-dimensional, tap-dancing vaudevillian, called "Project Little Man". Disney Imagineers filmed actor and eccentric dancer Buddy Ebsen performing tap-dance routines against a grid pattern for live-action reference. Sculpted by Charles Cristadoro and connected to a series of cams and gears like a music box, the little figure moved and was considered the beginning of Audio-Animatronics. Walt was disappointed with the lack of range of expressions on the carved face of the character, and explored using plastics to make it more realistic.

In June 1951, Walt and his team of designers and technicians began work on a third miniature display: a traditional barbershop quartet crooning "Sweet Adeline". The scene would include a barber, customer in a chair, and two more patrons waiting. Again, live actors were filmed for reference. Imagineer Roger Broggie recalled:

We got as far as building the guy in the chair and the barber. Then the whole job was stopped!

Walt became convinced that only a limited audience would be able to view these tableaus, and that his work would not generate enough income for their continued maintenance. Disneylandia, however, grew into Disneyland.

As Broggie recalled: "Walt said, 'We're going to do this thing for real!'"

In 1953, the sales pitch for Disneyland that Roy O. Disney presented in New York to raise money for building the theme park included a description of this never-built land that would have been located between Tomorrowland and Fantasyland:

Lilliputian Land. A Land of Little Things

... a miniature Americana village inhabited by mechanical people nine inches high who sing and dance and talk to you as you peek through the windows of their tiny shops and homes. In Lilliputian Land, there is an Erie Canal barge that takes you through the famous canals of the world where you visit the scenic wonders of the world in miniature.

Here a little diamond-stack locomotive engine seventeen inches high steams into the tiny railroad station. You sit on top of the Pullman coaches like Gulliver, and the little nine inch engineer pulls back the throttle taking you on the biggest little ride in the land. And for the little people who have little appetites-you can get miniature ice cream cones, or the world's smallest hot-dog on a tiny bun.

While Lilliputian Land, like many of Walt's other original ideas for Disneyland, was never developed, Disneyland did showcase a small-sized Storybook Land in Fantasyland.

Walt had been influenced by his visit to Madurodam, a tourist attraction in the Netherlands that featured landmarks in miniature size, and his initial idea was to create scale replicas of world-renowned landmarks. Eventually, Walt's idea evolved into miniatures of equally beloved, famous locations from his classic animated features. A majestic Cinderella's Castle overlooks a small world that includes Geppetto's Toy Shop, Mr. Toad's mansion, and the Seven Dwarf 's Cottage, with nearby a glittering, jewel-filled mine. Each structure was built with the same meticulous attention to detail that Walt lavished on his own miniatures.

Imagineer Ken Anderson, who designed Storybook Land, said he quickly discovered that it was:

> ... one of Walt's favorite rides. He'd make frequent visits to the model shop at the Burbank studio to provide comments and his expertise on the miniature models.

Walt also considered a plan to put Lilliputian-sized

replicas of famous American landmarks like Thomas Jefferson's Monticello and George Washington's Mt. Vernon on what would eventually become Tom Sawyer Island. Some early Disneyland souvenirs even show these tiny landmarks dotting the landscape. The decision was made to instead turn the Island into the domain of Mark Twain's adventurous young rascals, Tom Sawyer and Huck Finn, and so the miniature buildings were never built.

Walt's interest in miniatures didn't wane after the opening of Disneyland. While designing the Ford Pavilion with its soaring Magic Skyway for the 1965 New York World's Fair, something was needed for the Rotunda entry area to show that Ford was an international company. Walt suggested a miniature village. Soon, Imagineers had designed the International Gardens", a series of buildings on a scale of a half-inch to one foot that recreated world-renowned landmarks from eleven countries. Soon, scenes of Colonial America and "Merrie Olde" England, golden-hued Aztec temples and the half-timbered houses of Medieval Europe, invited visitors to imagine themselves small enough to walk the twisting lanes.

Still fascinated with the entire process of miniature making, Walt personally supervised the work. One day, as he was visiting the Imagineers' workshop, he saw six-foot eight-inch tall Imagineer Jack Ferges crawling around under his desk. As Ferges later remembered:

> Walt said, 'What are you doing?' I said, 'I just dropped the entire city of Copenhagen.' Walt laughed so hard, he had to sit down.

Eventually, shelves were built on two walls and enclosed by glass doors in Walt's office suite at the Disney Studio to showcase his amazing miniature collection. For Walt, good things did indeed sometimes come in small packages.

Horsing Around: Walt and Polo

The secret of success, if there is any, is liking what you do.
I like my work better than my play. I play polo,
when I have time, and I enjoy it, but it can't equal work!

— Walt Disney, San Francisco Chronicle, December 31, 1933

In the 1930s, polo was a very popular and expensive pastime, especially among members of the entertainment industry, despite it being an intense physical sport. This was an era when actors tried to emulate off-screen the macho characters they portrayed on-screen. While some of them were athletic, most were ill-prepared for the demands of the difficult and challenging game of polo.

Actor Spencer Tracy loved to saddle up his polo ponies, and during the early 1930s, he played whenever he was off the movie set. Studios pleaded with him not to play because of fear of injury, so Tracy played under aliases until he quit after his friend Will Rogers died.

Polo was also used for social networking in the Hollywood community. The famous Beverly Hills Polo Lounge was created at this time, and it still remains a popular and somewhat exclusive social gathering spot for Hollywood notables.

In the 1930s, there were more than twenty-five polo fields in Los Angeles. Walt played at such popular spots as the Uplifters Polo Field (now bulldozed and replaced with a street) and the Riviera Polo Field (now the home of the Paul Revere High School). The Riviera had three or four polo fields adjoining a golf course, and many celebrities also kept stables there.

In Hollywood, the strongest champion of the sport was humorist Will Rogers, who was introduced to polo in 1915. During the 1920s and 1930s, Rogers popularized the sport among Hollywood elites from Hal Roach and Darryl Zanuck to Walt Disney.

Walt had a personal friendship with Rogers. In fact, at one time, he was negotiating with Rogers to appear in Walt's first full-length, animated feature film. Snow White was not Walt's first choice for a feature project. He had developed several possibilities, including Alice in Wonderland with a live-action Mary Pickford as Alice interacting with animated characters.

When that project fell apart, Walt considered using the same concept but with Will Rogers as Rip Van Winkle interacting with animated characters. Walt sent some of his top Disney animators, including Grim Natwick, Art Babbitt, and Bill Tytla, to Rogers' Santa Monica ranch to sketch the popular comedian in action, but Rogers's untimely death put an end to the project.

The popularity of Mickey Mouse in the early 1930s brought great success and attention to Walt. However, it also brought great stress. Managing and expanding his studio as well as the many demands being made on him in other areas, from merchandising decisions to publicity requests, in addition to the tension at home where his wife Lillian struggled through two miscarriages, resulted in Walt suffering one of his infamous nervous breakdowns.

Walt's doctor suggested that he take up some form of exercise to help relieve the stress. Walt tried wrestling, boxing, and golf, but each attempt only frustrated him further instead of releasing tension. Walt had always loved horses, so next he took up horseback riding and joined a local riding club.

Always a multi-tasker, Walt decided to combine his love of horseback riding with his desire to mingle with Hollywood society by taking up the then popular sport of polo.

At the time, Walt quipped that polo seemed to be just "golf on a horse".

In the beginning, Walt enlisted Disney Studios personnel, including Jack Cutting, Norm Ferguson, Les Clark, Dick Lundy, Gunther Lessing, Bill Cottrell, and even his brother Roy to participate.

They studied the book *As To Polo* by William Cameron Forbes (1929), and had lessons and lectures by Gil Proctor, a polo expert. Eventually, they practiced in the San Fernando Valley at the DuBrock Riding Academy from 6:00 AM until they had to report to work at the Disney Studios at 8:00 AM.

Walt built a polo cage at the Studio so that, during lunch breaks, the men could sit on a wooden horse and practice hitting the wooden ball into a goal. He even installed a dummy horse in his backyard so he could get in early morning practice before heading to the DuBrock Riding Academy.

Walt's daughter Diane Disney Miller remembered:

> My sister and I grew up in a large playroom surrounded by framed head portraits of dad's horses and cases full of trophies. That is as close as we came to having a horse of our own and the shed on our back lot that was a sort of tack room for his polo saddles. It was always locked. So was the polo cage down at the bottom of what we called "the canyon". I always wanted to get into that cage and play on that horse, but was told that it was off limits because of Black Widow spiders.

Finally, the Disney team started having matches with other inexperienced teams at the stadium on Riverside Drive.

Walt and Roy would play regularly with their employees on Wednesday mornings and on Saturday afternoons. In addition, Walt and Roy joined the prestigious Riviera Club, where such Hollywood luminaries as Spencer Tracy, Leslie Howard, Darryl Zanuck, and others held court on the playing field. During this time, Spencer Tracy became a close friend of Walt's, and Tracy and his wife were often invited to Walt's home. Diane Disney Miller recalled:

> Many of dad's friendships came from polo. Some years ago, I was surprised to hear Bill Cottrell tell Rich Greene that he felt that Spencer Tracy was, perhaps, dad's best friend. Dad's friendship with Will Rogers was very important to him. He cherished being a part of the lunches that Mrs. Rogers would serve after a game. Other long-lasting polo friends were Carl Beal, who my mother told me was dad's

best friend on the occasion of Carl's death from leukemia when I was quite young, so it made an impression on me. Robert Stack, who was a teenager at the time; Russell Havenstrite, a wealthy oil man and eventual neighbor; and many others who played and loved the game were good friends as well.

In 1934, Roy Disney bought four polo ponies. At one point, Walt had nineteen horses in his stable. Polo players needed several horses because the horses would get hurt or tired, and if a player didn't have a good horse to get him to the ball, he couldn't hit it. Seven of Walt's ponies were named June, Slim, Nava, Arrow, Pardner, Tacky, and Tommy. As Walt wrote to his mother, however, purchasing good polo ponies was expensive:

> Don't fall over dead when I tell you I have six ponies now. After all, it's my only sin. I don't gamble or go out and spend my money on other men's wives or anything like that, so I guess it's okay. Anyway, the wife approves of it.

Roy Disney was a fair player; Walt was highly aggressive, but neither athletic nor coordinated. Director David Swift, then an animator, stated:

> He wasn't much of an athlete. I don't know how he played polo. I didn't see how he could stay on a horse and swing a mallet at the same time.

Unlike other young boys, Walt had never participated in sports. For most of his childhood, his spare time was filled with a morning and afternoon newspaper delivery route that was very demanding of his time and energy. While other young children played sports after school and on weekends, young Walt worked and never developed sports coordination skills.

Walt compensated for this lack of sports experience and coordination by being a focused competitor. Actor Robert Stack, who was a teenager at the time, remembered that Walt would:

> ... run right over anybody who crossed the line. Walt was a good polo player-and he loved the game. And I have a couple of trophies at home with Walt's name on them. We hadn't won the world's championships but we had an awful lot of fun.

Walt's wife, Lillian, would spend most of her Sundays sitting on the sidelines, munching a bag of popcorn while Walt played. She said:

> He would stop and buy me a big package of popcorn and I'd sit and eat popcorn and watch him play polo.

A program from 1937 declared:

> Benefit Polo Game Sponsored by Santa Monica Charity League and Santa Monica Junior Chamber of Commerce: May 9, 1937 Riviera Country Club. The first match was the Mickey Mouse Team against the Hollywood Team. The Mickey Mouse Team: James Gleason, Robert Presnell, Happy Williams, and Walt Disney. The Hollywood team included J. Walter Ruben, Mike Curtiz, Paul Kelly, and Dr. Percy Goldberg. Walt Disney captained the Mickey Mouse Team when it came to polo matches. However, many Disney fans may be unaware there was also a Donald Duck Team.

Walt Disney captained the Mickey Mouse Team when it came to polo matches. However, many Disney fans may be unaware there was also a Donald Duck Team.

Disney producer Harry Tytle was quite a polo player in college, but in the depths of the Depression, there were few jobs for polo players. However, he did get to play with Will Rogers in August 1935, a game which turned out to be Rogers' last.

Tytle also knew Harold Helvenston, then a professor of dramatics working at the Disney Studios. One night at dinner, through the kindness of Helvenston, Tytle met some Disney employees, including George Drake and Perce Pearce, and found himself hired as a messenger boy at the Disney Studios for the traffic department.

Once at the Studio, Tytle was introduced to Walt as a polo player, and was invited to play with Walt at the Victor McLaughlin Arena. Walt must have liked the competitive spirit of the young man, because Tytle soon found himself playing with Walt at the Riviera Country Club against Spencer Tracy and his family. Tytle, who didn't have the artistic skill to compete with other aspiring animators at the Studio, worked briefly in many different departments there.

However, he still had time to teach polo to a group of editors and cutters from other studios; play polo for the

Junior Chamber of Commerce; and form the Donald Duck Team (with members including Mel Shaw and Larry Lansburgh) which played a wide area as far distant as Arizona and even, in 1938, Mexico City, where they won their match.

Tytle thinks the team won because they were constantly underestimated due to the portrait of Donald Duck emblazoned on their shirts. "A clever touch suggested by Walt," remembered Tytle in his autobiography.

Walt's enthusiasm for polo inspired a popular Mickey Mouse cartoon, *Mickey's Polo Team*, released on January 1936 and directed by Dave Hand, whose attention was already focused on directing *Snow White*.

There isn't much of a storyline in the cartoon. It is just an interesting premise for physical gags in a polo game between four popular Disney animated characters against a team of four Hollywood celebrities.

The spectators in the stands are a mix of Disney animated characters and Hollywood celebrities. Clarabelle Cow kisses Clark Gable, Edna May Oliver sits next to Max Hare, and Shirley Temple cheers next to the Three Little Pigs, among other celebrity caricature cameos.

The Mickey Mouse team consists of Mickey, Donald Duck, Goofy, and the Big Bad Wolf. The Hollywood team is composed of movie stars Charlie Chaplin, Oliver Hardy, Stan Laurel, and Harpo Marx.

Modern audiences may struggle to identify the caricatures of some of the then famous stars in the cartoon — stars like Eddie Cantor, W.C. Fields, and Harold Lloyd — but even the most astute and knowledgeable classic films buff might have trouble identifying the referee.

The referee is a caricature of Jack Holt, a popular silent screen star who made the transition to talkies primarily in Westerns. In fact, Holt was the father of famous Western movie cowboy star Tim Holt. Jack Holt was well-known as a "manly man" and a strong supporter of polo as a terrific form of physical exercise. He played at the Riviera alongside Walt Disney, but unfortunately he is largely forgotten by modern audiences.

The cartoon was made at the height of the Disney Studios'

involvement in playing polo, but it was not the version that Walt originally intended. There was to be considerable footage devoted to a caricature of Will Rogers. It was Rogers' death in a plane accident in August 1935, while *Mickey's Polo Team* was in production, that resulted in the removal of his caricature.

The cartoon generated its own little controversy that has been forgotten over the years. The January 11, 1938, edition of the *San Francisco Examiner* ran a photo of Walt in Los Angeles looking pensive as he flipped through some papers. The caption and story stated:

Disney Faces Accuser in Court
Disney to answer charges of John P. Wade, writer and actor that *Mickey's Polo Club* [*sic*], was taken from a scenario submitted by Wade. "Mr. Disney told me the script could not be used. Then, several months later, I saw the film," Wade testified. Disney contends the idea was his own.

Time magazine for January 24, 1938, revealed the outcome of this particular court action, where Wade sued for a share of the film's profits:

Alleged plagiarism that the gag of the horses riding the riders had been lifted from author Wade's skit *The Trainer's Nightmare*. In court, attorneys for Cartoonist Walt Disney identified the device as a variation on "the reversal gag" easily traced to Aesop.

Said Superior Court Judge Thomas C. Gould, dismissing the suit and plagiarizing Ecclesiastes: "... it appears there is nothing new under the sun".

By 1938, Roy Disney was becoming worried that the combination of Walt's aggressiveness on the field and the inherent danger of the sport itself might rob the Disney Studios of its visionary leader. In fact, Roy himself had quit the sport that year and was getting rid of his polo ponies, and urged Walt to do the same. Walt resisted the suggestion to hang up his mallet even after he had seen matches where fellow horsemen had suffered severe injuries.

Always pushing himself, Walt eventually wanted to play with the better players. There was a South American team, the Argentines, who were practicing on a field at the Riviera, and Walt wanted to practice with them.

Actor Robert Stack remembered:

Any time the Argentineans would come in they would bring their horses with them. The reason they came, most of these great polo players came was to sell the horses and make a lot of money which they did. You could see some of them red-hots in our [movie] profession, and I think Walt was among them, bidding these fantastic sums for these magnificent horses.

Even then, it was almost impossible to tell Walt "no", so Walt took the field. One of the players hit the ball just as Walt, on horseback, was turning around, and the ball hit Walt hard enough to knock him from the saddle. Walt had four of his cervical vertebrae crushed, and was in tremendous pain. Instead of seeing a doctor, he went to a chiropractor, who manipulated Walt's back. Sadly, the injury might have healed if Walt had been placed in a cast.

Instead, it resulted in a calcium deposit building up in the back of Walt's neck that resulted in a painful form of arthritis which plagued Walt for the rest of his life. In his later years, Walt required a couple of shots of scotch and a massage from the studio nurse in order to get home at night. When the neck and back pain flared up, Walt was often unpleasant in interactions with his staff. When he went into St. Joseph's Hospital for the final time, no suspicion arose when employees were told Walt was just taking care of an "old polo injury".

In 1938, Walt sold off his ponies and resigned from the Riviera Polo Club. Walt loved to saddle up and socialize with Hollywood's elite on the polo fields, but it left him with a painful physical injury that influenced his moods for the rest of his life. Unfortunately, it was an unhappy ending to this interesting interlude in his colorful life.

Walt's School Daze

Walt and his younger sister, Ruth, graduated from Benton Grammar School in Kansas City, Missouri, on June 8, 1917. It was the only graduation Walt had from any school.

Walt graduated from seventh grade, and he surprised his parents by delivering a patriotic speech to the graduates. In later years, his sister remembered the speech was "something about national or international affairs".

During the graduation ceremonies, Walt drew cartoons in his fellow students' yearbooks. Even then, he was well-known as the boy who was going to grow up to be a cartoonist. The principal quipped to Walt's fellow students, "He will draw you if you like." Along with the diploma, the principal gave young Walt a seven-dollar award for a comic character he had drawn.

In May 1963, Walt received a Distinguished Alumnus Award from the Kansas City Art Institute. He had once taken a few Saturday morning children's art classes there, but he had never graduated. Three years earlier, in 1960, he had also received an honorary high school diploma from the Marceline School Board, since he had attended only one year of high school. At the Kansas City Art Institute ceremony, Walt said, laughing:

> Gosh. This goes along with my honorary high school diploma. I had honorary degrees from Yale, Harvard, and the University of Southern California before word got out that I didn't have a high school diploma. Now I have six high school diplomas.

Walt received honorary degrees from both Yale and Harvard

Universities on successive days in June 1938. Neither degree was a doctorate. They were both Masters of Arts.

After the Harvard ceremony, Walt told reporters:

> I'll always wish I'd had the chance to go through college in the regular way and earn a plain Bachelor of Arts like the thousands of kids nobody ever heard of who are being graduated today.

While Walt is rightly respected as an effective educator, he had a limited formal public school education. When the Disney family lived in Marceline, Missouri, Walt's dad, Elias, decided that Walt could not attend school until his younger sister, Ruth, was old enough to go as well, because it seemed to be the most practical thing to do. In that way, Walt could look after his little sister, and they could share the same classes. Walt recalled:

> My birthday came in the middle of the term and you had to be a certain age, so they just said, "Well, we'll just wait and send him when Ruth can go." And it was the most embarrassing thing that can happen to a fellow that I had to practically start in school with my little sister, Ruth, who was two years younger.

Walt's mother, Flora, a former grammar school teacher who had taught in the Central Florida area, home-schooled the children in basic arithmetic, reading, and writing. She was a good, patient teacher, and Walt loved being home-schooled by her.

At age seven, Walt was enrolled in the two-story, red-brick Park School that held close to two hundred children. He received a basic education from *McGuffey's Eclectic Readers*.

Walt was not an attentive student, always finding other things that captured his interest, especially cartooning.

His teacher, Miss Brown, arranged the children's seats according to their achievement in class. Walt was placed in a chair near the back door, and the teacher labeled him the "second dumbest" in the class, because he wouldn't pay attention. Miss Brown complained repeatedly, "He was always drawing pictures and not paying enough attention to his studies."

When the Disney family moved to Kansas City, Walt was enrolled at Benton Grammar School. He had to repeat second

grade, since the teachers felt he hadn't been provided a suffi-
cient education in Marceline. This meant Walt was almost two
years older than most of the other children in his class.

Walt's subjects included grammar, arithmetic, geography,
history, natural science, hygiene, writing, drawing, and
music. Walt was known to be a voracious reader, especially
enjoying the works of Robert Louis Stevenson, Horatio Alger
(who was famous for his many stories of young men who
rose from rags to riches by hard work and honesty), Sir
Walter Scott, Charles Dickens, and Mark Twain.

Supposedly, Walt read everything that Mark Twain wrote.
Walt also enjoyed Shakespeare, but only the parts with
battles and duels, he later told an interviewer. He also loved
the adventures of Tom Swift, a young boy who loved science
and technology, and who first appeared in print in 1910.

However, for the most part, Walt was a mediocre student,
with his worst subject reportedly being algebra. In Walt's
defense, he didn't have much time to study or sleep at home,
since he was also handling a newspaper route that required
him to get up at 3:00 AM each day to deliver the morning
newspapers, and then rush home after school to deliver the
afternoon edition. So, he sometimes caught up on his sleep
in class.

In 1940, Walt wrote to one of his former teachers, Daisy
A. Beck:

> I often think of the days I spent at Benton. I don't know
> whether you remember or not but I participated in several
> athletic events and even won a medal one year on the
> championship relay team. Do you remember the time I
> brought the live mouse into the classroom and you smacked
> me on the cheek? Boy! What a wallop you had! But I loved
> you all the more for it. And I can still plainly see the kids
> marching, single file, into the classrooms to the rhythm of
> the piano in the hall. I remember how [Principal]
> Cottingham would break in on any classes if he had a new
> story and all work would cease until he had his fun. He had
> his faults, but I think of him as a swell fellow.

One time, during a geography lesson, Principal
Cottingham discovered Walt not paying attention to the
class lesson, but instead hiding behind a big geography book
drawing cartoons. In front of the entire class, the principal

reprimanded Walt with the stern prediction: "Young man, you'll never amount to anything."

Walt didn't take offense nor did he hold a grudge. He always sent Mr. Cottingham and his family Christmas cards and autographed animation cels once he finally amounted to something. He even arranged for the entire Benton School student body to ride buses to downtown Kansas City and see *Snow White and the Seven Dwarfs* when it came out in 1938.

In fourth grade, Walt's teacher, Artena Olson, assigned the class to draw a bowl of flowers. Being very imaginative and creative, Walt drew human faces on the flowers, and he gave the flora hands and arms instead of leaves. He was reprimanded by his teacher that flowers do not have faces and hands, and the assignment was to draw a still life.

In fifth grade, on Abraham Lincoln's birthday, Walt dressed up as the former president, complete with home-made stovepipe hat, crepe hair whiskers, and his father's frock coat, and came to school having memorized the Gettysburg Address.

Friend and classmate Walt Pfeiffer remembered:

> He made this stovepipe hat out of cardboard and shoe polish. He purchased a beard from a place that sold theatrical things. He did this all on his own. Walt got up in front of the class and the kids thought this was terrific so Cottingham took him to each one of the classes in the school. Walt loved that.

After graduation, Walt enrolled in Chicago's McKinley High School in fall 1917. He would attend high school for only a year before volunteering as a Red Cross ambulance driver in France. Instead of continuing high school upon his return, Walt started his first animation studio, Laugh-O-Gram, and his formal public school education came to an end.

In 1956, the first elementary school in the United States to be named after Walt Disney was in Tullytown (now Levittown), Pennsylvania. The second was in Anaheim, California, where in spring 1958, Walt caused a commotion at the dedication when he spontaneously declared that school was out for the day and had buses take all the children to Disneyland.

The third was built in Marceline, Missouri, in 1960 to

replace the Park Elementary School that Walt attended as a child. That year, Disney artist Bob Moore designed and coordinated the installation of a series of Disney character murals for the school. Walt also donated: a Mickey Mouse flag, a flag that had once flown at Disneyland, a fifty-five-foot cast aluminum flagpole from the most recent Winter Olympics at which Disney had provided the entertainment, and school material like playground equipment and a filmstrip projection system.

The fourth Walt Disney Elementary School was in Tulsa, Oklahoma, in 1969.

It is ironic that a boy who struggled in school and for whom "getting through the seventh grade was one of the toughest trials of my whole limited span of schooling" ended up being universally acclaimed as a major educator who influenced and encouraged so many young minds.

In December 1955, after interviewing Walt for the *Journal of the California Teacher's Association*, the interviewer said:

> His impact as an educator may not be so widely appreciated. Yet he has done — and is doing — notable and lasting things in the field of education. His record and his plans establish him as a remarkable public educator. And like all successful people, he remembers his "good" teachers.

Walt's favorite teacher was Daisy A. Beck, a young woman with auburn hair who taught him in the seventh grade at Benton School in Kansas City, Missouri. By all accounts, she was an attractive, outstanding teacher whose encouragement of Walt's desire to draw was just another example of the support she gave to all of her students, especially in sports, where she felt winning wasn't everything but making a best effort was.

Daisy Beck's niece Helen recalled an anecdote about Walt that her aunt had shared with her:

> All [Walt] did was sit and draw and she recognized his talent. Now, a lot of teachers at that time didn't. So, she kept saying, "Walt, you've got to know more than just drawing. You've got to have something in your brain. When you get through with your arithmetic, I don't care how much you draw. You can draw any pictures you want, anything when you're through!" I don't think he was a very

good student by any means, but Auntie always said that he had a great mind.

Walt's affection for Beck didn't end at graduation, and in later years, after they reconnected, they continued to exchange letters until her passing. Walt eagerly shared each new letter with Disney storyman Walt Pfeiffer, who had been Walt's best friend and classmate during those Benton school years.

Beck also took the time to understand what Walt's life was like outside the classroom with his early morning and late afternoon paper routes.

One of Walt's classmates said:

If he was sleepy and had fallen asleep, she just let him sleep. She understood why the boy was so tired.

Walt's only participation in school athletics came as a result of Beck coaching the school's track team. As Walt recalled in a 1940 letter to his favorite teacher:

I often think of you and the days I spent at Benton. I can plainly see you ... coaching the athletic teams for the annual track meet. I don't know whether you remember it or not, but I participated in several events and even won a medal one year on the championship 80-pound relay team. I was kept rather busy with my paper route and I didn't have much time to train, but I did manage to get in on a few events.

In 1955, Walt wrote in a letter his memories of Daisy Beck:

The teacher I remember best, with affectionate respect, is Miss Daisy A. Beck. She taught the seventh grade in the old Benton Grammar School in Kansas City, Missouri. She later became Mrs. W.W. Fellers by marriage and she retired years ago after a rich full life of devotion to the hundreds of youngsters who moved through her classroom. And now she has passed on.

But persons like Miss Daisy A., as we called her, never retire from your memory. She remains as vivid today as she was in the days of her patient concern for a laggard boy more interested in drawing cartoon characters on textbook margins than in the required three Rs.

She gave me the first inkling that learning could be enjoyable — even schoolbook learning. And that is a great moment in a kid's life. She had the knack of making things I had thought dull and useless seem interesting and exciting. I never forgot that lesson.

Getting through the seventh grade was one of the toughest trials of my whole limited span of schooling. You've got to be good to teach the seventh. You have to know a lot about human nature in the bud. How to get into stubborn resisting young minds and how to make the classroom compete with everything that tends to lure a kid's attention to the world outside.

That's the kind of teacher Daisy A. was. I had little inclination toward book learning and very little time to study. When I was nine, my brother Roy and I were already businessmen. We had a newspaper route for the Kansas City Star, delivering papers in a residence area every morning and evening of the year, rain, shine or snow. We got up at 3:30 a.m., worked until the school bell rang and did the same thing again from four o'clock in the afternoon until supper time. Often I dozed at my desk, and my report card told the story.

But Miss Daisy A. wasn't discouraged. She knew our circumstances. She never slacked what she considered her teacher's responsibilities. I think I must have been a special challenge to her patience. She never scolded. And I don't believe she ever shamed any of us youngsters with discouragements.

Once only she lost patience with me. That was for a prank. I had rescued a field mouse from a cat and had brought it to school. Attached to a string, it had crawled to a nearby desk. A girl's shriek brought the teacher on the double, and boy, did I get it! She smacked me on the cheek so hard I felt it for several days. I deserved it. In a way, it was educational, too. One of my first "true life adventures", you might say.

It was always my inclination to think in pictures rather than words. I was already dreaming of becoming an artist — a newspaper cartoonist, at this point. I spent many study hours drawing flip-over figures on textbook margins — like the McGuffey readers — to entertain classmates.

Miss Beck understood this, too. She was not only tolerant about these extra-curricular activities, but actually encouraged them. She saw what she regarded as potential talents in other kids, too, and did everything she could to bring them out.

The point is, she tried to understand all of us as

individuals. But she never favored or pampered any of us. She managed somehow to promote our personal inclinations without neglecting the formal grade requirements.

She knew that the good students, the apt ones, who got their lessons easily would get along well without much urging or coaching. It was the laggards, like myself, who most needed encouragement. So with great patience and understanding, and incredible faith, she lavished her teaching genius upon the least promising of her charges.

Other teachers at Benton who often come to mind were Miss Katherine Shrewsbury and Miss Ora E. Newsome, art teachers, Miss Ethel Fischer, and by no means least, J. M. Cottingham, the principal, who acknowledged that I never had to visit his office in punishment. That, I must admit, was sheer luck.

To sum it all up, the outstanding teacher of my youth instilled in us a permanent sense of wanting to-do rather than having to-do.

Gospel According to Walt

Walt Disney was a deeply religious man who truly believed that good would triumph over evil, and that it was important to accept and help everyone no matter how different they were. He had a great respect for all religions.

Walt Disney's own name owes its existence to religion and the church. He was named after Reverend Walter Parr, who preached at the St. Paul Congregational Church in Chicago, where the Disney family attended services at the turn of the 20th century. When St. Paul's needed a larger church, Walt's father, Elias, who earned his living as a carpenter, volunteered to build a new church for the congregation. He put up a plain, serviceable structure with a tall, sloping roof.

Elias was close friends with Parr, and would occasionally step into the church pulpit to deliver the weekly sermon when Parr was out of town or indisposed. Elias's wife, Flora, would play the organ for the Sunday services. Parr baptized the young Walt Disney in the church on June 8, 1902.

Elias Disney has been portrayed as stern and straight-laced, although there is evidence that he was also a sociable, caring man who sometimes demonstrated a sense of fun playing his fiddle on Sunday afternoons. However, one of the things that Elias took very seriously was religion.

He didn't believe that adults should indulge in alcohol or tobacco, and disapproved of things he thought frivolous, including candy for children and certain books. He lectured his sons that, if they were determined to read before falling asleep, they should have their noses in the Bible, not in one of the popular books of the era. Each day in the Disney household began with a prayer session around the breakfast table.

This strong, religious upbringing had a definite effect on the young Walt, but not the one his father would have expected, because the adult Walt did not attend church.

Walt's daughter Sharon said:

> He was a very religious man, but he did not believe you had to go to church to be religious. He respected every religion. There wasn't any that he ever criticized. He wouldn't even tell religious jokes.

Walt's other daughter, Diane Disney Miller, recalled:

> Dad drove us to Sunday School every Sunday for some years. It was the Christian Science Church, because mother was dabbling in all that for a while. Then he'd pick us up and take us to Griffith Park, or to the studio or somewhere else. It was daddy's day. I attended a small Christian Science school up through third grade, and then went to Immaculate Heart, which I loved. The beauty of the campus, the grottos and shrines, the Stations of the Cross in the Chapel, the tangible yet mysterious faith really appealed to me, and I think that dad thought that I might want to become a nun. He always remained accessible to the sisters there, though, just as he was to the sisters of St Joseph's across the street from the studio.
>
> I do know that he had great respect for all faiths. Rabbi Edgar Magnin (Rabbi and Spiritual leader of Congregation B'nai B'rith/Wilshire Boulevard Temple, and was considered the "Rabbi to the Stars") refers to him as "my friend Walt Disney" in his book titled *365 Vitamins for the Mind*, or something like that. He was the B'nai B'rith Man of the Year for the Beverly Hills Chapter in 1955. My sister dated a Jewish boy for a while with no objections from either of my parents. One time, Dad said innocently but proudly, "Sharon, I think it's wonderful how these Jewish families have accepted you." … and it was a very sincere comment. And she was accepted. She knew about lox and bagels way before I was aware of them, went to several bar mitzvahs, etc.
>
> Jules and Doris Styne were good friends. Dad had so many very good Jewish friends, going back to his childhood. When I was asked by a young girl, one of my first friends when I entered Los Feliz Elementary School in the fifth grade if I was Jewish, I replied, "I don't know. I don't think so." I asked my parents that evening. Many of dad's strongest

supporters in his career in Hollywood were Jewish, weren't they? I have to conclude that dad was not guilty of any kind of anti-Semitism.

Jewish storyman and concept artist Joe Grant saw Walt's interaction with other Jewish staff, and said:

> As far as I'm concerned, there was no evidence of anti-Semitism. I think the whole idea should be put to rest and buried deep.

In January 1943, Walt wrote a letter to his sister, Ruth, about his daughter Diane, who was then about ten years old:

> Little Diane is going to a Catholic school now, which she seems to enjoy very much. She is quite taken with the rituals and is studying catechism. She hasn't quite made up her mind yet whether she wants to be a Catholic or Protestant. I think she is intelligent enough to know what she wants to do, and I feel that whatever her decision may be is her privilege. I have explained to her that Catholics are people just like us and basically there is no difference. In giving her this broad view I believe it will tend to create a spirit of tolerance within her.

Throughout his career, Walt purposely avoided any film material dealing with religion, reasoning that portions of the audience would be displeased by the depiction of a particular sect. For instance, the ending for the *Night on Bald Mountain* and *Ave Maria* sequences in *Fantasia* (1940) was originally going to take place inside a gothic chapel with multiple statues of the Virgin Mary, but Walt reasoned it would be more effective outdoors in a setting that merely suggested a church.

Diane Disney Miller told one minister that there are no churches on Main Street at Disneyland because her father did not want to favor any particular denomination, even though there were plans for a church in the original concept drawings, and even though (then) governor of California Goodwin Knight mentioned to a nationwide television audience on Disneyland's Opening Day that there was a church on Main Street.

The Reverend Glenn Puder, Walt's nephew-in-law, delivered the invocation at Disneyland's grand opening on July 17, 1955. Puder stood alongside representatives of the major American religions at that time: Catholic, Jewish, and Protestant. Individual invitees to the Opening Day ceremonies included Cardinal James McIntyre (Catholic), Bishop Francis Eric Bloy (Episcopalian), Bishop Gerald Kennedy (Methodist), Dr. Carroll Shuster (Presbyterian), and Rabbi Edgar Magnin.

Walt also had invitations sent to editors from eight different religious newspapers (Catholic, Jewish, and Protestant) as well as to representatives from nearby churches, including ten Baptist, nine Methodist, eight Catholic, eight Lutheran, seven Christian, six Church of Christ, six Episcopalian, six Presbyterian, five Free Methodist, two Congregational, one Nazarene, and one Jewish synagogue.

Over the years, Walt received many awards from various religious groups. In 1965, for example, he received the Amicus Juvenum (Friend of Youth) Award from the Catholic Youth Organization Federation of Single Adults Club, presented by Father William G. Hutson.

In 1955, writer Samuel Duff McCoy contacted several celebrities, including Lillian Gish, Herbert Hoover, Conrad Hilton, Burl Ives, Harry Truman, and Walt Disney, to write about how prayer had benefited them. He included their responses in his book *How Prayer Helps Me* (Dial Press). Walt wrote a three paragraph essay entitled "My Faith":

> I have a strong personal belief and reliance on the power of prayer for divine inspiration.
>
> Every person has his own ideas of the act of praying for God's guidance, tolerance and mercy to fulfill his duties and responsibilities. My own concept of prayer is not as a plea for special favors or as a quick palliation for wrongs knowingly committed. A prayer, it seems to me, implies a promise as well as a request.
>
> All prayer, by the humble or the highly placed has one thing in common, as I see it: a supplication for strength and inspiration to carry on the best human impulses which should bind us all together for a better world. Without such inspiration, we would rapidly deteriorate and finally perish.

Walt's brother Roy was so moved by these words that he had the Studio print shop produce a version entitled "Prayer in My Life" to give to selected visitors to the Disney Studios.

It was also reprinted as an insert for a 1978 record anthology, *Magical Music of Walt Disney*.

In 1963, religious writer Roland Gammon contacted fifty-five Americans, including J. Edgar Hoover, Steve Allen, Billy Graham, Eleanor Roosevelt, Roy Rogers, Bud Collyer, and of course, Walt Disney. He asked each of them the same question: "What is your faith and what part has it played in your life achievement?"

Gammon spent three years gathering the responses, and then included them in his book *Faith is a Star* (New York E. P. Dutton and Company).

Walt's contribution, "Deeds Rather Than Words by Walt Disney", repeats almost word for word what he had written for the previous book, but in addition, he greatly expands on the importance of his faith, mentioning his "study of the Scripture" and "my lifelong habit of prayer". Here is an excerpt:

> In these days of world tensions, when the faith of men is being tested as never before, I am personally thankful that my parents taught me at a very early age to have a strong personal belief and reliance in the power of prayer for Divine inspiration. My people were members of the Congregational Church in our home town of Marceline, Missouri. It was there where I was first taught the efficacy of religion ... how it helps us immeasurably to meet the trial and stress of life and keeps us attuned to the Divine inspiration.
>
> A prayer implies a promise as well as a request; at the highest level, prayer not only is a supplication for strength and guidance, but also becomes an affirmation of life and thus a reverent praise of God. Deeds rather than words express my concept of the part religion should play in everyday life.

Walt continued to write at length about how his commitment to his faith helped in the decisions that he and his brother Roy made about not only the films they produced but how they handled their business.

Walt ended his essay with:

> Both my study of Scripture and my career in entertaining children have taught me to cherish them. Most things are good, and they are the strongest things; but there are evil things too, and you are not doing a child a favor by trying to shield him from reality. The important thing is to teach a

child that good can always triumph over evil, and that is what our pictures attempt to do.

Thus, whatever success I have had in bringing clean, informative entertainment to people of all ages, I attribute in great part to my Congregational upbringing and my lifelong habit of prayer. To me, today, at age sixty-one, all prayer, by the humble or highly placed, has one thing in common: supplication for strength and inspiration to carry on the best human impulses which should bind us together for a better world.

Diane Disney Miller reflected:

It always seemed to me that dad wouldn't have been so pretentious about his attitudes toward prayer, and that he would have had more Lincolnesque views of religion and prayer, not just because of his reverence for Lincoln, but because they would have been his naturally. But there are things in this piece like his mention of DeMolay that wouldn't have come from a publicity person at the Studio if someone else had written it and maybe dad was just trying to be more deliberate because of the forum where it would appear.

Walt's wife Lillian added:

Every Sunday he took our daughters to Sunday school. Walt was very religious but he never went to church himself. He loved every religion and respected them, although he got upset with overly pious ministers. I never knew of his going to church but he was very religious.

Extra! Extra!
Read All About It!

Walt had a tendency to sentimentalize some of his childhood memories. The famous Kansas City paper route that Walt would talk about with such joy also caused him recurrent nightmares for the rest of his life. Yet, Walt never felt sorry for himself, nor did any of the hardships he faced as a child ever discourage him or make him angry and rebellious.

After selling their farm in Marceline, the Disney family moved to Kansas City, Missouri, where Elias Disney managed a paper route. The local papers, the *Star* and the *Times*, were reluctant to give the route to Elias because he was fifty-one years old, so the owner of record for the route was his son Roy Oliver Disney, who was then eighteen. One probable reason that Elias tried so hard to make the business a success and exceed his subscribers' expectations was to prove that he could handle the responsibility at his age.

Elias was firm that the newspapers were not to be tossed into yards or even onto porches by boys riding bicycles, but rather carried up the walk to the house. The papers couldn't be rolled or folded, and had to be anchored down with a rock or a heavy object if there was a chance that wind would blow the paper away.

In a 1966 interview, Walt said of his father:

> He insisted that it be delivered fresh and clean, without wrinkles. He was meticulous about it.

Route No. 145 was between 27th and 31st streets and Prospect and Indiana Avenues. The Disney family assumed control of the route on July 1, 1911. There were over 600 subscribers for the morning *Times*, 600 for the evening *Star*, and 600 for the Sunday *Star*. When the Disneys gave up the route, they had increased each paper's circulation by over 200 new subscribers.

Walt remembered there were tough kids along the route, including the Pendergast and Costello gangs, who in snowball fights would pack their snowballs with rocks. One time, they even threw a brick at Walt, and opened a nasty cut on his scalp.

Elias hired boys to deliver the papers, paying them roughly $2.50 a week. His sons Walt and Roy also delivered those papers but were paid nothing. Elias felt that the clothing, food, and shelter he provided his sons was compensation enough for the cash-strapped family.

Walt earned money by selling extra newspapers on street corners without his father knowing about it. During the noon recess at school, he swept out the candy store across from the school in return for a hot meal. Some days after school, he wasn't even able to steal a few minutes to play sports with his friends, because he had to deliver the afternoon edition of the newspaper.

For six years, Walt delivered the newspapers (missing only four weeks during all that time from illness). He delivered in drenching rainstorms and in icy blizzards. He got up around 3:30 AM to get the papers from the delivery truck by 4:30 AM.

Sometimes, after skinny, nine-year-old Walt had hauled over thirty pounds of newsprint through the neighborhood, he never made it home for breakfast. There was barely time to hustle off to school, where he struggled to stay awake during classes. And the Sunday edition, with all the inserts, made things even worse, since it was three or four times heavier than the daily edition.

In the morning, as soon as Walt got up to dress, he'd fall back asleep sitting on the edge of his bed while trying to tie his shoelaces. His dad would yell "Walter!", and he'd wake up with his heart racing and finish tying his shoes.

Walt delivered the papers to apartments first. He'd go up three floors and deliver to all the doors, then come down.

Years later, he could remember with clarity those chilly cold days when he was just a kid. One time, the snow drifts were higher than he was. The weather records for Kansas City at the time confirm that fact. On those freezing days, he'd sometimes have to crawl slowly up those icy, slippery steps. Walt once told his daughter Diane that he would occasionally slip down the steps and just cry because he was all alone and so cold.

In the winter, Elias would insist that every paper had to go behind its recipient's storm door. On those days, after Walt finally got home, people would sometimes look out on their porch but wouldn't open the front door. They'd see no paper on the porch, and so they'd phone Elias to complain. Elias would then sternly ask, "Walter, did you forget to deliver to so and so?" And Elias wouldn't believe him when Walt told his father where he'd left the paper.

Elias would say, "Well, they say they didn't find it. Now here, here's a paper." Young Walt would struggle back through the cold and go up and ring the bell. When the customer answered, they'd open the storm door and the paper would fall at their feet, with Walt holding another one outside. They'd say something like, "Oh, I'm sorry I didn't look there." No matter how often it happened, Walt claimed, people still forgot to look.

Walt had recurrent nightmares throughout his life, and one of them was that he had missed customers on his section of the paper route. He'd wake up in a kind of a cold sweat and think, "Gosh, I've got to hurry and get back. My dad will be waiting up at that corner." His dad really wanted to make that business a success after so many of his other business had failed, and Walt could sense that great anxiety.

The kids who lived along Walt's route were certainly much better off financially than the Disney family at the time. The kids would leave their toys out on the porch after playing with them the previous evening.

Walt didn't have any toys. If he got a top or marbles or some other toy, it was a big deal. Everything his parents gave him was practical, like underwear or a winter jacket. His older brother Roy set aside extra money from his job so that Walt and his younger sister, Ruth, could get some small toy.

At 5:00 AM, in the dark, Walt would put his sack of papers down and play with his wind-up trains and other toys. He'd sit there and play all alone with them. Once, he came to a porch where he found toys and a box of half-eaten candy. So he sat there and ate some of the half-eaten candy and played with the toys.

When Walt told about this time in his life, he always insisted that he left the toys in good shape and always carefully put them back in the same place so the families wouldn't know he'd played with them. Then he'd have to hurry and finish his route before school started.

Walt liked to recall how he, along with other Kansas City newsboys, were invited to the Kansas City Convention Hall over the weekend of July 27-28, 1917, for a special event sponsored by the Kansas City Star: a screening of the silent, live-action film version of *Snow White*, starring Marguerite Clark. The movie was projected on four different screens in the huge auditorium, and from where he was sitting, Walt could watch two of the screens (not quite synchronized) at the same time. It remained his most vivid early memory of attending the movies.

In 1963, Walt wrote:

> I'm genuinely glad that I had all this experience when I was a boy. In fact, sometimes I feel sorry for the boys who never have had the chance to carry papers or sell magazines or haven't had some way to earn their own money, because I think you'll all agree that it's a pretty swell feeling to know that the money in your pocket is there by your own efforts, and that you're getting experience in business that can't help but stand you in good stead later on.

Walt had shared some of those same thoughts a decade earlier in an article he contributed to a book written by Sid Marks and Alban Emley, *The Newspaper Boys' Hall of Fame* (House-Warven Publishers 1953). Among other things, the book contained accounts by former newspaper boys like Bob Hope, Al Jolson, Jack Dempsey, and Art Linkletter. Walt wrote:

> I have yet to meet a man who once was a newspaper boy who isn't proud of the experience. I myself look back upon the time when my brother Roy and I delivered papers in Kansas City, Missouri, with great appreciation for what this

daily chore meant then and what it has meant in all my grown-up life.

At the time, the sense of responsibility which goes with the job may seem like an onerous thing to a boy. Doing his work regularly every day, in all kinds of weather, often against his inclinations to loaf and postpone his accepted duties, gives a youngster a good foundation for his responsibilities as a man and a citizen later on. It helps greatly to equip him for the tasks and the satisfactions of business or professional life.

Walt wrote about how his father instilled in him and his brother the importance of customer satisfaction that served Walt so well in his future projects, including an innovative method of guest service at Disneyland that became the model for so many other businesses. Walt concluded:

Delivering papers to many homes and offices gives a boy an added feeling of being respected by his neighbors and of belonging to his town or community, as well as being an important and reliable member of his own family. In all this he builds a proper pride and confidence in his own abilities — a good self-reliance and competence which comes from earning his own money.

I believe that the benefits to a boy who carries newspapers on the neighborhood routes of his town or section, if he is not too young and the task is not too burdensome, are as generally sound and valuable today as they were in the days of my youth.

Walt's 30th Wedding Anniversary

Walt and Lillian Disney's 30th wedding anniversary was an out-of-the-ordinary celebration. Guests sipped mint juleps on the Mark Twain riverboat, followed by a lavish dinner at the Golden Horseshoe Saloon, complete with cancan dancers. Diane, their shy twenty-one-year-old daughter, wore a "sort of bare" red linen dress that her mother had bought for the occasion. "I never saw my Dad happier, ever, ever, ever," Diane Disney Miller now says.

During the early Summer of 1955, approximately three hundred people, including celebrities like Spencer Tracy, Cary Grant, Gary Cooper, Louis B. Mayer, and Joe Rosenberg, received the following invitation:

TEMPUS FUGIT CELEBRATION

Where: Disneyland ... where's there's plenty of room ...

When: Wednesday, July 13, 1955, at six o'clock in the afternoon ...

Why: ... because we've been married Thirty Years ...

How: ... by cruising down the Mississippi on the Mark Twain's maiden voyage, followed by dinner at Slue-Foot Sue's Golden Horseshoe!

Hope you can make it — we especially want you and, by the way, no gifts, please — we have everything, including a grandson!

Lilly and Walt

Although he was physically and mentally exhausted from preparation for the opening of Disneyland (just four days after this party), Walt decided to celebrate his 30th wedding anniversary at the park that had long been his dream.

It was a warm July evening. After a long day of inspecting the park with his small flip notepad, where Walt dutifully made notations of things to be changed or addressed, he ended his day by waiting cheerfully at the front gate to greet guests to his new magic kingdom.

An unexpected traffic snarl had delayed some of the guests, and Walt nervously smoked a cigarette or two as he impatiently waited for them to arrive. Horse-drawn surreys transported guests down the glittering lights of the almost completed Main Street and through the open gates of the wooden fort entrance into Frontierland. The guests were directed across the Frontierland Square to the mighty steamboat *Mark Twain*.

Admiral Joe Fowler, in charge of Disneyland construction, had arrived over an hour early to make a final inspection of the *Mark Twain* paddle-wheeler to ensure the evening would run smoothly. The boat had never been fully tested on the river, and Fowler later confessed to friends his nightmare of the previous night that the artificial river bed had once again sprung a leak and gone dry.

He was taken aback to encounter a woman on deck frantically sweeping sawdust and dirt with a broom. She handed him a broom and said, "This ship is filthy. Let's get busy and sweep it up." That woman was Walt's wife, Lillian, and the boat was swept clean by the time the first guests arrived.

Fowler recalled:

> I'll have to admit there were a lot of shavings and things around. That was Lilly. That's the first time I met Lilly. All of Walt's friends showed up. It was a great party! The *Mark Twain* never went around the track completely until the night of Walt's party.

By the time the guests arrived, the *Mark Twain* was shiny and white and new, with twinkling, old-fashioned light bulbs outlining the decks. A Dixieland band played lively New Orleans style tunes. Appropriately attired waiters wandered the decks with trays full of mint juleps.

A blast from the ship's whistle and it gently pulled away from the dock and began its journey in the approaching dusk around the Rivers of America. There was no distraction from anything on the darkened Tom Sawyer's island, since it would be another year before that location came to life. It was a festive mood as the boat glided effortlessly through the man-made waterway transporting guests to another time and place, and giving them a brief preview of what people would experience in a few short days.

After the leisurely cruise, the guests were ushered into the nearby Golden Horseshoe Saloon, designed by Imagineer Harper Goff. It was styled more as a typical turn-of-the-century opera house than as a rip-roaring Old West saloon. With its gilded wallpaper, ornate light fixtures, and carved wooden accents, it was a luxurious setting for the wedding anniversary celebration. The event included dinner and the cutting of a four-tiered cake, as Walt and Lillian's two daughters, Diane and Sharon, smiled broadly near their parents.

Diane told me:

> Mother and dad were not seated up in the balcony box, but down with their guests. Dad was so happy, and roamed around the room, which the photos indicate. All the invited guests were people he and mother liked. Everyone enjoyed him, and vice versa. I had come down from Monterrey for the event, with our infant son, Chris. Ron was in the Army stationed at Fort Ord. Mother had bought my dress. As I told you, everyone, my parents and their guests, were sitting at tables awaiting dinner and the show. I forget which came first. Dad was circulating throughout the room, greeting and schmoozing with his guests, which were all people he liked, longtime friends and family.

The stage show changed little over the decades, becoming the longest-running musical stage show in history, with tens of thousands of performances, according to the *Guinness Book of World Records*. Hostess Slue Foot Sue sang and introduced her dancing cancan girls. There was even a traditional Irish tenor. However, the heart and spirit of the show was the talented comic Wally Boag, who performed a hilariously corny vaudeville routine as a traveling salesman, and then reappeared in the finale as Sue's wild cowboy boyfriend, the famous Pecos Bill. With blazing six-guns (later supplemented with water pistols to squirt the audience), Boag and the entire cast filled the stage and brought the show to a raucous memorable ending.

In summer 1956, Diane recalled the event:

> The guests would come and they would ride around in their surreys which would bring them around to the steamboat dock. Then, they would ride around the river on the *Mark Twain* drinking mint juleps, or whatever they wanted to drink, and then we would all have dinner at the Golden Horseshoe. Dad had been out in the park all day prior to this. It had been a dream for so long and here it was. Everything was almost done. The planting was not quite in yet or anything and it was still a little dusty, but it was there. It was very concrete at that point.
>
> So when he got on the boat, I was with him most of the time and I don't think he'd had much to drink. I really don't. I think he had maybe two or three mint juleps at most on the boat. But he was completely relaxing mentally, physically, everything. He was so stimulated by this thing and by the hundreds of people that were there saying what a wonderful thing it all was. Everyone was surrounding him telling him what a wonderful thing he had. That stimulating response from everyone who was there plus what he was feeling himself, that just combined to have a very bad effect. Well, I don't know if it was good or bad. It was just very entertaining in retrospect.
>
> It was very entertaining for everyone there but disastrous for the family, I think. The finale of the floor show is Pecos Bill shooting off his guns and all the chorus girls are kicking up their heels and everything. So it is loud and chaotic and for a minute neither I nor my mother knew where daddy was. And all of a sudden, we see him hanging over the balcony trying to get down to the stage.
>
> You see, by this point Pecos Bill was shooting his guns and daddy was using his fingers to form a gun and he was shooting back. "Bang! Bang!" like that. And people noticed him and they shouted, "There's Walt!" There was a little applause and general recognition from the audience and that just spurred daddy on. I thought he was going to fall off the balcony but he made it to stage. He was just standing there and sort of beamed. Everybody started saying, "Speech! Speech!" or there was the clear expectation that he should say something. I just remember him standing there looking happy and pleased.

Then everyone applauded and shouted, "Lilly! Lilly! We want Lilly!" So mother got up and walked up the stairs to the stage thinking, "If I get up there, maybe I can get Walt down." Well, that wasn't the case. Mother dragged Sharon and I up there on stage as well and nothing was happening. My dad was firmly planted there just basking in the moment, loving every minute of it. I guess someone must have sensed our plight because the band started to play and Edgar Bergen came up on stage and started dancing with me. Someone came up and danced with mother and Sharon. Everybody started dancing on the stage and my father was gently elbowed off into the wings. He was quite content to just stay right up there. He loved every minute of it. He was just going to stand there and grin at the people, I think.

Everyone was so worried about him. They were worried about him driving himself home. Some people had chartered a bus to get to the park and they wanted Walt to go back with them on the bus. Somebody else volunteered to drive him back home. But I was going to drive him. It was fine with me. I didn't think daddy was that bad off but everybody was asking as if he was being belligerent and everything. "We've got to sneak the car keys out of his pocket" sort of thing. They were really, sincerely worried.

But I just went up to him and I said, "Daddy, can I drive you home?" "Well, sure, honey!" he said. No problem at all. He was just as meek and mild and willing. So he went out to the car and some people were still worried that he would try to abscond with the car himself. But he just climbed into the back seat of the car. He rolled up these plans, I guess it was a map of Disneyland, and he was tooting through it and into my ear like a little boy with a toy trumpet. Then he was singing a song or something. Before I knew it, all was silent. So I looked around in the back seat and there he was like a little boy with his makeshift trumpet sort of folded in his arms and sound asleep. It was really sweet. But I know he hadn't had too much to drink because the next morning, he didn't have a hangover. He bounced out of the house at seven-thirty and down to Disneyland again.

Performer Wally Boag remembered Walt's wedding anniversary performance:

Folks saw him [Walt] up there [in the upper stage left balcony box] and they started calling for him to come down to the stage. So he climbed out of the box and down onto the stage during the finale. I shot my final two rounds, and with his hand in the shape of a pistol, he "shot" back at me. Lilly joined him. Lilly loved to dance and Walt didn't. However, when the band began playing, he took her hand and danced around the stage. She didn't know it but he had taken some dancing lessons because he knew how happy that would make her. I don't remember exactly what he said once he got on the stage, but it was along the lines of finally realizing his long-held dream of an amusement park for the whole family. All of us there that night knew we were going to be part of something that was very special and wonderful, and that the adventure was just beginning.

Diane recently added:

It was a humorous, comic situation, not really an embarrassing one. The story was just as I told it. I thought it was sweet the way he just handed me the car keys. It was a "silly old dad" kind of thing.

It was during the show, when Wally Boag made his entrance, guns blazing, that we noticed dad up in the balcony. He exchanged fire with Wally — thumb and forefinger "bang bang bang" — do you know what I mean? And then decided, apparently, that he'd like to be down there sharing the stage with Wally, and began his descent which, I found, was well documented by the photographer. It was good theater, actually. One must remember that dad began his career that way, on the vaudeville stages of Kansas City, with his pal Walt Pfeiffer.

The following evening was a salute at the Hollywood Bowl honoring Walt Disney. Performers included Fess Parker, Buddy Ebsen, Sterling Holloway, and Cliff Edwards. At the end of the night's selection of Disney music, Goodwin Knight, governor of California, who would be an important guest speaker at Disneyland's opening in just a few days, declared Walt to be California's honorary governor and presented him with a Davy Crockett coonskin cap dipped in silver.

July 13, 2010, would have been Walt and Lillian's 85th wedding anniversary. While there have been many special parties and celebrations in Disneyland over the decades, none were as magical and heart-warming as that very first Disneyland party.

Eating Like Walt

In 1850, German philosopher Ludwig Feuerbach wrote the familiar phrase "Der Mensch ist, was er isst", which translates to "Man is what he eats".

If that is true, then what special foods created and sustained the unique genius of Walt Disney?

The answer is surprising.

Walt Disney's daughter, Diane Disney Miller, stated:

> Before he married mother, father had eaten in hash houses and lunch wagons for so many years in order to save money that he'd developed a "hash-house lunch-wagon" appetite.
>
> He liked fried potatoes, hamburgers, western sandwiches, hotcakes, canned peas, hash, stew, roast beef sandwiches. He's not keen for steak — or any of the expensive cuts of meat. He doesn't go for vegetables, but he loves chicken livers or macaroni and cheese.
>
> Father usually ate a big lunch at the Studio and then would pick at his dinner. Mother would say, "Why should [our housekeeper] Thelma and I plan a meal when all Walt really wants is a can of chili or a can of spaghetti?"

Walt often carried nuts and crackers in his jacket pockets so that he could have a simple snack if he felt hungry during the day. His wife, Lillian, recalled:

> Walt ate very simply. He liked basic foods. He loved chili. For breakfast he had eggs, toast, fruit juice, occasionally a sausage. Lunch was usually just a sandwich, milk, and coffee. He always wanted coffee for lunch.

When Walt had no visitors for lunch at the Disney Studios, he ate at his desk. His favorite meal was chili and beans. He would combine a can of Gebhardt's (which had much meat and few beans) with a can of Dennison's (which had less meat but more beans). The dish was preceded by a glass of V-8 juice and accompanied by soda crackers.

If visitors came to lunch, they were ushered into Walt's conference room at noon. He served them an apéritif of V-8 juice, which surprised some of his international guests who expected something stronger. Walt's secretary often warned visitors that if Walt offered them a glass of "tomato juice", they had best accept it. There is no documentation about the consequences for refusing.

When Walt traveled, he'd bring along cans of chili and beans and other canned foods he liked to eat. At the fancy Dorchester Hotel in London, the waiters would serve him chili and beans and crackers that he had brought from the United States, much to the embarrassment of Harry Tytle, the producer of a number of Disney films who was dining with Walt at the time.

In her book, *Kings in the Kitchen* (A.S. Barnes & Co. 1961 New York), Gertrude Booth collected "favorite recipes of famous men", including Walt Disney and also Bob Hope, J. Edgar Hoover, John F. Kennedy, Alfred Hitchcock, and many others. Booth presented Walt's special secret chili recipe to the public for the very first time:

WALT'S CHILI RECIPE

- 2 pounds ground beef (coarse)
- 2 whole onions (sliced)
- 2 whole garlic cloves (minced)
- 2 pounds pink beans (dry)
- ½ cups celery (chopped)
- 1 teas. chili powder
- 1 teas. paprika
- 1 teas. dry mustard
- 1 can solid pack tomatoes (large can)
- salt to taste

Soak beans overnight in cold water. Drain. Add water to cover 2 inches over beans and simmer with onions until tender (about four hours). Meanwhile, prepare sauce by browning meat and minced garlic in oil. Add remaining items and simmer 1 hour. When beans are tender, add sauce and simmer 30 minutes. Serves six to eight.

As part of the 100 Years of Magic Celebration at Walt Disney World, several restaurants wanted to offer special desserts based on Walt's favorites. One of his former secretaries, Lucille Martin, and his daughter Diane Disney Miller revealed that Walt's favorite desserts were very "home style" and included lemon meringue, apple, and boysenberry pies.

The Disney family's cook prepared a dessert every night. Walt's other favorites were Apple Brown Betty, custards, bread pudding, baked apples, red Jell-O with fruit, lemon snow pudding, and lemon chiffon with a graham cracker crust. He liked gingerbread and another type of cookie made with chow mein noodles and melted butterscotch.

When Dwight and Mamie Eisenhower published a cookbook, *Five-Star Favorites: Recipes from Friends of Mamie & Ike* (Golden Press 1974), and solicited recipes from their friends, the Disney family provided one of Walt's favorite desserts, which was also a favorite of Walt's first grandson, Christopher Disney Miller, for whom this lemon chiffon concoction on a graham cracker crust is named:

CHRIS' COLD PIE

- 4 eggs, separated
- ½ cup lemon juice
- ½ cup water
- 1 tbsp. unflavored gelatin
- 1 cup sugar
- ¼ tsp. Salt
- 1 tbsp. grated lemon rind
- 1 graham cracker crust (recipe on box)
- nutmeg

In a small bowl, beat egg yolks with lemon juice and water just until combined. Mix gelatin, half the sugar and the salt in the top of a double boiler. Pour in egg yolk mixture, blending well. Cook, stirring constantly, over boiling water (water should not touch top section of double boiler) until gelatin dissolves and mixture thickens. Remove top from boiling water. Stir in lemon rind. Let set 20 minutes in a bowl filled with ice cubes, stirring occasionally. Remove from ice when mixture thickens enough to mound when dropped from a spoon.

Meanwhile, beat egg whites (at room temperature) in a large bowl until soft peaks form when beater is raised. Gradually add remaining sugar, 2 tablespoons at a time, beating well after each addition. Continue beating until stiff peaks form when beater is raised. Gently fold gelatin mixture into egg whites just until combined. Turn into pie crust. Dust top with nutmeg and chill several hours. (If desired, omit nutmeg and serve topped with whipped cream.)

Lillian remembered that Walt:

… didn't like sweets very much. Sometimes he could be annoyed by something he was served. He didn't like cake. One time, Thelma Howard, who was the Disney family housekeeper, made a whipped cream cake and Walt was complaining about it. I got so put out that I picked up a piece of the whipped cream and threw it at him. It hit him right in the face. And he picked up some whipped cream and threw it at me. Then we started throwing it back and forth at each other. … I remember that I got some whipped cream on the wallpaper and it left a grease mark and I had to change it.

There is an oddball recipe for Macaroni Mickey Mousse that was supposedly Walt's favorite and appeared in the February 1934 issue of *Better Homes and Gardens*:

It is especially appropriate that Mr. Disney has this preference for a cheese dish, because it was partly because of his taste for cheese that he received the inspiration which led to the creation of Mickey Mouse. It happened like this:

Some years ago, working late at night for a Kansas City commercial artist, Mr. Disney used to feed bits of cheese from his midnight sandwich to the mice that scampered about the room in which he worked.

According to his story, one mouse finally became so friendly that he clambered up onto his drawing board, thus giving Walt Disney his first good look at the future Mickey Mouse.

Mr. Disney often serves Macaroni Mickey Mousse to his friends who visit him at his Hollywood bungalow. He sometimes varies this recipe by having his cook substitute 2 tablespoons of finely chopped celery for the 1 tablespoon of chopped parsley, and add 2 strips of finely chopped cooked bacon.

MACARONI MICKEY MOUSSE
- 1 cupful of macaroni broken into 2-inch pieces
- 1½ cupfuls of scalding milk
- 1 cupful of soft bread crumbs
- ¼ cupful of melted butter

- 1 pimiento, minced
- 1 tablespoon of chopped parsley
- 1 tablespoonful of chopped onion
- 1½ cupfuls of grated cheese
- 1 teaspoonful of salt
- ⅛ teaspoonful of pepper
- dash of paprika
- 3 eggs, beaten

Cook the macaroni in 1 quart of boiling salted water, drain, cover with cold water, and drain again. Pour the scalding milk over the bread crumbs, add the butter, pimiento, parsley, onion, grated cheese, and seasonings. Then add the beaten eggs. Now turn the macaroni into a well-greased loaf pan or casserole and pour the milk and cheese mixture over it. Bake about 50 minutes in a slow oven (325 degrees). The loaf is firm enough when done to hold its shape when turned out on a platter. Serves six.

In the early 1950s, when Walt was developing the concept for Disneyland, he would come home late in the evenings. He almost always entered his house through the kitchen, which was nearer the garage. He also used it as an excuse to check to see what his housekeeper, Thelma, had prepared for dinner.

If she was preparing steaks or lamb chops or broiled chicken, Walt would say, "You know I don't like that", with a sigh in his voice to indicate disappointment. It seemed that no matter what was being prepared for dinner, it was never what Walt wanted at that moment, and he would grumble.

Walt sometimes had a big lunch at the Studio (because he used that time for interviews or meeting with guests) and then would pick at his dinner. His grumbling still upset Thelma, even though she understood the reason. She would try to hide the dinner she was preparing if she heard Walt's car. Despite the pleas of Mrs. Disney not to enter the house through the kitchen because it upset Thelma, Walt continued to do so, because part of his evening ritual was to grab a raw hot dog wiener from the refrigerator. Walt called it a "weenie" based on what he heard it being called when he was growing up.

He would get one weenie for the family dog, a small white poodle, and another for himself. Walt loved that particular dog, and she even appeared with Walt on a few of the early

Disney TV show introductions. Wherever he went wiggling the hot dog, the poodle would follow. When Walt was building Disneyland, he used the non-architectural term of needing a "weenie" to get guests to go where he wanted them to go, such as Sleeping Beauty Castle, the TWA Moonliner, and the *Mark Twain* riverboat.

In a 1956 interview, Walt's daughter Diane remembered that her father loved:

> ... this old dog we had, the old poodle. She was just miserable during the day but she'd perk up in the evenings when Dad came home. In the evening, when Daddy came home, Dad would play with her with this hot dog.

In a more recent interview, Diane recalled:

> Over the years, we had a succession of cooks in the kitchen. Our last one in the Woking Way house, before we moved to the home on Carolwood Drive around 1948, was Bessie Postalwaite, a good cook, an intelligent woman and a Missourian. That fact established a special bond between her and dad.
>
> She knew how to prepare food that he liked to eat — really good hash made from the previous night's roast beef, bread pudding, apple Brown Betty, chicken pot pie (with biscuits on top), fried chicken, broiled chicken and chicken fried steak.
>
> When tomatoes were in season, she'd bring him a little side dish of them with vinegar and sugar. She was rather feisty, witty, and I think he really enjoyed her. During Bessie's time with us, Thelma Howard entered our lives, first as a cleaning girl coming once or twice weekly.
>
> When we moved to Carolwood, Bessie retired and Thelma moved in. She did everything, and did it well. She cleaned the house daily, fed us all breakfast, dinner and sometimes lunch, and did laundry perfectly. She was a superb cook. Her pies were the best.
>
> There were certain things that Dad liked to eat. He wasn't much interested in steak, but preferred hash, stews, soups, even out of a can. He became tired of mother's frequent meal plan of broiled lamb chops, baked potato, salad, and came downstairs for breakfast one morning and handed Thelma this list.
>
> He said, "Thelma, here's a list of things I like to eat." Somehow this list survived through the decades after his death and was found after mother's death in an old *LIFE*

magazine in the "maid's room" that had seen several different occupants since Thelma's retirement.

Walt had hand-printed "Walt Disney's Favorites" in blue ink on one side of two 5x7 pieces of paper, with several misspellings in his list of foods:

WALT DISNEY'S FAVORITES
- Chicken Fry Eube Stake [sp]
- Roast Lamb — Potatoes and Gravy
- Pan Fried Chicken with Dressing and Gravey [sp]
- Spam and Eggs with biscuits and honey
- Oyster Stew with crackers and cheese
- Breaded Veal Cuttlets [sp] — Bread and Gravey[sp]
- Chasens Chilli [sp] and Beans

Note — Only one vegetable with meals — corn — canned peas — leaf spinach-stewed tomatoes — etc.

Salads
- Carrot and Raisans [sp]
- Waldorf
- Tomatoes and Cucumber
- Chef's Salad

Desserts
- Jello — All flavors with pieces of fruit
- Diet Custards
- Pinapple [sp] — Fresh or Canned
- Fruit — Fresh or Canned

And written along the side of the second sheet, as if a last minute remembrance, Walt printed: "Homemade soups?"

Walt had simple culinary tastes, just like the vast majority of his loyal audience, but those types of dietary choices led to weight gain as he got older.

As Walt endured occasional diets to control his weight, one of his doctors urged him to stop eating egg yolks, butter, and milk. Diane Disney Miller remembered:

> Until then, Father had never cared for eggs, but after that doctor's edict, he insisted on having Thelma fry an egg for him every morning so he could trim the white away, discard the yolk, and eat the trimmings with an abused look on his face.

Part Two

Disney Film Stories

Every Disney film is somebody's favorite Disney film.

I learned this truth the hard way. I have always disliked the animated feature *The Aristocats* for a variety of reasons. I don't hate the film, but I am certainly upset by its many plot holes, the weak use of its recycled animation, and the general feeling that everything, including the kitchen sink, was tossed in, and it's still not soup.

However, once upon a time, I dated for several years a wonderful young lady whom I loved deeply and whose favorite Disney animated film was *The Aristocats*. As a result, I saw the film over and over and over, and while I never grew to love it, I did learn to accept it for what it was rather than compare it with what might have been. Surprisingly, after some research, I discovered it was intended to be a much different film.

Having worked as a professional actor and director, I know that every performance, stage production, television show, or movie has many colorful behind-the-scenes anecdotes of the trials and tribulations of bringing the show to its audience.

Some of the minor Disney films released on DVD have neither a commentary track nor a "Making Of " featurette to give insight into the movie. These unassuming, often formulaic productions are justly overshadowed by the critically lauded and financial blockbusters that come to mind when thinking of Disney films. But these smaller films brought delight to audiences for generations, and often were closely connected with Walt himself.

Let's Roll 'Em!

Lights!

Camera!

Forgotten Stories!

Disney's Ham Actors: The Three Little Pigs

Today, it is hard to imagine the impact of *Three Little Pigs*, one of Disney's *Silly Symphonies*. Not only did it win the 1933 Academy Award for Best Animated Film (the year after *Flowers and Trees* won the very first Oscar given to a cartoon), it was the most successful cartoon ever released up to that time.

The film was the 36th *Silly Symphony* (the seventh in Technicolor) and cost $22,000 (not counting prints and publicity), but earned over $150,000 in its first fifteen months of release. Until then, the average *Silly Symphony* grossed around $50,000 in its first year of release.

Three Little Pigs premiered on May 25, 1933, and was so popular that it ran for weeks. *Variety* stated:

> *Three Little Pigs* is proving the most unique picture property in history. It's particularly unique because it's a cartoon running less than ten minutes, yet providing box office draft comparable to a feature, as demonstrated by the numerous repeats.

United Artists could not supply enough prints to meet the demand. Some exhibitors had to share a print, running it back and forth between two or more theaters.

The song "Who's Afraid of the Big Bad Wolf?" replaced "Brother, Can You Spare A Dime" as the working man's anthem during the Depression. It was played constantly on the radio, and major record companies issued competing versions of the song. This was the first time that a cartoon had spawned a hit song which captured the fancy of the nation. The catchy tune even appeared in MGM's *Babes in Toyland* and Paramount's *Duck Soup*, as well as other non-Disney productions.

"Who's Afraid of the Big Bad Wolf" was composed by Frank Churchill, with Pinto Colvig (the voice of the Practical Pig) on the ocarina and storyman Ted Sears providing some of the couplets. A publicity release told the story of how, as a child, Churchill had been given three piglets by his mother to look after, and he played them tunes on his harmonica. A real-life big bad wolf came down from the hills one day and eliminated one of the pigs. An interesting fun fact is that the song never plays complete and uninterrupted in the actual cartoon.

There was a flood of merchandising for the characters, from stationery and playing cards to toothbrush holders, tea sets, radios, books, and even Christmas tree lights. References and images of the pigs and the wolf appeared in editorial cartoons, essays, and other places.

Walt felt trapped with his popular Mickey Mouse cartoon series, because audiences had certain expectations for those cartoons and for Mickey Mouse as well. Walt used the *Silly Symphonies* for the experimentation he couldn't risk in the Mickey Mouse cartoons, and that experimentation eventually resulted in *Snow White and the Seven Dwarfs*.

Although physically the three pigs were the same, they could be identified easily by the audience because of their different personalities. For example, notice how in the film each of the pigs' tails coils and uncoils, depending upon that pig's state of exhaustion or elation.

This type of animated acting was a turning point in the history of animation, distinct from the past where characters often were defined by what they looked like rather than how they acted. Disney later applied this lesson to the dwarfs.

In the original folk tale, the wolf eats the first two pigs after he blows down their houses, then he drops down the chimney of the pig with the brick house and ends up in a pot of boiling water — and gets eaten himself. It was Walt Disney who revised the story so that neither the pigs nor the wolf are eaten. Walt came up with the idea to give the pigs musical instruments and have them sing and dance.

When Walt first presented the idea of doing a cartoon based on this folk tale, his staff had no enthusiasm. Walt said:

> I think the reason they didn't like the idea was that at that time the thing wasn't very clear in my own mind frankly. I withdrew it and tried to forget it, but the pigs and the wolf and the little house kept haunting me. I thought about them until I saw the story clearly, and then I proposed it again. This time they liked it. I don't mean they threw up their hats, or that even I thought it would be a tremendous hit. We considered it a typical *Silly Symphony*.

In a 1932 memo to his staff in 1932, Walt stated:

> These little pig characters look as if they would work up very cute and we should be able to develop quite a bit of personality in them. ... Might try to stress the angle of the little pig who worked the hardest, received the reward, or some little story that would teach a moral. ... These little pigs will be dressed in clothes. They will also have household implements, props, etc., to work with, and not be kept in the natural state. They will be more like human characters.

Fred Moore was the primary animator on the pigs, although Dick Lundy did the sequences where they danced. Moore received coaching from Walt Disney, who regaled the young animator with tales of his riding a favorite sow into a mud puddle when he was a small farm boy in Marceline.

Another animation legend, Norm "Fergie" Ferguson, brought the memorable Big Bad Wolf to life, with voice work by Billy Bletcher, who was also the voice of Peg Leg Pete. Mary Moder voiced the Fiddler Pig, and Dorothy Compton was the voice of the Fifer Pig. Interestingly, despite all the attention and merchandising, the pigs were not officially given individual names until the short *Practical Pig* (1939).

United Artists, the distributor of the Disney cartoons, was unimpressed with *Three Little Pigs*, complaining to Walt that it was a "cheater", since there were only four characters, whereas *Father Noah's Ark*, the previous *Silly Symphony*, had featured dozens of animals.

Three Little Pigs premiered at Radio City Music Hall on May 25, 1933, and ran for one week. However, it did very well at local neighborhood theaters as well as at other New York theaters like the Roxy and the Translux. One New York theater played it so long that the manager added beards on the pigs in the lobby poster, and as the cartoon kept playing week after week, the beards grew longer and longer. Walt said:

> It was just another story to us and we were in there gagging it just like any other picture. After we heard all the shouting, we sat back and tried to analyze what made it good.

Theater owners requested more cartoons with the pigs, and these requests were supported by Roy O. Disney, who convinced Walt it would be good for business. Walt later regretted bowing to pressure and producing three more cartoons featuring the same characters: *The Big Bad Wolf* (1934), *Three Little Wolves* (1936), and *The Practical Pig* (1939). Though technically superior, these cartoons were not as memorable as the original.

During his speech for the Showman of the Year Award in 1966, Walt said:

> By nature, I'm an experimenter. To this day, I don't believe in sequels. I can't follow popular cycles. I have to move on to new things. So with the success of Mickey I was determined to diversify. We kept fooling around with the *Silly Symphonies* until we came up with the *Three Little Pigs*. I could not possibly see how we could top pigs with pigs. But we tried, and I doubt whether one member of this audience can name the other cartoons in which the pigs appeared.

Walt felt that he couldn't top the success of pigs with just more pigs. So, instead of sequels and repeats, the Disney Studios would devote itself to always finding something new. When theaters demanded Disney shorts featuring Dopey from *Snow White*, Walt didn't even consider those requests, remembering what had happened with the pigs.

Three Little Pigs has been parodied many times over the years, from Tex Avery's *The Blitz Wolf* (MGM) to Friz Freleng's *Three Little Bops* (Warner Brothers). The Disney pigs did pop up in cameos in other Disney cartoons like *Mickey's Polo Team* (1936), *Toby Tortoise Returns* (1936), *Mickey's Christmas Carol* (1983), and *Who Framed Roger Rabbit* (1988) as well as three World War II commercial shorts, including *Thrifty Pig* (1941).

One Disney *Three Little Pigs* cartoon has been mostly unknown to U.S. audiences for decades.

In fall 1962, Walt Disney introduced Bill Justice and X. Atencio to Carlos Amador and Amador's movie star wife, Marga. Disney fans may know Justice as the primary animator of Chip'n'Dale in their classic cartoons, and Atencio as the lyricist for both the Pirates of the Caribbean and Haunted Mansion theme park attractions. Their other projects for the Disney Company could fill books.

Amador was preparing a live-action movie about the life of a famous south-of-the-border writer. Since one of the stories was about the three little pigs, Amador wanted to use Disney's three little pigs in a four-minute animated segment.

Walt agreed to donate the animation. He assigned Justice and Atencio to the project, because half of the profits would help provide poor Mexican children a free lunch each school day. The charity was the favorite of the Republic of Mexico's First Lady, and it was the only way many Mexican children could be persuaded to attend school.

Amador wrote the adaptation, with Justice and Atencio doing the production work.

In the film, a live-action young boy and girl on their bed look at a framed picture of three sleeping pigs. As they gaze at the picture, it comes to cartoon life. The three little pigs are tucked into bed and given a kiss by their mother.

One pig dreams of being a king and having lots of tasty treats brought for him to gorge upon. Another dreams of having his own rowboat, but with disastrous results when he ends up in the water and then back in bed, where a tear trickles down his face.

The Practical Pig, however, dreams of the Big Bad Wolf threatening the Pig's mother that she must pay the rent by tomorrow. La Fiesta de las Flores (with animation re-used from *The Three Caballeros*) offers the pigs a chance to win money to pay the rent by performing a musical number.

Of course, they win the contest, and return home late at night, whistling "Who's Afraid of the Big Bad Wolf", when they are attacked by the wolf but escape as the wolf shakes his fist. The wolf is standing by a palm tree, and a coconut drops from its palms to bonk him on the head. The pigs give the money to their mother, who hugs all three of them at once. The film then shifts back to the live-action children.

A few months later, after the finished film had been shown to Walt for his approval, Amador invited Justice, Atencio, and Gene Armstrong of the Disney Studio's Foreign Department, along with their wives, to visit Mexico for ten days. The Disney staff was treated like royalty. At the Mexico City airport, they were greeted by a mariachi band and their wives given bouquets of roses. One evening at a special dinner, as guests of honor of the First Lady of Mexico, Justice and Atencio were given gold medals for their work.

A Disney press release from fall 1963 announced:

> *The Three Sleepy Pigs*, a new four-minute segment of animation in Spanish, has been produced by Walt for incorporation in a live-action Mexican feature called *Cri-Cri, El Grillito Cantor*, or in English, *Cri-Cri, the Little Singing Cricket*. The feature itself is based on the life of Gabilondo Solar, a famous south of the border song writer, while Walt's contribution to it is based on Solar's popular ballad "Los Cochinitos Dormilones".
>
> Proceeds of the feature, which is set for widespread theatrical release throughout Mexico beginning in October, will go to the Institute for the Protection of Mexican Children, an organization that maintains thirty-two plants engaged in the packaging and shipping of food to millions of school-age youngsters all over the country.

Justice and Atencio were invited back to Mexico again in November 1963 to attend an international film festival, where the completed film was to be given an award. Tragically, the screening was during the same time that President Kennedy was assassinated. Justice and Atencio attended, and the film festival continued, but Bill told me that he still remembers how deeply the people at the festival expressed their sympathy when they discovered he was a citizen of the United States.

In December 1933, Walt told an interviewer:

> These cartoon comedies last for a long time. They are still showing the first Mickey Mouse comedy after nine years. Maybe ten years from now the big bad wolf will still be huffing and puffing before the door to the house of bricks.

Although they have been eclipsed by other Disney animated stars, at one time the Three Little Pigs were cartoon superstars whose huge success allowed the Disney Studios to briefly live high on the hog and create even greater triumphs.

Snow White
Christmas Premiere

*Who says there is no Santy Claus? It seems to me that
Walt Disney tonight in giving this feature to the
children of the world is indeed the modern Santa Claus.*
— Jesse Lasky, film pioneer, with credits
that include *The Covered Wagon* (1923) and
The Ten Commandments (1923), December 21, 1937

*One thing I do know is that this picture is the best Christmas
present the children of Hollywood could possibly have.*
— Louella Parsons, Hollywood columnist, December 21, 1937

*Walt Disney ... brings to motion pictures a new medium for a greater
art. It looks like a Snow White Christmas for all.*
— Narrator, RKO Pathé newsreel, December 1937

Snow White and the Seven Dwarfs premiered at the Carthay
Circle Theater in Hollywood on the night of December 21,
1937. Countless articles and several good books have been
written about this innovative film, but never a detailed look
at its memorable premiere at the Carthay Circle Theater.

The first cleaned-up animation drawings for *Snow White*
were taken to Ink and Paint on January 4, 1937, and were
put under the camera nine weeks later to be filmed. The last
cels were painted on November 27, 1937, and final
photography took place on December 1, 1937. There was a
sneak preview at a Pomona theater on December 6, 1937.

Wilfred Jackson, one of the sequence directors, recalled:

> The preview was unsettling. The audience seemed to be enjoying the film, laughing, applauding. But about three quarters of the way through, one-third of them got up and walked out. Everybody else kept responding enthusiastically to *Snow White* right to the end, but we were concerned about that third. Later we found out they were local college students who had to get back for their ten p.m. dormitory curfew.

The Carthay Circle Theater was a movie palace designed in Spanish Mission Revival style by architect Dwight Gibbs. The 1,500 seat theater opened in 1926 at 6316 San Vicente Boulevard in the mid-Wilshire district. Along with Grauman's Chinese Theater, the Carthay Circle hosted more big West Coast movie premieres than any other Hollywood theater (*Gone With the Wind* premiered there in 1939).

A glimpse of what the theater looked like at the time of *Snow White* can be seen in the *Our Gang* film *The Big Premiere*, released March 9, 1940. The first five minutes of this film was shot on location at the Carthay Circle, where the gang of children tried to crash a film premiere.

In 1929, Walt decided to produce a new animated series, the *Silly Symphonies*, with its first installment entitled *Skeleton Dance*. However, Walt's distributor didn't want to release the cartoon, but wanted more Mickey Mouse cartoons, instead.

Walt found a salesman he knew at a local pool hall, gave him a copy of *Skeleton Dance*, and convinced him to contact Fred Miller, owner of the Carthay Circle Theater. Miller liked the cartoon and booked it into his theater for August 1929. It was a huge hit and gave Walt plenty of positive reviews to convince his distributor to book the film in other theaters.

This success convinced Miller to take a chance on the first feature-length animated cartoon, *Snow White and the Seven Dwarfs*, which premiered at his Carthay Circle Theater in December 1937. The film had already been booked, sight unseen, as the Christmas attraction at Radio City Music Hall, but for his peers Walt wanted a Hollywood premiere to demonstrate that his work in animation was comparable to the work done in live-action films. Walt remembered:

> All the Hollywood brass turned out for my cartoon! That was the thing. And it went way back to when I first came out here

and I went to my first premiere. I'd never seen one in my life. I saw all these Hollywood celebrities coming in and I just had a funny feeling. I just hoped that some day they'd be going in to a premiere of a cartoon. Because people would depreciate the cartoon. You know, they'd kind of look down.

Ken Anderson, talking to Disney historian Paul Anderson, remembered that night, when the Disney animators in tuxedos were completely unprepared for the reaction of the celebrities:

So then there came the premiere of the film. It was a big deal. We all had monkey suits the first night. We were wearing these; we were really dressed up in clothes that weren't ours. We were standing around trying to listen to what the big shots were saying. And these stars were all coming. We were looking at these stars. And they were coming to this thing to see it and they were pretty off-hand about it. They came, "Oh, what the hell. It's a damn cartoon. We wouldn't waste any time on this damn thing or not if it was up to us to do it." And so they were kind of put upon to do this thing.

And they came, they walked in the theater, did this kind of down their nose thing. And they filled the theater. When they left, they were all talking about the story. In fact, you can't really begin to convey what they felt. Because they were astounded. They stood and they clapped and they had a terrific time at the end of the thing. And they were all kids again. These people were just moved by this thing, this cartoon. They could not understand it. We were never prepared for this type of reception. And, boy, they were crowding around Walt. And each of us. They crowded all around, "What did you do?" And such and such. We're standing out there in the foyer and these people just went on and on and on and on about this marvelous picture. And I, for one, and I know everybody must have felt the same way, was thrilled.

That bright starlit night was fairly cold. Animator Marc Davis, who was not invited to the premiere nor could he afford a ticket, remembered trying to dress up warmly to stand with over thirty thousand other people to see the celebrities and top Disney staff enter the theater, and then quickly left once the film started. There were approximately one hundred and fifty policemen there to maintain order.

A long canopy stretched from the theater to the edge of the sidewalk. It covered a deep blue carpet for the many film executives and glamorous celebrities who had come out for a premiere that was unusual even for Hollywood. A small elevated platform was there so that celebrities like Charlie Chaplin, Ed Sullivan, Joe Penner, and the actors who portrayed Amos'n'Andy could be interviewed briefly for the radio. The glare of floodlights surrounded the theater, as searchlight beams waved across the sky.

An RKO Pathé newsreel proclaimed:

> Blasé Hollywood accustomed to gala openings turns out for the most spectacular of them all, the world premiere of the million-and-a-half-dollar fantasy *Snow White and the Seven Dwarfs*.

Those celebrities included Marlene Dietrich, Preston Foster, Shirley Temple, Bob "Bazooka" Burns, Charles Correll and Freeman Gosden (Amos'n'Andy), Joe Penner, Helen Vincent, Fred Perry, George McCall, Charlie Chaplin with Paulette Goddard, Gail Patrick, Ed Sullivan, Clark Gable and Carol Lombard, Norma Shearer, Judy Garland, Charles Laughton and Elsa Lanchester, Jack Benny and Mary Livingstone, George Burns and Gracie Allen, Cary Grant, and many more.

Roy O. Disney had cleverly invited Joseph Rosenberg (who had arranged for the Bank of America to loan money to the Disney brothers for the film) and the board of directors of Bank of America.

The distributor, RKO, teamed with the Disney Studios to promote the film. In the weeks before the premiere, more than a thousand posters decorated billboards around the Los Angeles area. There were promotional visits by Walt and his characters to such radio shows as the Lux Radio Theater and Charlie McCarthy to make audiences aware of the film.

Bleachers were erected to accommodate four thousand fans, though almost ten times that number showed up. Hundreds of people waited long hours in the brisk night air to catch a glimpse of the stars. The show had been sold out for many, many days, but a long line of people were at the ticket box office buying tickets for future shows thirty minutes before the premiere.

There was a full orchestra, including the singers who had recorded the movie's songs and who performed under the direction of Manny Harman. Usherettes wore Snow White costumes. NBC radio was there for a coast-to-coast half-hour broadcast with announcer Don Wilson. A special display on the street was described on the radio like this:

> Believe it or not, ladies and gentlemen, Dwarf Land was moved to Hollywood. Down at the corner of Wilshire Boulevard just outside the Carthay Circle, Walt Disney built a replica of the dwarf cottage that appeared in the film. The cottage is only ten feet high and not quite so wide but every kid in this town has been through it. Outside are mushrooms three feet tall painted yellow and blue and pink. Weird looking trees with eyes that light up and long arms that reach out and grab at you just like the way they grab at Snow White.
>
> There's a little Dwarfs' mill wheel and a diamond mine sparkling in the spotlights that illuminate the entire scene. The Dwarfs garden stretches for about two blocks. It's filled with all sorts of strange looking statuary and stumps and toadstools and flowers by the hundreds and hundreds. A stream flows through the garden that turns the mill wheel. The crowds stand around watching the antics of the seven little dwarfs. Actual dwarfs dressed in quaint medieval costumes who work the diamond mine, rake the garden, run in and out of the house, putting on a great show.

An article from *Movie Mirror* magazine in 1938 discussed this "Snow White Island":

> Snow White Island: Maybe you think that the dwarf's cottage, their mine, the mountain climbed by the wicked queen, and all those strange scenes you saw in Snow White and the Seven Dwarfs exist only on paper, just so many colored lines drawn by a cartoonist. Actually all these things existed to be touched, felt, and photographed by some half million people who visited The Island during the four months' run of the movie at Carthay Circle in Los Angeles.
>
> Since so much interest was aroused by travelers to the dwarfs' country, we delved into the matter and came up with some pertinent information. The Island is a park, surrounded by a road, which is owned by the Native Sons and Daughters of California. It is almost 900 feet long, and on this was built the land of the seven dwarfs. It cost nearly

$10,000 to erect, and bills for lighting and watchmen (there were four) ran $6,500.

You could see the mountain, the wishing well, the fantastic forest—all real as life and twice as exciting. The first day it was finished, a guard counted 1,010 cars circling the display in one hour. That was just a starter.

The gnomes were first made of plaster, but inquisitive kids, poking Dopey to see if he'd talk, forced Disney to remake them all in more enduring concrete. Souvenir hunters were a constant menace, one fellow stealing a bat out of a tree and flying off with it before the guard could catch him.

Thousands of requests came in offering to buy sections; all were refused. When the movie ended its run at Carthay Circle, the entire forest, the mountain, the cottage—all disappeared to be stored away. In three days, like magic, green grass covered the park and the Island once more dozed in the sun, as if Snow White and her crew had never been.

This was probably the first time that the Disney Studios attempted to do costumed characters for such a star-studded event. Mickey Mouse, Minnie Mouse, and Donald Duck were there looking as if the famous three-dimensional Charlotte Clark dolls had been blown up to life size.

Mickey and Minnie had the famous "pie-eyes", but the missing "slice" was used by animators to indicate a highlight to show where the round eye was looking. Both slices should be pointing in the same direction. On these faces, the slices were facing each other so Mickey and Minnie looked cross-eyed.

The costumes were typical "pajama" costumes, meaning that the costume followed the shape of the person's body. The costumes for the dwarfs were even worse and looked like blow-up dolls from a mail-order company, with mouths frozen open in an oval shape and dead eyes not anchored but staring straight out.

Animator Bill Justice, who attended the premiere and who, decades later, would be in charge of designing Disneyland character costumes, remembered

When Snow White was finally completed, all employees were invited to the premiere at the Carthay Circle Theater. Everybody went, and as it turned out, enjoyed a success beyond anyone's dreams. My most vivid memory of the evening, however, was the dwarf costumes. To help generate some atmosphere the Company made one of its first attempts at costumed characters. They must have been an after-thought because they sure weren't close to the model sheets. It's a wonder those dwarfs didn't scare people away.

To explain the process involved in making *Snow White*, a large display of original art was set up in a gallery-type setting around the corner from the Carthay entrance. The outdoor display included black-and-white photos as well as cels, backgrounds, and layout drawings. Above the protective lattice work were huge three-dimensional heads of the dwarfs.

Clarence Nash, the voice of Donald Duck, was also there, with one of his early Donald Duck ventriloquist dummies. Looking at stills from the premiere, it is amusing to see that everyone's eyes are focused on the small dummy and not on Clarence, who was happily quacking away.

Mickey Mouse, Minnie Mouse, and Donald Duck were interviewed by Wilson on the radio. Mickey was nervous and Donald was upset that someone seemed to have stolen his ticket. Donald starts singing for the radio audience as Mickey, Minnie, and Pluto try to shut him up and take him away.

Donald wasn't the only one who didn't have a ticket; neither did Adrianna Caselotti, who voiced Snow White, nor Harry Stockwell, father of actor Dean Stockwell, who voiced the Prince. Caselotti loved telling this story:

> When we got to the door, the girl said, "May I have your tickets, please?" I said, "Tickets? We don't have any tickets — I'm Snow White and this is Prince Charming!" She said, "I don't care who you are, you don't get in unless you've got tickets!" So, we sneaked in when she wasn't looking and we went upstairs to one side of the balcony and I stood there watching myself on the screen and all those movie stars clapping for me. Boy! Did I get a thrill out of that!

Walt was interviewed for the radio:

> Well, I'm very happy about everything. It's been a lot of fun making it and we're very happy that it's been given this big premiere here tonight and all these people turning out to take a look at it and I hope they aren't too disappointed. Well, our favorites are the little dwarfs. There's seven of them. We got names for them all that sort of fit their personality such as Doc whose the pompous leader and then there's old Happy, the smiling little fellow and

Grumpy, the old sourpuss, the woman hater and ... I can't remember them all here tonight. [Laughs] And little Dopey. He's sort of our pet, you know. He hasn't any lines. He doesn't talk. Well, I don't know. I guess he just never tried.

Announcer: "Are you going in to watch the premiere?"

Walt: "Yes, and have my wife hold my hand."

Amazingly, since all the publicity emphasized only Walt's name, another Disney staffer was also interviewed. Dave Hand, introduced as the supervising director of *Snow White and the Seven Dwarfs*, the general manager of Disney Studios, and "Walt Disney's right-hand man", told the radio audience:

At times it appeared to be an almost impossible task. The fact that we did it is a tribute to the guiding genius of Walt and the whole-hearted efforts and perfect cooperation of the seven hundred artists and technicians of the studio staff. We found we have only scratched the surface of the wonderful possibilities of the full-length animated feature. We have recently started work on two new feature-length features. Our staff thrives on tough assignments. We are hoping to produce things far above anything imaginable.

Animator Ward Kimball. who had worked many months on a scene of the dwarfs eating soup that was cut from the final film before it went to ink and paint, attended the premiere with his wife, Betty, and shared these memories:

I was at the premiere in 1937. We were worried. It was being shown at the Carthay Circle Hollywood. We didn't know how it would go over. Walt was on pins and needles. We sat down. Movie stars were sitting in seats. Betty and I sat behind Clark Gable and Carol Lombard and he got upset when Snow White was poisoned. He started to sniffle and borrowed a handkerchief. That type of reaction is hard to get with a cartoon because after all you are exaggerating and caricaturing and the tendency is to do a put on. Not Walt! I think that was the key to his secret.

In the beginning the audience warmed up to the first little gags. Gradually, there was this buzz that arose with the whole theater. They laughed at the gags, especially that dancing thing with Dopey on Sneezy's shoulders. It just tore up the place. You knew what was going to happen. Sneezy lets go and off goes Dopey. That was Walt's timing. He criticized the first version. He said, "Blow Dopey out of the screen and then you don't go and see what happened to him. You cut to Snow

White and she's laughing and all the dwarves are laughing. And then go to Dopey and he's up there swinging and wiggling his ears." On the night of the premiere, that scene got the biggest laugh. That was Walt's timing.

Anyway, when Snow White is laid out on the marble bier and in comes the prince and everybody in the audience is sniffing and I heard people blowing their noses. It was weird. It really got to them. I knew the picture was a winner because they laughed at the gags and cried at a silly thing of a cartoon of a girl who comes to at the prince's first kiss.

It's hard to believe but the people in the audience were really blowing their noses. I heard all this noise and I said, "Betty, let's run out and watch them come out in the lobby." They came out and they were rummaging around putting on dark glasses so no one would know they had been crying and their eyes were all red. They were wiping their eyes. It was a very moving experience. We knew it was a winner then.

Layout artist Ken O'Connor shared with Steve Hulett:

The audience was wildly enthusiastic. They even applauded the background and layouts when no animation was on the screen. I was sitting near John Barrymore when the shot of the Queen's castle above the mist came on with the Queen poling across the marsh in a little boat. He was bouncing up and down in his seat he was so excited. Barrymore was an artist as well as an actor, and he knew the kind of work that went into something like that.

Animator Wolfgang Reitherman recalled:

The audience was so taken by the magic of what they had seen that they applauded after individual sequences, just as though they were watching a stage play. I've never seen anything quite like it since.

As the house lights came up, the audience — which was already applauding, rose to its feet. "It was the most receptive, enthusiastic audience I have ever seen," animator Shamus Culhane remembered.

Walt, who appeared on stage with his wife, said

I always dreamed that one day I would attend a gala premiere in Hollywood of one of my cartoons. Tonight you've made it come true. You make me feel like one of you.

Snow White played at the Carthay Circle for four months. The Spanish-language version, *Blanca Nieves y los Siete*

Enanos, was unveiled at the Carthay Circle on Sunday, February 27, 1938, and became a regular Sunday afternoon feature during the remainder of *Snow White's* run there.

Animator Woolie Reitherman recalled:

> I ran into Walt the next morning after the premiere. Instead of talking about how he could now take a little rest, he began talking about the next animated feature, and how he wanted to get started right away. There was only one Walt Disney.

The Disney connection with the Carthay Circle doesn't end with *Snow White.* The Carthay Circle was one of only fourteen theaters to be fitted with the full Fantasound equipment for the presentation of *Fantasia* just a few years later in 1940.

At the Academy Award ceremony on February 23, 1939, Walt received a special Oscar for *Snow White and the Seven Dwarfs.* It was one large statue and seven small Oscars. The inscription read:

> To Walt Disney for *Snow White and the Seven Dwarfs* recognized as a significant screen innovation which has charmed millions and pioneered a great new entertainment field for the motion picture cartoon.

It was presented by nine-year-old Shirley Temple, who at the premiere had posed for pictures with the costumed dwarfs who were almost exactly her size.

The final box office gross for the first release of *Snow White* was close to $8.5 million, making it the highest-grossing Hollywood film up to that time. This was when adults in general paid a quarter and children a dime to see a movie. That record-breaking gross would be broken two years later with the release of *Gone With the Wind,* but at that moment in time, it really was a Snow White Christmas.

Destino

According to a 2008 Disney press release:

> *Destino* began in 1946 as a collaboration between Walt Disney and the famed surrealist painter Salvador Dali. A first-hand example of Disney's interest in avant-garde and experimental work in animation, *Destino* was to be awash with Dali's iconic melting clocks, marching ants, and floating eyeballs. However, *Destino* was not completed at that time. In 2003, it was rediscovered by Walt's nephew, Roy E. Disney, who took on the challenge of bringing the creation of these two great artists to fruition.

Dali contacted Walt Disney as early as 1937 while on a trip to Hollywood. During that era, Walt was always bringing high-profile artists, writers, and other creative people to the Disney Studios to share ideas with his artists.

However, it was a dinner party nearly a decade later, in 1945, that resulted in an official collaboration between Disney and Dali. At the time, Dali was in Hollywood to design sets for a dream sequence in the Alfred Hitchcock film *Spellbound* (1945), and he was staying with Warner Bros. Studio head Jack Warner and his wife to paint their portraits. Walt attended a dinner party at the Warner home, where he and Dali bonded immediately, beginning a friendship that would last until Walt's passing two decades later.

Besides the mutual respect each man had for the other's innovative art, Dali and Disney were workaholics who loved controlling their work, were terrific self-promoters, and were filled with a seemingly endless supply of ideas, optimism, and humor. So this unusual friendship began with a good many strong connections already in place.

Dali officially moved into a room on the third floor of the Animation building at the Disney Studios in 1946. Originally, the project was top-secret, because they had not settled on exactly what that project would be. At the time, due to financial and labor restrictions, Walt was producing "package films" — a feature comprised of several short, self-contained segments. Walt had purchased a romantic Mexican ballad by Armando Dominquez entitled "Destino" that he thought might be a good vehicle for South American singer and dancer Dora Luz, who had recently appeared in *The Three Caballeros* (1945). "Destino" was intended to be a segment in another upcoming package film, and Walt felt Dali could provide interesting backgrounds for the piece.

Dali disliked the song but loved the word "destino" ("destiny"), and his imagination began to run wild as he created an entire elaborate scenario. Dali visualized two lovers in an ever-changing dreamlike landscape, and the effect of time and other obstacles on that relationship. It would combine animation, live action (ballet dancers in a Dali-esque landscape), and special effects, with a running time of six to eight minutes. As work progressed, Dali added new ideas and symbolism so that the story became ever more complicated and unwieldy.

"It is a magical exposition of the problem of life in the labyrinth of time," proclaimed Dali. (Walt added that it was really "just a simple story about a young girl in search of her real love".)

Upon Dali's arrival in 1946, Walt announced:

> We have to keep breaking new trails. Ordinarily, good story ideas don't come easily and have to be fought for. Dali is communicative. He bubbles with new ideas.

Dali declared, "I have been given absolute freedom! That is paradise for the artist!" In *Dali News*, his own publication, he wrote:

> Dali and Disney will produce the first motion picture of the "Never Seen Before", and the most rigorous secrecy on this subject will prevail.

Walt assigned artists John Hench and Bob Cormack to assist Dali so that his visions could be adapted to the necessities of animation. Dali painted the key scenes, while Hench and Cormack made continuity sketches to segue from one image to another. Dali painted some key scenes in water-color, a medium he never used for his exhibition paintings.

As Hench remembered:

> Walt came in and looked at the work from time to time. He saw the storyboards in progress and decided to let Dali go ahead and see what would happen. Dali was given complete freedom.

But, Hench said, that didn't prevent Walt from con-tributing ideas.

> Well, they had a Roman god and it represented a blockage to a labyrinth, but the hummingbird opened it and it became a passageway. I don't know if people got that or not but that was Walt's suggestion.

Perhaps that explains why Dali's painting of the head of Jupiter from the film was framed and hung in Walt's office until Walt passed away. Dali said that Jupiter determined the course of all human affairs, which is why a giant sundial emerged from that great stone face in the film.

As the cryptic and flamboyant Dali put it:

> Now the metamorphosis! We see the face of Jupiter, which becomes a big stone sun dial. His hair is a magical arch. Time stops the way into the labyrinth of life, and true love is not possible until time is destructed.

The film is filled with Dali symbolism. The ravaging ants signify humanity's desolation. The crutches suggest that mankind cannot live without support. The famous melting watches denote the death of time. The idea of a sculpture coming to life was something Dali originally proposed for Hitchcock's *Spellbound*. However, actress Ingrid Bergman vetoed the idea in the dream sequence, because Dali wanted to cover her with live ants when she came to life. Dali was not adverse to borrowing ideas from his previous work. The heroine in *Destino* seems similar to the woman from his painting *Suburbs of the Paranoiac-Critical Town* done nearly a decade earlier.

There were scenes of the girl running up a cliff pursued by a horde of figures whose heads were eyeballs, representing the eyes of public opinion trying to prevent her from achieving happiness. There are drawings of these eyeballs flaring like giant flashbulbs on contemporary cameras — just like today's paparazzi. To further emphasize that theme, there are drawings of newspapers with scorpion legs chasing the helpless girl.

For more than two months, Dali arrived by 9:00 AM each day at the Disney Studios to diligently work at his easel. He often was accompanied by his wife Gala, who not only helped inspire him but interpreted for him, since he often chatted away in an odd mixture of French, Spanish, broken English, and his own unique language. Dali sometimes had lunch with Walt and Hench in the Disney Studios' Coral Room restaurant. Disney Legend Ward Kimball remembered that Gala would sometimes pin directions to Dali's house on Salvador's jacket when he came to the Studio by himself, so that if he got on a bus, someone would be able to help him find his way home.

For several months, Dali also worked out of his own studio at Monterrey, California, near the old Del Monte Lodge Hotel. Hench would commute there on weekends.

As interest in the project was starting to wane at the Studio, Hench put together what might be considered a fifteen-second "animatic" of a scene to help everyone visualize what the finished film might look like. He explained:

> I thought I'd shoot this one scene because I thought it was so astonishing. It was an appearance of the female character, the ballerina, and it was an empty field with just a white ball floating on a field and then two turtles, one approaching from the left and then the right, and I used sliding fills because I didn't have an animator that I could use. But we pulled these slides across and then when they met, the negative space turned into the ballerina and the ball was her head. And I thought, yeah, I can show that to Walt. He may just go ahead with the thing anyway. But it was very surprising and I thought it would interest him. And it did interest him too but he put it aside, though. Years afterward, whenever Walt and I talked about Dali, he always said we should have made that thing anyway.

Hench further recalled:

> Salvador was back in Monterrey, so once I finished filming the test, I drove up to show it to him. I tipped the manager of this little theater that was showing some B Western to

show it after the film was over and the audience had left. The lights went out, and Salvador saw his artwork in full motion. He loved it. Just then the projectionist came out and practically roared, "What was THAT?" Dali and I looked at each other, and we both knew that it was a unique moment in art.

There were two completely different storyboards and five different written treatments, and none of them give any clue to what Dali intended the narrative to be.

Walt told Dali that *Destino* was unfortunately canceled because Walt felt — supposedly urged by his film distributor RKO — that the market for package films was gone. This didn't prevent Walt from releasing *Melody Time* two years later, considered the last of the package films.

Actually, the true final package film, little-known *Music Land*, was released on October 5, 1955. Disney had by then created its own company to release its films to theaters, but still owed its current distributor, RKO, one more film under their existing contract. To fulfill that commitment, Disney took a combination of four sequences from *Make Mine Music* and five from *Melody Time* to create a new compilation film, *Music Land*. The poster boldly declared that the film was "The Big Parade of Mirth and Melody!" *Music Land* was never shown again, except once during a retrospective called "Tribute to Walt Disney" at the National Film Theater in 1970.

Walt said:

> It was certainly no fault of Dali's that the project we were working on was not completed. It was simply a case of policy changes in our distribution plan.

Diane Disney Miller recalled:

> Salvador Dali came to our home and rode Dad's train, and although it was the middle of summer, he was dressed in a black overcoat, with a collar and cravat. He sat on a little boxcar with his cane upright in front of him.

Dali remained convinced that he and Disney would collaborate on something eventually, perhaps even reviving *Destino*. Walt did, in fact, visit the artist at his home in Spain several times during the 1950s. They talked about a possible animated sequence from Dante's *Divine Comedy* (which Dali had illustrated for the Italian government), an animated feature version of *Don Quixote*, and even El Cid — Dali supposedly developed a story concept — possibly with a live-action Errol Flynn. Walt told people he thought that Dali was "a friend, a very swell guy, and a person whom I thoroughly enjoyed working with."

Walt prepared an Art of Animation museum exhibit in 1958 that would tour the United States, Europe, and Japan, then eventually end up as a display attraction in Tomorrowland at Disneyland. This exhibit was to promote the upcoming release of *Sleeping Beauty* in 1959. To put the exhibit together, Walt sent people to the animation "morgue", where animation art was kept. Walt wanted some specific pieces, and not just cel setups but backgrounds, concept art, story sketches, and more. There were three versions of this exhibit, each featuring different original art.

Walt felt the inclusion of art done by Dali would add another dimension to, and generate more publicity for, the exhibit. He was shocked to discover that practically all of the major Dali art had disappeared from the morgue. Walt never had the heart to tell Dali what had happened.

When Dave Smith started the Disney Archives in 1970, he appealed to Disney employees to donate any Disneyana in their possession. Five Dali paintings mysteriously re-appeared, and they were cleaned and put safely away. Also, in the 1970s, Albert Field, a New York-based appraiser, approached Dali and showed him some unsigned, newly discovered artwork from *Destino*. Dali couldn't distinguish the drawings by Hench from his own work, so he signed them all. Roy E. Disney stated:

> They [Hench and Dali] worked closely together to the point where they couldn't tell each other's drawings apart. John was the only one in the world, until he died, who could sit down with us and say: "That's mine; that's his."

There is some dispute over how much *Destino* artwork was recovered by the Disney Studios, although at least one reliable source indicated that fifty-five sketches by Dali and seventy-five by Hench were preserved at the Studio in the early 1990s. Supposedly, the original portfolio for the project had almost 375 sketches and twenty-two completed paintings.

Robert Descharnes, one of the foremost experts on Dali

artwork, has pointed out that some enterprising seller has faked Dali signatures on some of the unsigned *Destino* originals, and even painted some phony *Destino* artwork that has been sold over the years.

In 1997, John Hench said:

> Walt abandoned *Destino* very regretfully. He hoped to pick it up later. He had gotten a great kick out of the project and besides admiring Dali's talent, he liked him personally.

While working with actress Bette Midler on the interstitial in *Fantasia 2000* that referenced Dali's art, executive producer Roy E. Disney thought about using that art to promote the film:

> During the filming, I learned from one of the attorneys that we actually didn't have legal possession of the Dali art, because the contract signed in 1945 stated that it wouldn't become the company's until the film was made. When I've told this story, some people think my motivation was to make a lot of money by acquiring the valuable artwork. The fun of it was the idea of finishing something that had grown to almost mythic proportions, and getting it out to the public.

Roy Disney decided to complete the film with input from Hench. Approximately twenty percent of the finished film had computer-generated art to help move the virtual camera around objects. It was directed by Dominique Monfery and produced by Baker Bloodworth, who explained:

> Some of it [the art] was incomprehensible. Dali had always said, "If you understand this, then I've failed." We pulled together the love story and compressed. And yet there is a long baseball sequence that no one could make sense of that we only touched on. We were true to the look that Dali painted. Dali would start with an image, which would become another one, and just when you thought it would hold on that image, it would become something else. Monfrey took the best of the drawings and then went back to the Dali works to find patterns.

About the infamous extended baseball sequence, Dali said:

> Baseball, it is fascinating. About the game, I know nothing. But as an artist, I am obsessed!

Destino played at several film festivals in 2003, including the Telluride Film Festival, the New York Film Festival, and the Chicago Film Festival, and it was nominated for an Academy Award but did not win. Some people love the film, while others find it incomprehensible and boring, but there is no denying it is a unique achievement of two distinct artistic innovators.

The Alice in Wonderland That Never Was

It [Alice in Wonderland] fascinated me the first time I read it as a schoolboy and after I started making animated cartoons, I acquired the film rights to it. Carroll with his nonsense and fantasy furnished a balance between seriousness and enjoyment which everybody needed then and still needs today.

— Walt Disney, *American Weekly*, August 11, 1946

There were three silent film versions of *Alice's Adventures in Wonderland* (1903, 1910, 1915), and while Walt Disney never mentioned seeing any of them, it is possible that he might have seen at least one, either upon its release or in preparation for his own film version. But he *had* read the book.

He had also not only read but studied and recommended *Animated Cartoons* (1920) by E.G. Lutz. In that book's final chapter, Lutz discusses the future of animation:

> Lewis Carroll's *Alice in Wonderland* is a good example of the type of fanciful tale on the order of which animated cartoons could be made for children. The Mad Hatter would make an admirable figure to pace across the screen. An artist desiring to be the author of an animated story built on the model of Carroll's classics would need a gleeful imagination and a turn for the fantastic. And he would require, besides, if he hoped to draw characters of a par with Tenniel's depictions, more than the ordinary qualifications of a screen draftsman.

This suggestion might have inspired Walt to title his successful animated series about a live-action little girl interacting with a fantastical world of cartoon characters the *Alice Comedies*, and call its first installment *Alice's Wonderland*.

The year 1932 marked the centennial of the birth of Lewis Carroll (the pseudonym for the Reverend Charles Dodgson), who wrote the adventures of Alice, inspired by the child Alice Liddell. That year, Liddell, who grew up to be Mrs. Alice Hargreaves, visited the United States to receive an honorary degree and make personal appearances. In June 1932, she viewed three Mickey Mouse cartoons on a theatrical screen, and was quite pleased. She felt that Carroll would have enjoyed the new medium in which to tell stories.

At the time, silent screen star Mary Pickford, one of the founding members of United Artists, asked Walt Disney to film a feature-length version of *Alice in Wonderland*, with Mary playing the role of Alice in an animated Wonderland created by Disney and his artists. Pickford was hugely excited about the project, did costume tests for the character, and issued press releases. The film was planned for black-and-white, although some of the costume tests that survive were done in three-strip Technicolor. Walt did not appear to be equally enthusiastic, and when he heard that Paramount Pictures was producing an all-star, live-action film for release in December 1933, he ended work on the project.

Walt told *The New York Times Magazine* (June 3, 1934):

> We have been asked to make *Alice in Wonderland* with Mary Pickford. We have discouraged the idea, for we aren't ready for a feature yet.

Prompted by the success of *Snow White and the Seven Dwarfs*, Walt purchased several projects for future animated features, including the rights to *Alice in Wonderland* in 1938 — in particular, the rights to reproduce the original Tenniel drawings. Again, Walt told *The New York Times Magazine* (March 1938):

> *Alice in Wonderland* should never have been done in the realistic medium of motion picture [referring to the 1933 Paramount film] but we regard it as a natural for our medium.

Between December 1938 and April 1941, Walt held at least eleven documented meetings with members of his staff to discuss the possibilities of making *Alice in Wonderland*.

In a January 4, 1939, story meeting, Walt said:

I'll tell you what has been wrong with every one of these productions on Carroll. They have depended on his dialogue to be funny. But if you can use some of Carroll's phrases that are funny, use them. If they aren't funny, throw them out. There is a spirit behind Carroll's story. It's fantasy, imagination, screwball logic ... but it must be funny. I mean funny to an American audience. To hell with the English audiences or the people who love Carroll ... I'd like to make it more or less a 1940 or 1945 version-right up to date. I wouldn't put in any modern slang that wouldn't fit, but the stuff can be modernized. I want to put my money into something that will go in Podunk, Iowa, and they will go in and laugh at it because they have experienced it. They wouldn't laugh at a lot of English sayings that they've never heard or that don't mean anything to them. Yet, we can keep it very much Carroll — keep his spirit.

Disney storyman Al Perkins researched Carroll and his work, and produced a 161-page analysis of *Alice in Wonderland* that broke the book down chapter-by-chapter, pointing out the possibilities for animation. Some of his suggestions were later used in the final animated feature, including the idea that the White Rabbit should wear glasses because Carroll once commented that he thought the White Rabbit should have spectacles, even though Tenniel never drew the character that way. Perkins also felt that the Cheshire Cat should be expanded and appear in other scenes of the story, and that the watch fixed by the Mad Hatter and the March Hare should belong to the White Rabbit.

Beginning June 1939, British artist David Hall spent about three months to produce roughly four hundred paintings, drawings, and sketches using Perkins' analysis as a guide. Hall had a background as a production artist in the film industry, with such credits as DeMille's *The King of Kings* (1927). Story conferences at the time were not helpful to Hall, because Walt felt that his people didn't understand the spirit of the story.

For instance, they had suggested changing the croquet match into a football game. According to the story conference notes, Walt considered this approach at humor to be "Donald Duck gags" and that:

> I think the book is funnier than the way you guys have got it. Get in and study characters and personalities, and that's where the real humor will come from.

In November 1939, the Disney Studios filmed a Leica reel (a film of the concept drawings and story sketches with a soundtrack to get an idea of story continuity and flow) using Hall's artwork. The soundtrack included Cliff "Jiminy Cricket" Edwards doing the voice of the Talking Bottle (later changed in the final film to a talking doorknob). After viewing the reel (which has since disappeared), Walt said:

> There are certain things in there that I like very much and there are other things in there that I think we ought to tear right out. I don't think there would be any harm in letting this thing sit for a while. Everyone is stale now. You'll look at it again and maybe have another idea on it. That's the way it works for me. I still feel that we can stick close to Alice in Wonderland and make it look like it and feel like it, you know.

David Hall left the Disney Studios in January 1940.

At a meeting on April 8, 1941, Walt brought up the project again:

> I've been wondering if we could do this thing with a live-action girl. Here's the value in the live girl over trying to animate it — we can animate a girl, make her run around and things — but carrying this story is different. There's a lot of story here with the girl, and trying to carry the story with a cartoon girl puts us in a hell of a spot. We might, in the whole picture, have, say a dozen complicated trick shots, but the rest of them would be close-ups and working around it. We can get some good characters and good music. There's so much stuff in this business, we could work around the girl.

At the meeting, it was suggested that actress Gloria Jean, who was fourteen at the time and had just appeared as W.C. Fields' niece in *Never Give a Sucker An Even Break*, should be considered for the role of Alice.

The outbreak of World War II halted further work on the project. In 1944, the Disney Studios provided cover art of a massive mushroom and the famous caterpillar for a record album based on *Alice in Wonderland* and read by actress Ginger Rogers, who then was thirty-three years old. The album featured original music composed by Frank Luther and conducted by Victor Young. Besides Rogers, voices on the album included Lou Merrill, Bea Benaderet, Arthur Q. Bryan, Joe Kearns, Ferdy Munier, and Martha Wentworth.

In fall 1945, Walt brought in writer Aldous Huxley to work on the live-action/animation script for what was to become *Alice and the Mysterious Mr. Carroll*. The idea was that the film would star actress Luana Patten, who later appeared in Disney's *Song of the South* (1946) and *So Dear To My Heart* (1949). Huxley was a well-known and prolific English writer best remembered for his novel *Brave New World*, written in 1932 about the anti-utopian London of 2540 A.D., where the human spirit is subjected to conditioning and control.

Highly regarded for his ideas as well as for his writing, Huxley — through his friend novelist Anita Loos — spent time in Hollywood in the 1940s working on such screenplays as MGM's *Madame Curie*, *Pride and Prejudice*, and *Jane Eyre*, although his work was not always credited or used in its entirety.

The Disney Studios agreed to pay Huxley $7,500 to write the treatment for the *Alice* film. They paid him $2,500 on October 18, 1945, with the balance to be paid upon delivery of the final treatment, no later than January 15, 1946. Huxley delivered his fourteen-page treatment on November 23, 1945. The Disney Studios also took out an option for Huxley to do the final screenplay for $15,000, a job which would have included "all additions, changes and revisions". Huxley delivered the first draft of the script on December 5, 1945.

Walt Disney had been seriously thinking of diversifying into live-action, since World War II had shown him the vulnerability of his business when his talented animators were drafted into the service and when foreign markets were closed to his films. It became apparent that the time-consuming and costly process of creating animated features would not supply a steady income for the Studio. It was thought that live action could be done quicker and with less upfront investment.

One result of this thinking was *Song of the South*, primarily a live-action film but with animated segments to support the story. Huxley's script was in this same style, with the story of

Carroll and Alice told in live action supported by animated segments of Alice seeking safety from her troubles in her imaginary Wonderland. Huxley tried to set a premise that Carroll and Alice were alike in their love of fantasy, but their personal happiness was thwarted by very stern, no-nonsense people who controlled their lives.

Here is a paraphrasing of Huxley's synopsis for *Alice and the Mysterious Mr. Carroll* from November 1945:

> A letter states that the Queen of England wants to know and meet the author of *Alice in Wonderland*. She has been told he is an Oxford don and that she wishes the vice chancellor of the University, Langham, to discover his identity.
>
> Langham tosses aside the request, since he has other concerns, including the Reverend Charles Dodgson lobbying to become the new librarian. Dodgson loves books and wants to be relieved of his lecturing duties, since he stutters badly when nervous. (The Dodo in Wonderland was named after Dodgson, who sometimes — because of his stutter — would introduce himself as "Do-Do-Dodgson".) Langham is not inclined to endorse Dodgson for the new job, because he feels it is inappropriate for the good reverend to be interested in the theater and in photography. Langham's assistant, Grove, who knows Dodgson quite well and considers him a little eccentric, tries to plead Dodgson's case, to no avail.
>
> Grove is the weak-willed guardian of a little girl named Alice, whose parents are temporarily off in India. Grove has hired Miss Beale to take care of Alice. Miss Beale, a strict, no-nonsense person, dislikes Dodgson because he fills Alice's mind with nonsense. Huxley points out that it is important to establish Alice as "temporarily an orphan at the mercy of a governess and an old man who do not truly understand her or love her."
>
> Dodgson has invited Alice to join him for a theatrical performance of *Romeo and Juliet*, featuring one of his former students now grown into an attractive and talented young woman, Ellen Terry. Miss Beale is outraged and orders Alice to write Dodgson and inform him that she cannot attend because of her "religious principles".
>
> Dodgson visits Terry in the theater, and she immediately guesses that he is the mysterious author Lewis Carroll, because he used to tell her stories of the Cheshire Cat when she was younger. Dodgson begs her to keep his secret, since he is up for

the job of librarian and that, if it were revealed he was the one who wrote the children's book, it would go badly for him. He also talks about bringing Alice to the play the next day.

Mrs. Beale discovers that Alice has not posted the letter to Dodgson but hidden it so she could sneak out and attend the theater with him. Enraged, Beale locks Alice in the garden house. When Grove expresses concern about the severity of Alice's punishment, Miss Beale assures him that this is how it was always done in the best and most pious families. Grove ends by agreeing, as he always does when confronted by a personality stronger than his own.

Miss Beale raises the question of her pension that must be submitted to the Bishop within days (or else wait another two years for the next opportunity). Grove advises her that the Bishop was good friends with Dodgson's father, and so perhaps the reverend could write a recommendation. Miss Beale appears visibly shaken.

Alice is terrified at being locked in the garden house, but Miss Beale informs her that if she does not stop her screaming and pounding, she will remain locked in there both day and night. To escape her terrors, Alice starts to imagine that a hanging rope is the caterpillar from the book and that a stuffed tiger's head is the Cheshire Cat. Eventually, by remembering that in Wonderland there "is a garden at the bottom of every rabbit hole", she finds a small shuttered window and escapes.

She rushes down the street towards the theater, but has some horrendous adventures, including being robbed by street urchins and trying to escape from a policeman after remembering "Miss Beale's blood curdling accounts of what happens to children who fall into the clutches of the Law".

Alice eventually finds her way to the theater, and rushes tearfully to Ellen Terry and the surrounding performers taking a break on stage. She incoherently blurts out her tale. Terry sends for Dodgson, indignant about the way Alice has been treated. Alice confesses her "system of overcoming fear is pretending to be in Wonderland".

Ellen Terry says that is the purpose of theater — to "take people out of Dull Land and Worry Land and carry them into Wonderland".

Terry, joined eventually joined by the other actors, recounts the story of the Red Queen's croquet game, and the film transitions into animation. Dodgson arrives to take Alice home, but Terry insists that Alice stay until Terry has had an opportunity to talk "with that old dragon" who has been persecuting Alice. Dodgson agrees, and joins in on the storytelling that transforms into another animated segment.

At the point in the animated story where the Red Queen yells "Off With Her Head!", the film returns to live action with the appearance of Miss Beale followed by Grove and two policemen. Grove is persuaded to dismiss the policemen, and Terry eloquently convinces Beale of the need to be kinder to Alice. During the discussion, Alice blurts out that Dodgson is really Lewis Carroll. A disgusted and frustrated Grove proclaims that this is the final straw why Dodgson is unfit for the job of librarian, and leaves to confront Langham with the news.

But Langham has no time for Grove, because he has been informed that the Queen is arriving that very afternoon to meet the author of *Alice in Wonderland*, and he fears her reaction to his failure in finding the author. Grove announces he can produce the author and returns to the theater. There, without telling them the reason, other than Langham needs to see them immediately, he gathers Beale, Alice, and Dodgson, and takes them in a cab back to the University.

Langham and the other dignitaries are paying their respects to the Queen. As Langham is about to admit he does not know who Carroll is, Grove arrives and shoves Dodgson forward. Alice is terrified the Queen will cut off his head, but the Queen is quite pleased. When she leaves, Dodgson finds himself lionized by those who had previously looked at him askance.

Even Miss Beale apologizes, and shyly asks for Dodgson's recommendation to the bishop about her pension. Once assured that a pension would retire Miss Beale from teaching any more children in the future, Dodgson warmly agrees.

As the new-found flatterers cluster around Dodgson, they all appear in Alice's eyes to transform into residents of Wonderland, with only Dodgson himself remaining human.

A brief epilogue shows a gothic doorway with the word "Librarian" painted on the door and Dodgson seated comfortably inside at a table, writing, and surrounded by walls of books. A scout comes in and announces the carriage is ready, and Dodgson leaves to visit a nearby park, where children are having a party that includes a Punch and Judy show. Alice runs up to Dodgson to introduce her new governess, a "young and charming girl" who seems to be enjoying the party as much as Alice herself is enjoying it.

A stout, middle-aged woman approaches Dodgson to tell him how much she loves his wonderful book. Dodgson bows, smiles, and hands her a printed card from his pocket, then walks away. The card states: "The Reverend Charles L. Dodgson takes no responsibility for any publication not issued under his own name." The woman looks back up to see Dodgson walking away with Alice and animated characters from Wonderland.

On December 7, 1945, the fourth anniversary of Pearl Harbor, Walt and Huxley met at the Disney Studios (along with Dick Huemer, Joe Grant, D. Koch, Cap Palmer, Bill Cottrell, and Ham Luske) to discuss Huxley's script, completely oblivious to the historical significance of that day.

Huxley had made some significant changes to the screenplay. For example, the transition into Wonderland was shifted from the theater to Dodgson's studio, where Alice is looking through proofs of the *Alice in Wonderland* book. As Dodgson begins to tell her the story, the film would dissolve into a scene of Alice entering Wonderland. With only the first thirty-one pages from the screenplay extant, whatever other changes that Huxley made may never be known.

Joe Grant suggested Harold Lloyd for the Carroll/Dodgson role, but Walt preferred Cary Grant. Walt also wanted to play up a suggested romantic interest between Carroll and actress Ellen Terry in the script because:

[W]e don't want him to look like a "queer". I don't want to see us build up any sex story here. ... We don't bring sex into it all at.

Cap Palmer added:

Just a healthy interest in a grown woman.

Walt insisted the importance of nonsense be made clear:

We are driving toward another underlying point, which is that, often times, the best sense is non-sense. I'd like to finish the whole thing by coming out with some bit of nonsense that makes very good sense — and the implication would be — "There, that's what we've been trying to tell you." ...

I'd like to work it so that there's only one heavy in the picture and that's Beale and we can lay everything on her.

> Have no other heavy, you see? The thing that makes the whole story pay off is that there is a conflict between Beale and her theory on how children should be handled — there should be no nonsense at all — everything has to drive toward something practical.

There were vast differences of opinion on how to show Miss Beale's villainy: jealousy of Ellen Terry, pleasure in the merciless domination of Grove (whom some wanted to turn into Alice's uncle or father, rather than just her guardian), inhumane punishment of Alice, or just discovering Carroll's identity to blackmail him from helping Alice. Walt stated:

> But to strengthen the whole thing, Beale is trying to bring this child up in a certain way. When she comes back from Dodgson's, the child has come back with a certain amount of nonsense and a certain philosophy along those lines. If he has said, for example, "Going through life with nothing but Sense is like trying to run a race with one foot." Well, now that's a heck of a philosophy to give a child — in other words, it clashes with what Beale is trying to do.

For the final scene, Walt suggested:

> Maybe in the last scene we see Mr. Carroll with all these little characters around him and all of a sudden he turns into the little character we want him to be. We can just make a tag ending. Suddenly, the whole thing changes. We make an overlap right on into this fantasy and don't go into any other scenes. Everybody's happy. Grove is all right and when the Queen comes you can bring Miss Terry and her mother in. Everybody can be happy while this is happening. It's a natural place to bring everybody together.

Earlier, however, Walt had suggested:

> There is this chance to have a scene in the end where they all go on a picnic-there is Dodgson, Grove, Alice, Terry, Mrs. Terry, and the new governess. And the new governess is not so bad to look at, and it is quite a change for Grove, so Grove becomes a sort of comic figure in a way. Or there is another play. There could be a suggestion that Mrs. Terry and Grove become rather friendly. But we could do the same thing through the new governess who is an entirely different character. That could be a very happy setting and you would leave with a very happy thought.

Some believe Walt rejected Huxley's script because it was

too "literary", and he could only understand every third word. Based on the notes from the story meeting, it is more likely that Walt just felt the script didn't capture what he wanted. Apparently, Walt did comment that the approach was "too literary" for his tastes, but he was excited about shaping the story into something workable.

Huxley's wife, Maria, later stated, "This was the first movie he [Huxley] liked doing."

Unfortunately, a massive fire in 1961 destroyed more than four thousand of Huxley's annotated books and documents, including his involvement with the Alice project. Fortunately, the Disney Archives has some of the story meeting notes, some memorandums, the fourteen-page treatment, and thirty-one pages of Huxley's script.

At the end of World War II, Walt was eager to get into production of full-length animated features, and began work on *Cinderella*, *Alice in Wonderland*, and *Peter Pan*. So, instead of a live-action/animation mix, *Alice* became full animation and veered from the original Tenniel illustrations to the more modernistic design work of Mary Blair. When the animated feature was released in 1951, it contained no elements from Huxley's work.

Ward Kimball, who animated the Cheshire Cat and the Mad Tea Party scene for the film, revealed:

> I think perhaps the decision to make *Alice* was based fifty percent on the fact that we sorely needed another feature at the time because a lot of animators had to be kept busy. Disney had many, many artists on the payroll during this period, and he preferred to keep them working on his own projects rather than to let them seek employment elsewhere between features.
>
> Surely an economic factor here was the combination of Alice's good name as a famous property and the fact that many animators were out of work. Also, because of the story's episodic nature, Walt could quickly assign different people to different sequences or characters without worrying too much about hook-ups between the sequences.

Audiences and critics didn't care for the film on its initial release, and even Kimball referred to it as a:

... loud-mouthed vaudeville show. There's no denying that there are many charming bits in our *Alice*, but it lacks warmth and an overall story glue."

Storyman Winston Hibler stated:

Walt thought it didn't have any emotional appeal. As he said himself, there was no heart in *Alice*. You really didn't pull for her. She was a mischievous, adventuresome gal and you never really felt sorry for her. I really think that he made *Alice* almost out of a sense of duty to the public, that he was expected to make it, so he made it. I think he worked extremely hard on it, and probably gave it as much or more of himself in an effort to make it satisfying and rewarding to himself.

What did Huxley think of the final animated film? Hibler said:

He was a real *Alice* fan and he was particularly complimentary about the talking doorknob sequence. After he had said how really "Carrollesque" it was, Walt said, "But we invented that. There was no talking doorknob." Which is true.

Secret Origins of The Aristocats

The Aristocats premiered on December 24, 1970, over forty years ago, and is rarely discussed, even though it was the first animated film made entirely after Walt's death. *The Jungle Book* was released a year after his death, but since it was in production during Walt's lifetime, the perception was that it reflected his spirit and direct input, and was a final tribute to his art.

In a movie review for the *Los Angeles Times* (April 9, 1987), animation historian Charles Solomon wrote:

> *The Aristocats* reveals how essential Walt Disney was in shaping the studio's animated features — and how significant a gap he left. *Aristocats* was the first film made entirely after his death. The plot does little more than link a string of vaguely related episodes.

Certainly, there are major story issues from the presence in Belle Époque France of two giddy English geese along with their drunken uncle (basted in white wine and the last voice work of the talented Bill Thompson, known as the Little Ranger, the White Rabbit, and Mr. Smee) and two dimwitted Deep South dogs (voiced by well-known country performers Pat Buttram and George "Goober" Lindsey). What the devil do all these diverse characters contribute to the story or the growth of the main characters, anyway?

How did a Sixties cat with love beads and indoor sunglasses end up in an all-cat jazz band with distasteful stereotypes (remember the Chinese Cat with slanted eyes and buck teeth voiced by Paul Winchell?) when American jazz didn't become popular in France until after World War I? Remember that this story is supposedly set in 1910 pre-war Paris, France.

There seems to be extensive "borrowing" of moments from other Disney films, including the feeling that "Ev'rybody Wants to Be a Cat" is desperately trying to ape the song hit "I Wanna Be Like You" from *The Jungle Book*. Also, the defeat of one of Disney's weakest villains ever, Edgar the Butler (Why does he feel the desperate need to kill the cats when the Duchess is still in fine health? Does he also plan to kill the Duchess?) by the animals is strongly reminiscent of Horace and Jasper's downfall in *101 Dalmatians*.

The film was released in December 1970. Though a box office success, critics were more than a little under-whelmed, especially after the charms of Disney's previous release, *The Jungle Book*. Today, the little white kitten named Marie is a huge favorite of Japanese Disney fans, and there is a ton of merchandise featuring her. In 2003, the Disney Channel considered making Marie and her brothers into teenagers, and using them in a syndicated television series. In 2005, Disney announced a direct-to-video sequel of the film, but canceled the project in 2006, along with several other proposed sequels.

The Aristocats proves that every Disney movie is somebody's favorite, and the film has many ardent fans. Perhaps the most fascinating thing about the film is its genesis.

The Aristocats originally was planned as a two-part, live-action story for *Walt Disney's Wonderful World of Color* TV show. Walt was deeply involved, and it was he who decided the story would be better in animation.

It all begins with a gentleman named Harry Tytle, who spent forty years at the Disney Studios, eventually becoming a producer of live-action films. He was well-liked and close to Walt.

On December 9, 1961, Tytle was in London, where Tom McGowan, who had directed *The Hound Who Thought He Was a Raccoon* (1963) and other animal films for *Wonderful World of Disney*, lived with his family. (McGowan also developed *Born Free* and offered it to the Disney Studios, which passed on the project.) Walt was in London at the time, and suggested that Tytle make a deal with McGowan to find animal stories for the Disney Studios.

By the New Year, McGowan had found several stories, one of them a children's book about a mother cat and her kittens set in New York City. Tytle felt that a London location had added a significant element to the story of *101 Dalmatians*, and suggested setting the story of the cats in Paris.

McGowan and Tytle worked out a rough storyline, assuming it would be done in live action and run as a two-part television show, then combined into a theatrical release as had been done with previous two-part television episodes.

Originally, the story revolved around two servants, a butler and a maid, who were in line to inherit the fortune of an eccentric mistress after her pet cats died. The story focused on their feeble and foolish attempts to eliminate the felines. Then there was an extended section of the mother cat hiding her kittens in a variety of different homes and locales in Paris to keep them out of danger.

The concept was that the live-action cats talked to each other, much like the popular talking horse in the *Mr. Ed* television program. Walt was in favor of the animals talking, as long as it was not in the presence of humans. He felt it helped develop the animals' personalities and moved along the storyline.

About two months later, when Tytle was in Rome to supervise the shooting of *Escapade in Florence* (1962), starring Annette Funicello, McGowan brought him the story, which had been written by Tom Rowe, an American writer then living in Paris. McGowan had paid out of his own pocket for all of Rowe's expenses. Rowe had an interesting career as a writer: he started as a film reviewer for *Variety*, then wrote scripts for television shows like *Fantasy Island* and films like *The Green Slime* (1968) and *Tarzan the Ape Man* (1981). He was also a painter, with several exhibitions in Paris.

Tytle and McGowan spent a few days revising Rowe's script. By August, they sent the completed script to Burbank, where it was returned as "rejected" by the Disney Studios.

The rejection did not come from Walt, who had not seen the treatment, but by underlings. Tytle was hesitant to contact Walt, but that didn't stop McGowan, who tracked

Walt down in London and slipped the treatment into an envelope that he had delivered to the front desk of Walt's hotel, the Conaught.

Walt liked the story and called McGowan at his home before McGowan had even returned from dropping off the envelope. Walt said he would be seeing Tytle in Lisbon, and they would go over the treatment. Tytle did meet with Walt in Lisbon, and on the plane trip back to London, Walt told Tytle to buy the story and prepare it as a live-action feature that McGowan would direct and Tytle would produce. Walt suggested eliminating the musical kitten from the script, which he felt had too much material, and he specified other cuts and revisions as well.

Beginning on August 30, 1962, Tytle and McGowan worked for six straight days on a contract. The London Disney office amended the contract to cut McGowan in on merchandising royalties. (This wasn't a problem when the film was a live-action project, but when it became an animation project, Disney purchased merchandising rights back from McGowan.)

In January 1963, Tytle was in a London hospital for surgery. During his recovery, he worked in his hospital room with McGowan and Rowe on revisions. The script was finished on February 1, and Tytle returned to Burbank to prepare for shooting in Paris.

In June, Walt showed Tytle a letter from Rowe. Apparently, Rowe was unhappy with the revisions to the script, and in particular with Tytle, whom he felt was a "minion" of Walt's sent to corrupt the work. Walt, however, was happy with Tytle's work, and allowed Tytle to respond to the letter himself. Tytle informed Rowe that it was just a difference of opinion, and that he was sorry about Rowe's feelings on the matter, but that Walt liked the changes and so they would remain.

For various reasons, the Disney Studios shelved the story. McGowan attempted to buy back the rights, but Disney refused.

Since stories for animated films were becoming more difficult to come by, Tytle suggested to Walt that *The Aristocats* might make a good Disney animated feature. The idea was run past Woolie Reitherman, then supervising director on the animated features, and some of the key animators. They all agreed.

In August 1963, Walt asked for a copy of *The Aristocats* script. Two days later, Card Walker announced it would be Disney's next animated feature, although work on the project didn't resume until May 1964.

In a diary entry dated November 25, 1964, Tytle recounts a discussion he had with Walt:

> We spent some time discussing the idea. I told him of various gags and bits of business that were not in this script because when we were planning live-action, we had felt they were too "cartoony", but now could be used. For instance, where the mother cat uses her whiskers as radar, protecting her from the two servants. The other one I told him about was when the servants were in the cellar. They get locked in (the mother cat pushes the door shut) when digging a hole to bury the cats, they hit the water main, flooding the wine cellar. The butler grabs for a floating wine bottle, can't pour the contents into the already rising water, so drinks it, puts in a note (for help), then floats it out the cellar window. After doing this a couple of times, he gets "high" and doesn't care about help coming. Walt felt *The Aristocats* should follow the same tack as *Dalmatians*. He said it would be good if the cats could talk amongst themselves, but never in front of humans. He seemed to especially like the various artists in the story, and the characters. He says when we get started, he would like the Sherman boys to come in and write songs. We discussed Waterloo (one of the kittens) and some of the earlier business that Walt had cut out. We have to stay to (just) three kittens, as there is too much business in the original treatment. Walt seemed to agree that the (family) history of the cats that was written by Tom Rowe was good, but extraneous.

Studio nurse Hazel George asked for a copy of the script (apparently at Walt's suggestion), read it, and returned it a few days later saying that she liked it very much and told Walt so. Walt valued George's opinion. Grace Bailey, head of the Ink and Paint department and another Disney employee whose opinion Walt respected, also read the script and liked it.

This leisurely process of delays on the film while work focused on other projects caused some problems after Walt's passing. Tytle was told he was to centralize his efforts on live action, and that Winston Hibler would take over *The*

Aristocats project. When Hibler ran into production troubles, Woolie Reitherman took over, and Hibler was never again involved with animation projects. Major changes to the story were made.

Tytle remembered:

> The part of the story that most intrigued Walt, that is, adoption into homes befitting the kittens' talents, was cut. In my opinion, the resulting film lost the very element we tried to build, the Parisian atmosphere and characters, all the French charm. I honestly think the original story that Walt bought was much better. We didn't have a mouse in the original story; I, for one, felt it was a cliché and not vital to a cat story. For once, I wanted to do a cat story without a mouse.

Elsa Lanchester, whose many film credits included *Mary Poppins*, had been cast as the voice and live action reference for Elvira the maid, who wanted to eliminate the kittens. However, after Walt's passing, the voice cast was shuffled, and Elsa's role eliminated. Much of the original business was thrown out and replaced with other things, including the geese.

Tytle said:

> It would have meant much more if the story that McGowan, Walt, and I wrote had reached the screen, and had been left for the audience to judge. Thus ended my working on any cartoon product.

After Walt's death, Rowe sued the Studio, claiming that, because he had written sections of the film, French law entitled him to the rights to those characters, even though he acknowledged the original idea was not his own. He lost.

In the final film, Tom McGowan and Tom Rowe are given credit for the story, along with Disney storymen Larry Clemmons, Vance Gerry, Ken Anderson, Frank Thomas, Eric Cleworth, Julius Svendsen, and Ralph Wright.

Walt did do some work on the story for *The Aristocats*, but it was tossed aside in the final version. The publicity for the film claimed it was in production for over four years and had cost over four million dollars.

Perhaps if the film had included some of the earlier work done on the story, it could indeed have been the cat's pajamas, an old-fashioned term meaning incredible, rather than what some people consider kitty litter.

So Dear to My Heart

Come One! Come All! To the Walt Disney County Fair!
Filled with music, laughter and heartwarming drama!
— Theatrical poster for Disney's feature film
So Dear To My Heart

It was the film that inspired the creation of Disneylandia and eventually Disneyland. There were plans for it to be the first all live-action Disney film. Part of it ended up in the backyard of animator Ward Kimball, but resulted in some unusual problems. A significant part of Walt Disney's personal childhood in Marceline is physically represented in the film, including a classic structure that gave Walt countless hours of private pleasure at his own home until his death. The film featured an Academy Award-nominated song performed by "America's favorite balladeer" — his first hit single. The book adaptation of the film was the first children's book with illustrations by legendary storyman Bill Peet, who later would have a successful career as a children's book writer and illustrator.

Yet, this simple story of a boy and his black lamb is mostly forgotten today, even though it won the *Parent's Magazine* Box Office Award. *So Dear to My Heart*, released nationwide on January 19, 1949, by RKO Radio Pictures, is a sentimental snapshot of a bygone period close to the heart of Walt Disney. It was meant to be an affectionate and respectful look at country life at the turn of the century, not an opportunity to snicker at the antics of country yokels.

There is no huge melodramatic conflict. No villain is

foreclosing on the farm. No natural disaster or illness threatens the family. There is no trauma over the young boy's parents apparently having been dead for quite some time. Although the grandmother is practical and God-fearing, the young boy gets whatever he wants and overcomes with relative ease obstacles like bees, bogs, a lost pet, and poverty.

In comparison with other Disney films, and despite being pivotal in many ways, *So Dear to My Heart* has been ignored and undocumented, yet surprisingly, the film influenced many other areas of Disney history.

Sterling North was an acclaimed American author of such books as 1963's bestselling *Rascal*, the autobiographical story of raising a baby raccoon that was eventually made into a Disney feature film. North's 1943 book, *Midnight and Jeremiah*, was the source material for *So Dear to My Heart*.

Set in 1903, in the fictional Fulton Corners, Indiana, *So Dear to My Heart* tells the tale of a young boy named Jeremiah Kincaid (Bobby Driscoll, fresh from his appearance in *Song of the South*), who adopts a rejected and mischievous black lamb called Danny (named after the famed champion race horse Dan Patch, who was also black). Jeremiah's dream of entering Danny at the Pike County Fair is almost crushed by the objections of his loving but strict grandmother, Granny Kincaid (twice-nominated Academy Award actress Beulah Bondi).

Jeremiah's only adult ally seems to be the blacksmith, Uncle Hiram Douglas (Burl Ives in one of his very first film roles), although Jeremiah also gets encouragement from his animated daydreams, featuring the Wise Old Owl, that magically spring to life from his scrapbook. He is also supported by his best friend, Tildy (Luana Patten from *Song of the South*), although we never see her parents, even at the Fair. Of course, there are tough challenges along the way, especially when the grown Danny — in typical Disney film fashion — becomes comically destructive and wreaks havoc on the farm and the local store. Eventually, Jeremiah earns enough money to enter Danny at the Fair, and there is a clever and satisfying ending.

In a publicity release for the film, Walt claimed:

I knew I had found the perfect story for a new kind of motion picture when I read the book.

In 1945, Walt first met with screenwriter Edwin Justis Mayer about adapting the story. The final credits list the screenplay by John Tucker Battle (the same screenwriter responsible for 1953's still frightening *Invaders from Mars*), with adaptation work by Maurice Rapf and Ted Sears (both of whom had done some preliminary story work on *Song of the South*). That same year, in summer 1945, producer Perce Pearce had gone to Indiana to get a sense of the atmosphere for *So Dear To My Heart*. Pearce later would do some second unit directing on the film.

The early scripts, including one from December 1945, did not feature any animation. However, scripts from 1946 did include sections for animated inserts, which were reflected in the official budget for the film. An article in the June 30, 1946, *Los Angeles Times* stated the film would be:

> ... about 90 per cent live action. In that one, Walt will resort to cartoons only when nature can't provide his needs.

RKO salesmen argued that it would be hard to sell a Disney picture without cartoons, so some believe that Walt was pushed into adding short animation sequences that can seem intrusive. In actuality, Walt's contract with RKO required that the features he would make for RKO distribution "shall be animated cartoon or may be part animated cartoon and part live action." There was no provision for a wholly live-action feature. When the public sees the name "Disney", they expect animation, and that may be why the first two minutes of the film are animated.

In a later interview, Walt said:

> I saw the cartoon characters as figments of a small boy's imagination, and I think they were justified.

Disney Legend Hamilton Luske was the supervising director of the animation that, according to the pressbook, amounted to only fifteen percent of total film footage. Story was credited to Marc Davis, Ken Anderson, and Bill Peet; animation to Eric Larson, John Lounsbery, Hal King, Milt Kahl, Les Clark, Don Lusk, and Marvin Woodward; and art direction to Mary Blair, John Hench, and Dick Kelsey.

Many of Blair's concept paintings, done in a primitive

quilt-inspired pattern, still exist, and there is a strong connection between these drawings and the designs of the completed film, such as the appearance of the Grundy store.

It's interesting that the surprisingly good animation sequences are never discussed. Besides the standard character animation, featuring everything from a Scottish dancing spider and a threatening sea serpent to a professorial Wise Old Owl, there are some intriguing, impressionist scenes that stand out in an animated feature. While the film itself is often forgotten, it is puzzling why some of these self-contained animated "lessons" didn't get re-used on other projects like the Disney television shows.

Walt Disney was fond of the film *My Friend Flicka* (1943) directed by Harold Schuster, who over the years had risen from actor to cameraman and finally to director. In fact, Walt's wife and daughters loved the film so much that they ran it many times in their home theater. Under contract to 20th Century Fox, Schuster was lent to the Disney Studios to do the live-action scenes for *So Dear To My Heart*. "The idea of working with Walt Disney appealed to me greatly," stated Schuster when he signed on to the project.

Schuster later claimed that the lamb was hardest to direct, even though it was often tempted with food to provide appropriate responses. The lamb stole so many scenes that actor Burl Ives described the animal as "a ham in sheep's clothing". After he had finished filming a scene at the County Fair sheep judging, little Bobby Driscoll remarked, "Sheep and actors back to their pens!" It greatly amused the crew. Driscoll was awarded a special Oscar as "Outstanding Juvenile Actor" both for his work on this film and on a non-Disney thriller, *The Window*.

Cinematographer Winton Hoch would later film *Darby O'Gill and The Little People* (1959), but Walt was familiar with his work as director of photography for the live-action sequences in *Reluctant Dragon* (1941) and the live-action "Pecos Bill" segment with Roy Rogers in *Melody Time* (1948).

Filming for *So Dear to My Heart* began on April 30, 1946, and continued until August 23, 1946. Additional shooting was done between February 5, 1947, and March 28, 1947, with still more filming done in May and August 1947. Since initial filming went into late summer, the landscape had started to dry up, so every night twenty-seven greensmen watered the soil and plants to make them look fresh and green for the next day's shooting. Temperatures exceeded 100°F, and while the cast and extras suffered in their heavily layered period costumes, cool air was pumped into the animal paddocks.

The movie was filmed, according to the official pressbook, around the homes and farms "amidst the grain fields, the orchards and vineyards, the alfalfa pastures, the cattle corral under the great spreading elms near Tulare, Visalia and Porterville" in the San Joaquin Valley about 250 miles north of Hollywood. Supposedly, some photography was done in Sequoia National Park, too. Director Schuster described the San Joaquin Valley as "one of the loveliest valleys in the world."

Schuster suggested Beluah Bondi for the role of Granny. Though only fifty six years old at the time, Bondi had the reputation of playing care-worn matriarchs such as the mother of Jimmy Stewart's characters in four films, including *It's A Wonderful Life* (1946) and *Mr. Smith Goes To Washington* (1939). She played her first "old lady" part when she was just twenty years old. For *So Dear to My Heart*, Bondi learned to take care of sheep, plow a field, spin wool, and work a loom. In the final film, she does these and other activities as if she had been doing them all her life.

Schuster also chose beloved character actor Harry Carey for the part of the County Fair judge. Carey was well-known for his work in silent Westerns, and had the persona of a man of integrity and authority, which is why Schuster wanted him. Sadly, Carey died before the film was released but after all principal photography had been done.

Unusually, some interior sets like the Grundy store were actually built on location, since the Disney Studios then had only one small stage.

Schuster told noted film historian Leonard Maltin:

> They found an old, and I mean old, hardware store near the town of Porterville. It was closed, and the various wares inside were bought lock, stock and barrel and moved into the Grundy store. Both the barn and Granny's house were built on the location. The railroad station was already there as were the railroad tracks. We rented the old engine and cars from Paramount, who had used them for *Union Pacific* (1939).

According to Disney publicity:

> Old No. 99 of the Evansville and Indianapolis Railroad as it is labeled for the [Technicolor film] was actually one of the Virginia and Truckee Railroad's venerable engines, long since retired.

Reportedly, it first saw service in 1875.

Close to five hundred local residents gathered daily at the set to perform as background extras "dressed in the period clothes of their forbears [sic], providing the familiar farm chores and animals and the behavior of farmers at their fairs and picnics half a century ago. Disney personally supervised much of the action." At least Walt supposedly "supervised much of the action", according to the publicity releases that also pointed out how Walt helped supervise the train scenes.

Shuster told Maltin:

> Walt would come up sometimes on weekends. We would have Sunday breakfast, and talk over the rushes. He was a very enthusiastic gentleman, and a joy to be around. His suggestions were always presented as suggestions only. He left the reins firmly in my hands.

When the film was released, Walt claimed:

> *So Dear* was especially close to me. Why, that's the life my brother and I grew up with as kids out in Missouri. The great racehorse, Dan Patch, was a hero to us. We had Dan Patch's grandson on my father's farm.

To promote the film, Walt, Beulah Bondi, and the child stars went on a tour that included stops in Nashville and Chicago. While the film itself was not as profitable in its initial release or re-releases as some other Disney films, it inspired many pivotal moments in Disney history.

Here are just a few:

The barn from the film was recreated in Walt's backyard and provided him endless hours of pleasure.

At the time, John Cowles Jr., son of Dr. John Cowles, a financial supporter of Walt Disney's first animation studio that produced the Laugh-O-Gram cartoons, worked as an architect at the Disney Studios. In addition to his set designs, Cowles Jr. also helped plan many of the permanent buildings at the Studio, as well as the blueprint for the layout of Walt's backyard railroad, the Carolwood Pacific.

Cowles Jr. designed the authentic red barn in *So Dear To My Heart* that reminded Walt of the one from his own childhood on a farm in Marceline, Missouri. Walt had Cowles Jr. adapt that same structure for Walt's backyard workshop. The only variations were a concrete slab foundation, windows along the east wall, and a small room housing the central track control board for Walt's railroad. This piece of *So Dear To My Heart* remained close to Walt until his death, and it was one of his favorite locations to get away from the burdens of work and just have fun.

The railroad station from the film ended up in the backyard of animator Ward Kimball.

A long-time railroad buff, Kimball designed the railroad depot in *So Dear To My Heart* based upon a Lehigh Valley Railroad flag depot in Pottsville, New York. After the filming, Walt (perhaps in a good mood after a trip with Kimball to the Chicago Railroad Fair) decided that Kimball's backyard Grizzly Flats railroad needed a train station, and so a Disney Studios truck delivered the disassembled train station building from the film to Ward's home in San Gabriel. It was an unexpected and appreciated gift — until Kimball tried to reassemble it.

Kimball claimed it was like trying to put the unmarked pieces of a jigsaw puzzle back together on a concrete foundation. He was even more frustrated when he had a big crane put the roof on the final structure and the whole thing collapsed. It was only a movie set, so it only had three sides without enough framing to support the roof. Kimball had to start over from scratch, but was able to salvage the roof, the windows, and the doors. Kimball never revealed to Walt at the time how much extra effort and expense it took to rebuild the depot.

Years later, Walt decided that the depot would be perfect for the railroad stop in Frontierland in the Disneyland theme park then under construction, and it would save some money to have Kimball simply return the train station. Kimball refused, and finally revealed how he had to completely rebuild it. Walt ordered the station built in Frontierland according to the same blueprints, but with the addition of double doors, covered loading platforms on both ends, and a separate freight office. Decades later, it was used as one of the sets for the *Two Brothers* short film shown at the Disney theme parks, as a segment in the American Adventure pavilion film at Epcot, and in the Great Moments with Mr. Lincoln pre-show film at Disneyland.

Before Disneyland, Walt had toyed with a concept called Disneylandia which would entail several three-dimensional, mechanical, miniature exhibits in train baggage cars that would travel the country. Walt imagined people, especially schoolchildren, visiting their local train station to learn about their history and heritage. The first tableau was inspired by the film.

Walt was skilled at making miniatures. Working from plans that Imagineer Ken Anderson adapted from *So Dear To My Heart*, Walt personally built Granny Kincaid's cabin as a 1/8 scale mockup now showcased in the One Man's Dream attraction at Disney's Hollywood Studios. Walt displayed his hand-built model at the Los Angeles Pan Pacific Auditorium in November 1952 as part of the Festival of Living show.

To build the chimney, Walt picked up pebbles at his vacation home, the Smoke Tree Ranch, in Palm Springs. Inside, a hand-braided rag rug warmed a floor of planks not much larger than matchsticks. A china washbowl and pitcher, guitar with strings thin as cat whiskers, and a small family Bible sat on the table. A tiny flintlock rifle hung on the wall and a spinning wheel with flax sat in the corner. The scene looked as if Granny herself had just stepped away from her small rocking chair to go outside, but viewers heard Granny's voice describing the cozy scene. Walt had recorded a narration by Beulah Bondi, who had played Granny in the film.

In a 1953 interview, Walt explained:

> This little cabin is part of a project I am working on, and it was exhibited as a test to obtain the public's reaction to my plans for a complete village.

Walt was later convinced that Disneylandia would not be able to generate enough income to maintain the exhibits, and that only a handful of people at a time could enjoy the experience. Disneylandia evolved into the full-sized Disneyland.

So Dear To My Heart provided legendary storyman Bill Peet his first opportunity to illustrate a children's book.

In 1950, Simon & Schuster released a one-hundred-and-twenty-six-page Golden Story Book (GS-12) of the film, with text by Helen Palmer and illustrations by Bill Peet. (It was one of a series of twenty books that included two other Disney titles: *Mystery in Disneyville* and *Donald Duck and the Hidden Gold*.) Peet would later find success and acclaim as a children's book writer and artist. His first book is usually considered *Hubert's Hair-Raising Adventure* (1959), but actually this Golden Story Book contained his first published art in any children's book. He provided ink and watercolor drawings for almost every page of the book in the same style that he'd later use for his own books. It was not unusual for Disney artists to moonlight as illustrators, especially for Disney-related storybooks and comic books. Other Disney artists, including John Hench, Mary Blair, Bill Justice, and Retta Scott did outstanding work for Disney-related children's storybooks. Unfortunately, the lack of success of *So Dear to My Heart* resulted in its Golden Story Book adaptation never being reprinted.

So Dear To My Heart gave "America's favorite Balladeer" (as the pressbook described singer Burl Ives) his first hit single.

Burl Ives was a collector and performer of authentic American folk songs, and at the time of the film, best-known for his appearances on radio and at various concerts. He had been performing for well over a decade when he recorded songs for *So Dear to My Heart*. "Lavender Blue (Dilly Dilly)" was a 17th century English folk song and nursery rhyme that Disney song writers Eliot Daniel and Larry Morey adapted for the film. Sung by Ives, it was nominated for an Academy Award for Best Song. It was Ives' first hit single.

Daniel and Morey contributed two other songs to the score: "Ol' Dan Patch" and "Stick-To-It-Ivity". (Daniel was later responsible for the *I Love Lucy* theme song.) The film's title tune, "So Dear To My Heart", was from Ticker Freeman and Irving Taylor. Mel Torme provided the lyrics for Robert Wells' music for "County Fair". Bondi and Ives duet on the traditional folk song "Billy Boy". While the publicity for the film proclaimed that Ives would also sing the traditional folk song "Sourwood Mountain", that song does not appear in the final film. Apparently, other folk songs were cut as well.

The most important thing about *So Dear to My Heart* is its stated moral: "It's what you do with what you got." Certainly that philosophy was important back then, in a kinder, more innocent time, but even more so today. Animation historian John Culhane has claimed it was a phrase that Walt said frequently. It's easy to imagine it as part of Walt's philosophy.

One of the reasons Walt wanted to recapture the nostalgic memories of his youth with this film was to remind himself of what he did with what he had been given.

And the Oscar Goes to...
Walt Disney

During his lifetime, Walt Disney won the most individual Oscars in the history of those prestigious film awards. It is an amazing accomplishment still unbroken nearly five decades after his death.

The Academy of Motion Picture Arts and Sciences was conceived by late movie producer Louis B. Mayer, who felt such an organization was necessary to give status and respect to the motion picture industry. With help from other prominent figures in Hollywood, the Academy was created, and gave its first, then nameless, awards at a banquet on May 16, 1929.

The Short Subjects Awards were first handed out in 1932 in three categories: Cartoon, Comedy, and Novelty. Supposedly, the cartoon category was established primarily to honor the work of Walt Disney. For several years, most of the nominees and winners in this category were Disney cartoon shorts, with a token nomination or two of other animation producers like Leon Schlesinger.

For example, in 1938, four Disney cartoons were nominated: *The Brave Little Tailor*, *Mother Goose Goes Hollywood*, *Good Scouts*, and the eventual winner, *Ferdinand the Bull*, a cartoon which also spawned a good deal of merchandise. Disney won in the cartoon Short Subjects category every year from 1932 (*Flowers and Trees*) through 1939 (*The Ugly Duckling*).

The streak was broken in 1940, when MGM's *The Milky*

Way, about three little kittens who lost their mittens and dream of visiting the Milky Way in a balloon basket, took the award. There were no Disney cartoons nominated that year. The other two nominees were MGM's *Puss Gets the Boot* (arguably the first Tom and Jerry cartoon) and Warner's *A Wild Hare* (arguably the first "official" Bugs Bunny cartoon).

Academy Awards Ceremony 1932
Mickey Mouse and Flowers and Trees

In 1932, besides *Flowers and Trees*, the other two nominees in the cartoon Short Subject category were Disney's *Mickey's Orphans* and Warner's *It's Got Me Again*.

Also that year, Walt received a special Oscar for the creation of Mickey Mouse. Actor Charlie Chaplin was supposed to present the statuette, but decided to stay home. This moment was a milestone in Oscar history, since it was the first year that one man was given two awards at the same ceremony, and only the second time a special Oscar had been awarded. (The first such award went to Chaplin.)

Walt Disney knew that he was going to receive two awards. Until 1941, winners were informed beforehand to help reporters meet their news deadlines.

On November 18, 1932, the fifth annual Motion Picture Arts and Sciences' banquet was held in the Fiesta Room of the Ambassador Hotel on Wilshire Boulevard. Nine hundred people attended.

As part of the festivities, and to show appreciation for the honors he was to receive, Walt produced a short color cartoon for the attendees. Entitled *Parade of the Award Nominees*, it was a two-and-a-half-minute film starring Mickey Mouse that featured caricatures of performers nominated in the Best Actor and Best Actress categories.

Mickey Mouse, in green shorts, led the parade of nominees (with some recycled animation from *Mother Goose Melodies*, a 1931 *Silly Symphony*) down a red carpet. It was Mickey's first color film appearance, pre-dating *The Band Concert* by several years.

In order, the caricatures were Wallace Beery for *The Champ* (with supporting actor Jackie Cooper trailing along behind him), Alfred Lunt and Lynn Fontanne for *The Guardsman*, Helen Hayes for *The Sins of Madelon Claudet*,

Fredric March for *Dr. Jekyll and Mr. Hyde*, and Marie Dressler for *Emma*.

One newspaper reported that the cartoon garnered a "huge laugh". Another newspaper reported:

> Judging by the applause, the greatest enthusiasm was for Walt Disney, creator of Mickey Mouse, and for Helen Hayes (who won Best Actress).

Academy Awards Ceremony 1939
Snow White and the Seven Dwarfs

On February 23, 1939, a nervous Walt Disney waited at the Biltmore Hotel in Los Angeles. He'd already been the recipient of seven Academy Awards from previous years. That night, Walt was to be presented with an Honorary Academy Award for *Snow White and the Seven Dwarfs*, a "significant screen innovation, which has charmed millions and pioneered a great new entertainment field for the motion picture cartoon".

Snow White was then the top-grossing film of all time, and had become so hugely popular and critically lauded that the Academy felt it deserved some sort of recognition, but didn't want to award a Best Picture Oscar (or a nomination in that category) to an animated cartoon.

According to his autobiography, Academy President (and legendary film director) Frank Capra came up with the idea of a special award in the shape of a full-sized Oscar statuette with seven smaller ones descending in a row. Even though Walt was adamant that he didn't make films just for children but for the entire family, it was felt that the top child star of the time, Shirley Temple, best represented Walt's young fans and should make the presentation.

A photo distributed to newspapers by Wide World Photos' Los Angeles Bureau had the caption:

> Long applause greeted Shirley Temple when she walked to the rostrum to present a special award to Walt Disney for *Snow White and the Seven Dwarfs*, which is recognized by the industry as a screen innovation that pioneered a new entertainment field.

Capra swore this exchange "brought down the house":

> Shirley Temple: I am sure the boys and girls in the whole world are going to be very happy when they find out that

the daddy of Snow White and the Seven Dwarfs, Mickey Mouse, Ferdinand, and all the others is going to get this beautiful statue [removes the fabric covering the award]. Isn't it bright and shiny?

Walt Disney: Oh, it's beautiful.

Shirley Temple: Aren't you proud, Mr. Disney?

Walt Disney: I'm so proud I think I'll bust. You know I think that Mickey Mouse, Ferdinand, Snow White and all the dwarves are going to be very proud that you presented it.

Shirley Temple: I'm glad.

The references to Ferdinand were to the main character in *Ferdinand the Bull*, the Disney short cartoon that had won that year.

Interviewed by Animation Historian John Culhane in February 1988, Shirley Temple Black remembered:

I thought that the big statue was for Walt and that the Seven Dwarfs were the little ones going down the side and that Snow White herself hadn't gotten anything. I was eleven years old. And I was worried about Snow White at the time, that she hadn't gotten an Oscar. It's just that the big one is the one usually presented to who the person is. I mean Snow White wasn't there. ... He [Walt] was a very special guy and I enjoyed him very much. I am just sorry I never worked for him.

Academy Awards Ceremony 1942
Thalberg Award

The Irving G. Thalberg Memorial Award is presented to "[c]reative producers, whose bodies of work reflect a consistently high quality of motion picture production".

The award was named for the late Irving Thalberg, legendary vice-president and head of the Production Division of Metro-Goldwyn-Mayer, who was responsible for developing MGM's top productions. The award, a bust of Thalberg attached to a rectangular base, is considered an "honorary Oscar", though it is not given every year. The first recipient was Darryl F. Zanuck at the 1937 Academy Awards ceremony (held in 1938). Three other honorees received the award between 1939 and 1942: Hal B. Wallis (1938), David O. Selznick (1939), and Walt Disney (1942), who was the youngest ever to win it.

Producer David O. Selznick presented Walt with the award. Walt was so overcome with emotion that he wept openly. From a story headlined "Walt Disney Weeps as He Gets Oscar" in the February 27, 1942, issue of the trade newspaper Daily Variety:

> [Walt] found it difficult to speak and was only able to say with great emotion: "I want to thank everybody here. This is a vote of confidence from the whole industry."

Actually, Walt said a little more. Presenter Selznick praised Walt for using classical music by Bach, Beethoven, and Tchaikovsky in *Fantasia*, stating that it "contributed to the musical education of the public". In his acceptance speech, Walt replied:

> Thank you so much for this. Maybe I should get a medal for bravery. We all make mistakes. *Fantasia* was one but it was an honest one. I shall now rededicate myself to my old ideals.

Actress Norma Shearer, Thalberg's widow, went over to Walt when he returned to his seat and gave him a kiss. She did not care for the rendering of her late husband's head on the trophy so, at her own expense, commissioned a new sculpture. She sent the new version to the first four winners, including Walt, and it became the standard for many years.

Academy Award Ceremony 1949
Seal Island

Even in the 1940s, Walt was worried about the vanishing frontier, so he asked husband-and-wife photographers Alfred and Elma Milotte, who owned a camera store in Alaska, to venture into the Alaskan wilderness and shoot everything they could — from Eskimos to businesses to whatever — in an attempt to capture the spirit of this disappearing outpost of civilization.

Studying reels and reels of unrelated shots, Walt zeroed in on footage of seals, and asked the Milottes to emphasize the life cycle of those seals with no indication of man's presence.

The resulting film, the first of the *True Life Adventures* series, did not appeal to RKO, Disney's film distributor at the time, who felt audiences would not sit still for a nature film. In addition, they felt the Disney name was so closely connected to animation that the small audiences who might show up for the film would be disappointed by seeing only the live animals.

Walt asked a friend, the owner of Pasadena's Crown Theater, to show the film, *Seal Island*, for one week in December 1948, so it would qualify for a possible Academy Award nomination.

At twenty-seven minutes, much longer than the usual short subject film, *Seal Island* was not only nominated for but won an Oscar that year for Best Documentary.

The very next day, Walt took that Academy Award to his brother Roy O. Disney's office and said:

> Here, Roy. Take this over to RKO and bang them over the head with it.

Confronted with the impressive Oscar, RKO distributed the film.

Academy Award Ceremony 1953
Music Presenter

Walt Disney himself was a presenter three times. In 1937, he presented the Short Subjects awards, and in 1943, he presented the Thalberg Award to producer Sidney Franklin.

On March 19, 1953, Walt Disney presented the music awards at the 25th Academy Awards held at the RKO Pantages Theatre in Hollywood. It was the first year the ceremonies were televised. Host Bob Hope introduced Walt:

> You know when we called Walt Disney and asked him to present the music award tonight, we said, "Walt, with all the songs you've commissioned for your pictures and what with *Fantasia* and all, you would be the right man to do it. After all, think about how much you have done for music and Hollywood."
>
> And his warm reply was, "I would have thought it was the other way around." In any case Walt fought his way through all the Oscars in his living room to our stage tonight. One of the great theatrical inventors of modern times, Mr. Walt Disney.

Walt mangled the names of several nominees. Miklos Rosza became "Miklos Rosca". Orchestra conductor Adolph Deutsch tried to loudly whisper to Walt the correct pronunciations from the orchestra pit, but it didn't help. Walt changed the song title "Am I in Love?" to "I Am in Love!", and couldn't make it all the way through Dimitri Tiomkin's name. The highlight was when Alfred Newman, who won for Best Scoring of a Musical Picture, walked away from the podium, leaving his Oscar behind.

Academy Award Ceremony 1954
Four Awards

Walt Disney achieved a milestone at the March 25, 1954, awards ceremony by becoming the person with the most Oscar wins (four) in a single year, up to that point. He won the Oscar in four award categories (all for films released in 1953):

- Best Cartoon Short Subject: Toot, Whistle, Plunk and Boom
- Best Documentary Short Subject: The Alaskan Eskimo
- Best Documentary Feature: The Living Desert
- Best Two-Reel Short Subject: Bear Country

Disney Legend Ward Kimball, director of *Toot, Whistle, Plunk and Boom*, had hoped to accept the Oscar, but he was told that, since Disney was nominated for multiple awards, "it would be a better show to have Walt go up each time. And it was," grumbled Ward when I interviewed him in 1996.

After receiving his fourth Oscar that evening, Walt told the audience:

> Just gotta say one more word. It's wonderful, but I think it's my year to retire.

Walt's niece-in-law Patty remembered:

> Tom Jones, a Studio publicist, was assigned to take Walt to the Academy Awards one year. Walt told [his wife] Lilly not to bother coming to the event because he didn't think he was going to win anything. So Walt went to the awards and got so many that the press took photos of him holding all these Oscars. When Tom drove Walt home, Lilly wouldn't let him in the house because she was so mad that he told her to stay home. She was furious because it had been a big night and she wasn't with him. So Tom had to drive Walt back to the Studio and [Walt] had to sleep in his apartment at the Studio that night.

The largest single collection of Oscars outside of Hollywood is at the Disney Family Museum in San Francisco. Its lobby showcases many of the awards that Walt won in his lifetime, including his Oscars.

In the early 1960s, Walt had a very special 18K gold bracelet fashioned with twenty miniature Oscar statuettes, each engraved underneath with the name of the film for which it was awarded. Walt had to get permission from the Academy to duplicate the trademarked statuettes. Originally, he wanted to give his wife, Lillian, a necklace with these charms, but Lilly said she preferred a bracelet, and she wore that bracelet often. It is now on display at the Disney Family Museum.

The only feature film Walt produced that was nominated for Best Picture was *Mary Poppins*. It was nominated in 1964 for thirteen awards, and won five of them on Oscar night, April 5, 1965, including Best Actress for Julie Andrews. About the win, Walt said:

> Knowing Hollywood, I never had any hope that the picture [*Mary Poppins*] would get it. As a matter of fact, Disney has never actually been part of Hollywood, you know. I think they refer to us as being in the cornfield in Burbank.

Part Three

Disney Park Stories

Whenever I visit Walt Disney World with a good friend who is also a recognized Disney authority, he is enthralled by the stories I share about the history of the various attractions. He is fond of telling the thousands of fans of his podcast that these are the stories that "only Jim Korkis knows".

At first, I was flattered by the compliment, but as I thought about it, I became increasingly frightened. Over the decades, I've been able to interview many of the Imagineers who created the Disney theme park attractions. I've worked with and talked with Cast Members who helped open Disneyland and Walt Disney World. They shared many terrific stories and facts that I later discovered were never documented. Thankfully, I took good notes and often recorded the conversations.

Was it true that I might be one of the last people left who knew the stories about these attractions? Was that why arbitrary changes have been made to the Disney theme parks with no regard to original story lines? Was there no one left working at the Disney Company as the "keeper of the stories" or in a position to share those stories with decision-makers?

Suddenly, I felt the need to share these stories with as many people as possible to keep that history alive. Rather than rely solely on the memories of those whom I have spoken with over the years, I tried to confirm their stories from other sources. I was shocked to discover that some documents had been destroyed to save on storage costs or because an attraction closed or never was built. Fortunately, Cast Members often saved this material as personal souvenirs, and I was able to access it to verify information.

But some facts had never been recorded at all, because in the heat of final deadlines, no one had the time, especially if something had to be changed at the last minute. There has always been a tradition of "oral history" at the Disney Studios and the Disney Parks. The belief was that if someone had a question, someone would be available with the first-hand knowledge to answer it. No one thought what would happen when the people with first-hand knowledge died or retired. The situation grew worse year after year as talented people left the company.

So, here are some of the stories about the Disney theme parks that I may be one of the few people to know. I do not want these great tales to go with me to the grave. I am grateful that people shared these (and so many other) stories with me, but I regret that I was not more aggressive and astute to retrieve even more information when it was available. Perhaps these stories will bring new appreciation for Disney theme park attractions to those who have visited them countless times.

Cinderella's Golden Carrousel

On June 1, 2010, the Disney Company created a new storyline for the popular Cinderella's Golden Carrousel in Walt Disney World's Fantasyland. As part of the new storyline, the name of the attraction was changed to Prince Charming Regal Carrousel. No physical changes were made, except for a new sign.

In a press release, Disney explained:

> Following their fairy-tale romance and happily ever after wedding, Cinderella and Prince Charming took up residence in Cinderella's Castle. With peace throughout the kingdom, Prince Charming had time to practice for jousting tournaments. In the countryside near the castle, he built a training device of carved horses, on which he could practice the art of ring-spearing, a tournament event in which a knight rides his horse full speed, lance in hand, toward a small ring hanging from a tree limb, with the object of spearing the ring. This event was known by various names throughout the lands, but generally came to be called "carrousel".
>
> The carrousel device drew the attention of the villagers, who wanted to take a turn on this amazing spinning contraption. So Prince Charming had a second carrousel constructed closer to the Castle, where everyone could take a spin on this wondrous invention. Instead of a working knight's training device, however, this new carrousel is more befitting its regal location in the Castle Courtyard — its rustic training horses replaced with ornately decorated prancing steeds adorned with golden helmets and shields, flower garlands, feathers and other festoons. Prince

Charming invites one and all to test their horsemanship skills and to enjoy their own happy ending.

Some Disney fans debate the need for such re-branding, since for forty years the beloved icon at the entrance to Fantasyland in the Magic Kingdom had a rich history, beginning with Walt Disney's own fondness for carousels.

In 1963, Walt revealed where he got the notion for Disneyland:

> Well, it came about when my daughters were very young and Saturday was always Daddy's day with the two daughters. So we'd start out and try to go someplace, you know, different things. I'd take them to the merry-go-round and I took them different places and I'd sit while they rode the merry-go-round. Sit on a bench, you know, eating peanuts. I felt that there should be something built where the parents and the children could have fun together. So that's how Disneyland started.

The famous merry-go-round that inspired Walt still operates in Griffith Park in Los Angeles. Located in Park Center between the Los Angeles Zoo and the Los Feliz park entrance, the Griffith Park Merry-Go-Round has been a family attraction for over five generations. It was built in 1926 by the Spillman Engineering Company, and is the only Spillman-built carousel still in existence. It has most of its original parts and paint.

The Spreckles family originally purchased the merry-go-round for its amusement park in Mission Beach, near San Diego, but when attendance dropped during the Depression, the carousel was moved to nearby Balboa Park for the California Pacific International Exposition. When the Exposition ended in 1936, Ross Davis purchased the carousel, and then in 1937 brought it to Griffith Park, where it has operated ever since. Davis helped Walt obtain and refurbish another carousel for Disneyland that became the famous King Arthur's Carousel.

The Griffith Park Merry-Go-Round boasts sixty-eight elaborately hand-carved horses, every one a jumper. All four rows of horses boast jewel-encrusted bridles, detailed draped blankets, and are decorated with sunflowers and lion's heads. In addition, there are two chariots supposedly depicting Adam chasing Eve, with a plaque on one of them stating:

> Restored in memory of Walt Disney through the generosity
> of the Walt Disney Family Foundation.

A Stinson 165 Military Band Organ, claimed to be the largest band organ accompanying a carousel on the West Coast, plays over 1500 selections of marches and waltz music.

In 1984, the merry-go-round was purchased by Rosemary West and Warren Deasy, who together began the enormous, painfully slow task of restoration, using the profit from operating the carousel to pay for its restoration. The ravages of time are very evident on this vintage attraction.

At the Disney Gallery in Disneyland, against the wall in the front entrance of the Main Street Opera House, sits a green wooden park bench (on loan from Imagineer Tony Baxter's personal collection) with a plaque that reads:

> The actual park bench from the Griffith Park Merry-Go-
> Round in Los Angeles, where Walt Disney first dreamed of
> Disneyland.

The most magnificent carousel at any Disney theme park may be the one at Walt Disney World's Magic Kingdom. Its rich history and fine detail are unsurpassed.

Every day, unsuspecting guests at Walt Disney World ride a genuine antique by mounting a horse that might be valued at more than $100,000 and decorated with 23-karat gold leaf. For two minutes, they are transported to the joy of their youth or to a royal fantasy, where they heroically ride round and round through a land of enchantment. That experience originally cost just an "A" ticket, or ten cents, the lowest price for any Walt Disney World attraction. Today, it is free.

Most historians agree that the concept of a carousel began in the 1100s, when Italian and Spanish crusaders watched Arabian and Turkish horsemen play a very serious game on horseback (actually a cavalry training preparation exercise) that the crusaders dubbed "little battles" or "little war". In Italian, that means "garosello, and in Spanish, "carosella".

The French adapted the game into an extravagant display of horsemanship to replace jousting and called it "carrousel" (with a double "r"). Both riders and horses wore elaborate costumes and performed choreographed routines to entertain royalty. One routine had a man on horseback use his lance to spear a small ring dangling from a tree limb or pole.

Roughly three hundred years ago, the French built a rotating device that moved up and down, and which featured carved horses and chariots suspended by chains radiating from a center pole. It was used to train young nobleman for the event without tiring their horses.

By the late 1700s, there were numerous carousels (powered by men, mules, or horses) scattered throughout Europe and used solely for amusement at fairs and special venues. In the 1860s, Gustav Dentzel pioneered the modern carousel in America, inspiring other talented craftsmen.

The American carousels were bigger and more elaborate. Their horses and chariots were extravagantly decorated in keeping with the tradition that a carousel was meant to entertain royalty. American carousel horses are much more active than their European counterparts, with expressive eyes, tossed manes, and extreme poses of movement. It truly is an art to bring the illusion of life to a piece of wood.

Technological advances brought a stationary circular platform for people to walk on, and the addition of stationary animals (standers or prancers), with bevel gears and cranks to give up-and-down motion to other animals around a center pole.

During the Great Depression, the decline of amusement parks resulted in many carousels being abandoned or destroyed as the few companies still producing them shifted their manufacturing focus or went out of business. Carousels were now considered just a children's ride rather than something for adults to enjoy. With the huge interest in collecting the carousel animals as antiques during the 1970s, many of the remaining carousels were dismantled to sell the individual figures for profits in the thousands of dollars.

During the Golden Age (before the Depression), there may have been more than four thousand operating carousels. Today, in the U.S., just over one hundred remain intact.

The sole Disney craftswoman who supervised and maintained the Walt Disney World carousel for over two decades since its installation was a delightfully talented woman named Isle Voght. About ten years ago, Disney removed her from that responsibility, but I visited her many times in the late 1990s at Central Shops to see her at work. She was always eager to share information with me about the history of the WDW carousel and about her job. I watched in awe as she worked her magic.

Isle composed a memorandum dated September 18, 1990, about the history of the WDW carousel, and sent it to multiple recipients, including Disney University, so that the true story could be saved and documented. At the time, Isle was involved with the carousel for Euro Disneyland. That carousel's outer ring had new wooden horses carved by an artist in Ohio, while the inner rings had fiberglass horses cast from molds of the wooden horses on the Walt Disney World carousel. As she had done with Imagineer John Hench for the WDW carousel, Isle was in charge of the color selection for each horse.

Two paragraphs from her two-page, single-spaced memo were excerpted for publicity and used over and over during the past twenty years. The document itself has disappeared.

As background, it helps to know that the Golden Age of American Carousels featured three primary styles: Philadelphia (inspired by the work of Dentzel and the Philadelphia Toboggan Company), Coney Island, and County Fair.

Isle told me:

> The Walt Disney World Carousel in the Magic Kingdom was produced in 1917 by the Philadelphia Toboggan Company, which created some of the most beautiful horses of the era. It was carved by German and Italian carvers to express the patriotism that was prevalent in the United States after the First World War. The carousel was named Liberty, and was one of the largest carousels ever built, being some sixty feet in diameter.
>
> The first home of the Liberty Carousel was at the Detroit Palace Garden Park where it stayed until it was rehabilitated in Philadelphia in 1928 and set up in Olympic Park in Maplewood, New Jersey for the next 39 years.

The Liberty Carousel originally had seventy-two horses and two chariots (not four as is reported in some articles). The distinctly American horses were black, brown, gray, and white. Their saddles included items that celebrated the American frontier, including images of buffalo and bison now painted silver or gold, faces of Native Americans, bows and arrows, and even holsters with pistols or rifles.

Carved figures of Lady Liberty holding shields that featured a red, white, and blue flag emblem decorated the interior top circle. There were eighteen landscape paintings of American scenery. Just below was a running board decorated with golden American eagles. Over the years, less skilled craftsmen slopped coats of paint and lacquer over the horses, eventually obscuring the intricate and uniquely engraved features underneath.

The Philadelphia Toboggan Company built only eighty-nine carousels before 1929 and the Great Depression. The Liberty Carousel (#46) is one of only a dozen or so of those classic original carousels still in operation.

In 1965, when Olympic Park closed, the Liberty Carousel had fallen into a state of disrepair and was slated for demolition. Antique carousel horses are in such demand that owners often sell them and the decorations individually. Studies have shown that when an entertainment venue sells off or removes its carousel, the venue usually closes permanently within a year. By 1967, Disney had located and acquired the Liberty Carousel, an antique masterpiece, for the Magic Kingdom.

Isle shared with me:

> All of the horses were shipped to Disney Shops where craftsmen were surprised by the detail and artistic grace uncovered when all the years of paint and grime was removed down to the gleaming Maplewood of the horses. Months of Disney artistry went into the rehabilitation. The chariots were removed and the carousel was filled out to the present number of ninety horses when Disney purchased some antique horses that were made by two other well-known producers of carousels, the Dentzel Co. and the Parker Co.

The horses were sanded down carefully to the original wood so that no detail was lost. Sanding down to the actual wood could have resulted in damage and loss of detail, so standard practice today is to sand down only to the level of primer and no further. Then the horses were primed and painted white.

The horses are white for two reasons. First, since it is Cinderella's carousel, the white horses reference the white horses that pulled Cinderella's pumpkin carriage. Second, one of the things Disney discovered with the King Arthur's Carousel at Disneyland was that when people ride a carousel, they first try to get on a white horse because it is considered the "hero" horse. For over a decade, the Disneyland carousel featured horses of different colors, until Imagineer John Hench decided to make them all Arctic white, because at a Disney theme park, every guest — no matter their size — gets a chance to be a hero. Walt also wanted each guest to have a "jumper" rather than a "stander", so some horses on the Disneyland carousel were refitted into running horses.

For the WDW carousel, John Hench and Isle Voght selected the unique color palette for each horse. Each horse's tack has a different color scheme numbered on its bridle. One time, Isle tried to test my color awareness, and asked me to look carefully at the saddle she was painting and tell her its color. I immediately responded that it was blue, a dark royal blue. She laughed and said I was not looking carefully enough because, while it *was* blue, it also had a touch of red — not enough red to turn the color to purple, but enough so that it was different from another blue saddle horse she showed me nearby. Once she pointed it out, it was very obvious.

One of my many regrets is that when I knew Isle, I was transitioning into a different job with new responsibilities, and so I wasn't able to spend as much time with her as I would have liked. She told me that she and Hench had determined the sex of each horse (no, you do not look underneath), and whether each was a young horse or a mature horse. She was planning to teach me how to tell the difference between male and female, and young and old, but I never followed up on that opportunity. Isle might still have that documentation somewhere.

She was also going to teach me how to determine whether a horse was wood or fiberglass. All the horses are wood, but Disney made fiberglass molds of eleven of the antique wood horses (and then painted them using the same process for painting the wooden horses) as "understudies". These understudies replace horses on the carousel when the originals are pulled off for repair and repainting. The horses do suffer wear and tear from the guests. Usually, a complete row of five horses are pulled, although each might be pulled from different rows. Isle indicated that knocking at the right location on the upper chest near the horse's neck was one way to determine the difference, since fiberglass is hollow but the wood is solid.

A "row" of horses does not go around the carousel, but goes from the outer edge of the carousel toward the center. On the WDW carousel, a row is five horses deep with the largest "A" horse on the outside and the smallest "E" horse on the inside.

Since the "A" horses are the ones facing the crowd, they are more elaborate in their design and detail. The horses progressively get less intricate as they move toward the center. In addition, the side of the horse (whether "A" or "E") that faces the audience is more elaborate than the side that faces the center, and is known as the "romance" side. It is similar in concept to the set of a play or a movie. While the difference between the two sides of the smaller "E" horses are not as noticeable as the much larger "A" horses, the difference still exists.

Isle told me (for a class that I was teaching in 1998):

> Each year between fifty to sixty horses are completely redone at a cost between $2500-$3,000 to refurbish each horse. All the horses are hand-painted and everything that looks like gold really is gold. Only 23-karat gold leaf is used, along with silver, copper, and aluminum leaf. The antique wood horses of the Walt Disney carousel are valued between $20,000-$100,000, depending upon size, intricacy of carving, and age.

Smaller horses can take two to three days to refurbish, but "A" horses can take one week or more. When the Disney Company obtained the carousel, almost all of the original wooden working parts were replaced by metal, but the horses, decorations, and band organ (from one of Italy's most famous factories) were saved.

While the Magic Kingdom was being built, Walt's brother Roy O. Disney would inspect the park. At the train station, he looked down Main Street and saw through the open castle gate that the carousel seemed off-center. Subsequent measurement showed he was right, so the ride was recentered. According to legend, the carousel had been off only a foot or two.

When the carousel opened, it was an "A" Ticket attraction called Cinderella's Golden Carrousel (with the double "r" to reference the French word for the original, and also because it was the French version of the Cinderella tale that inspired Disney's animated feature). On the sign were the two mice, Gus and Jacques ,perhaps waiting for the Fairy Godmother to return and transform them back into white horses. Or perhaps it was a playful reminder that those magnificent white steeds may be mice, and Gus and Jacques are there visiting their friends, who preferred to remain noble horses.

About ten years ago, the urban myth arose of a "Cinderella horse", possibly from Cast Members trying to create magical moments for guests. At the time, I asked Isle if there was a Cinderella horse, and she laughed. She assured me it was never planned for Cinderella to have a special horse. Cinderella never rode one in the animated feature. And the horses on the carousel were all distinctly American steeds. If Disney had wanted a Cinderella horse, it would have created a special one, or done extensive surgery on an existing horse to include details like Cinderella's crest on the saddle.

The horse with the gold ribbon on its tail — often identified as Cinderella's horse — is a "B" horse, and certainly Cinderella would be riding a much more elaborate "A" horse, astride which she could be seen by her subjects, not hidden in the second rim on a less elegant steed. However, like most Disney urban myths, this one persists with such intensity that sadly it now appears in officially approved Disney books and websites.

The carousel at Disneyland does feature a special "Julie Andrews" horse called Jingles. This horse sports an elaborate emblem on its saddle that includes Julie's initials and a silhouette of a flying Mary Poppins. It is an "A" horse, clearly seen and easily found on the carousel, and Disney had a formal dedication ceremony declaring it the Julie Andrews horse.

Fortunately, Isle was still working when there was a "happy ending" story for Cinderella's Golden Carrousel. When the carousel was being prepared for Walt Disney World, the two authentic chariots were removed so that more horses could be installed for guests. As often happens, those chariots disappeared, and Isle was unable to locate them years later.

Times change, and Disney felt that small children or guests with mobility issues might enjoy riding in a chariot. There was discussion about creating fiberglass replicas based on existing photos and artwork of the chariots, but Isle was adamant that she wanted the originals, since everything else on the carousel was original. She posted pictures in her work area, contacted as many people as possible, and tried everything she could to locate the lost chariots.

In 1996, a Cast Member who was a friend of Isle's and familiar with her hunt was walking through a Disney warehouse in California looking for something else. For a reason he is still unable to explain, he looked up and behind where he was standing. There, in the rafters, he saw what seemed to be one of the chariots, unlabeled and apparently "lost" on the books. He took a photo and sent it to Isle, who immediately confirmed it was one of the missing chariots.

It was quickly recovered. John Hench was involved in selecting the color scheme for the chariot, and it was then repaired, repainted, and installed on the WDW carousel in 1997. When I asked Isle if she would use this original as a mold for a fiberglass model to use on the other side of the carousel, she looked at me firmly and said, "Only originals." She felt that the other chariot would pop up somewhere in one of the many Disney warehouses. "After all, it only took twenty-five years to locate this one," she joked. The chariot took up the space of four horses, so the carousel now has eighty-six horses and can be enjoyed by all guests.

Whatever its official name or storyline, the carousel provides enjoyment for guests of all ages who, for two minutes, are transported into a land of imagination, where mighty steeds carry noble people on magnificent adventures.

Circarama 1955

An advanced motion picture development, Circarama, consisting of a continuous image focused on a 360-degree screen, will be introduced at Disneyland Park on July 17 by American Motors Corporation, producer of Hudson, Nash, and Rambler automobiles. and Kelvinator appliances.
— Disney Press Release, June 27, 1955

In 1960, Disney Legend Ub Iwerks was honored with the Herbert T. Kalmus Gold Medal from the Society of Motion Picture and Television Engineers (SMPTE) for his outstanding contributions to the technology used in the equipment and processes for making color motion pictures. These achievements included creating the double-headed optical printer, the color correction masking process, the xerographic process for animation, and the 360-degree Circarama system.

Circarama! Like so many early Imagineering achievements for Disneyland, this was another innovative experience sadly taken for granted and poorly documented over the years.

The original Circarama film, *A Tour of the West*, ran from 1955 to early 1960 in the building at the entrance to Tomorrowland, just to the left of the infamous clock that told the time around the world.

As Iwerks remembered it, one afternoon, while working on the Disney live-action film *Westward Ho, the Wagons!* (1956), he paused in a hallway of the Disney Studios in Burbank to talk with Walt Disney about the challenges in adapting certain films to the Cinemascope process.

Supposedly, Walt encouraged Iwerks to develop a new format for presenting movies that would completely surround an audience with a series of screens.

Disney Legend Roger Broggie remembered that after Walt had seen the new process of Cinerama at the Hollywood Pantages theater, where three large screens were synchronized to present motion pictures like *How the West Was Won* and *It's a Mad, Mad, Mad, Mad World*, he called Broggie and special effects expert Eustace Lycett into his office and wondered: Since three screens could be put together, would it be possible to extend it so there would be screens entirely surrounding the audience?

Walt's speculation resulted in the creation of the first Circarama theater, one of the few Disneyland attractions working properly for guests on Opening Day, July 17, 1955.

Even though an early version of a 360-degree film had debuted decades ago at the 1900 Paris Exposition, the Disney process was so unique that Walt and Iwerks shared a patent on Circarama that they filed on the one-year anniversary of Disneyland and received four years later on June 28, 1960.

They called it Circarama not only as an allusion to Cinerama (which later resulted in Disney renaming its process "Circle-Vision" in 1967 because the words were too similar), but also because the film was sponsored by American Motors, which used the Disney Studios to produce animated television commercials for its product and which also sponsored both the weekly Disneyland television show and Circarama itself. The original sign outside the attraction had the word "Circarama" in large dark black letters, except for "car", which was in red.

(American Motors Corporation, or AMC, was formed on January 14, 1954, by the merger of the Nash-Kelvinator Corporation and the Hudson Motor Car Company. It has been defunct since 1988.)

Nomenclature used at Disneyland during the early years was often casual. For example, in newspaper stories, internal publications, maps, guides, and other documentation of the time, Circarama has been called the American Motors Circarama Exhibit, American Motors Exhibit, American Motors presents Circarama, and Circarama, U.S.A.

No matter its official name, Circarama was the American Motors show for Disneyland. Sponsorship from Richfield, Kaiser Aluminum, Monsanto, and other companies provided funds for Tomorrowland, which was built only six months before the park opened. Without money from those lessees (as participants were known in the early days), Tomorrowland wouldn't have been built at all, since Walt had spent all of his money — and more — on the rest of the park.

In a June 27, 1955, press release about Circarama, American Motors President and Chairman George Romney said:

> This combination of photographic skills and entertainment talents promises an unusual spectacle for visitors to Disneyland. We're happy to have a part to play in making Circarama possible. As it represents added pleasure and value for the public, sponsorship of the Circarama is another forward step in our program to make American Motors mean more for Americans.

On the floor inside the attraction, five AMC automobiles were prominently displayed alongside such Kelvinator appliances as the futuristic Foodarama refrigerator ("the last word in foodkeeping") capable of holding 166 pounds of meat in its freezer, and featuring a breakfast bar for eggs, bacon, and two pitchers of juice; cheese and butter chests; an aluminum foil dispenser; and even an unrefrigerated bin for bananas!

How was this unique movie experience filmed?

Eleven 16mm Cine-Kodak Special cameras with two hundred feet of pre-threaded film magazines were mounted on a circular platform covering 360 degrees of arc. The drive shafts of all the cameras were linked mechanically via a single sprocket chain.

The tachometer permitted precise control of the shooting speed for a full range of adjustments from eight to twenty-four frames per second. The driving power was supplied by batteries and a push-button device inside the car to start, stop, and control the cameras — basically, the push button controls for the camera were on the dashboard.

This unique camera set-up was strapped to the top of an American Motors Rambler to record a travelogue down the new Los Angeles freeways to Monument Valley, the Grand Canyon, and even a visit to Las Vegas.

Disney Legend Peter Ellenshaw, art director of the original show, remembered:

> It was a travelogue in the round of Southern California and the West. They mounted eleven cameras on a circular platform atop a station wagon. I was the art director. My greatest problem is I would find this lovely composition, just beautiful, but the cameras behind this vista would show all this trash and junk. It was horrible. I had nothing to do with the mechanical side of the process. That was all Iwerks. On Wilshire Boulevard we ran the cameras at half-speed so when it was run at normal speed it seemed like we were demons going at tremendous speeds and somehow amazingly stopping just in the nick of time. That's the scene that most people remember. That film lasted until around 1959 and then they replaced it.

The filming was plagued with challenges from the start. On the way to Utah's Monument Valley, an unexpected bump sent the whole camera system lurching forward. Finding good, smooth roads in the desert was next to impossible. Pictorially, it was also a challenge when in front of the crew was a magnificent mesa or butte, and along the side or behind were electric power lines, billboards, or similar visual disturbances.

A press preview of Circarama held at the end of June was favorably reviewed in the *Los Angeles Times*, which stated, in part:

> Spectators located on a so-called island in the center of the stage where Circarama was shown at the Disney plant were able to look out in every direction and observe views of the Grand Canyon, Monument Valley, Las Vegas, Balboa Bay, and even the heavily traveled streets of Los Angeles.

The original design for the Tomorrowland theater was a central gondola from which twelve images would be shown on twelve screens surrounding the audience. With a working area only forty feet in diameter, extremely wide-angle, short focal length projection lenses would have been required, and probably would have caused image distortion. A "doughnut" type of arrangement with an odd number of screens resulted in the 360 degrees of arc being serviced perfectly.

William McGaughey Jr. recalled:

George Romney [American Motors Chairman] and Dad [Romney's assistant] were hosts of the opening of the Circarama Exhibit which opened at 8 p.m. on the preview day. A line of people were standing at the door. Dad spotted Frank Sinatra and invited him in. A black man with Sinatra was hanging back. Dad invited him to come in, too. This man turned out to be Sammy Davis Jr. After viewing Circarama, Sinatra remarked to Dad that this was the ultimate in motion pictures.

What was the experience like for *A Tour of the West*? Here's what Disneyland guests saw in 1955, after surrendering a "C" Ticket worth thirty cents.

In a twelve-hour day, Disney scheduled three showings per hour, each approximately twelve minutes long, and separated by eight-minute intermissions during which audiences were loaded into and out of the theater. The film, of course, was shown in commercial Kodachrome.

The audience stood in an asphalt-paved circular area forty feet in diameter, with the eight-foot-high screens elevated about eight feet off the floor. There were no "lean" rails in those early days. As mentioned, AMC cars and Kelvinator appliances were placed around the outside of the perimeter.

The circular screen was divided by six-inch wide vertical black strips into eleven 8x11 foot sections onto which the continuous surrounding motion picture image was thrown by eleven Eastman 16mm Model 25 projectors with self-loading take-up reels (which required no rewinding) in perfect synchronization.

Those projectors were equipped with a variable focus 15mm lens. Attendants were not needed to operate the projectors, merely to replace burnt-out bulbs in the automatic lamp changer, as well as torn film reels. Both project and sound recording were synchronized by Selsyn motor controls. The projectors were located between the black, six-inch-wide strips dividing the eleven screen sections.

The black separating panels added to the illusion of continuity between adjoining sections of the picture, because they eliminated the disturbing jiggle between adjacent screen sections on the Cinerama three-screen image, as well as making it seem the viewer was in a car looking out the windows.

This early system did have its "blind spots". A person or landmark could suddenly disappear into a blind spot only to magically reappear on the adjacent screen. The strip of black between each screen helped solve that visual problem.

Since the projectors were about twelve feet apart, it was impossible to link them together mechanically, as was done with the Cinerama system. Instead, the projectors were equipped with slotted-rotor synchronous drive motors that kept time with each other via the alternating cycles of the AC electricity that drove them. To compensate for voltage fluctuations, which might slow down or speed up one or another of the projectors, and also to synchronize the projectors with a four-track sound reproducer, a Selsyn motor control unit was superimposed on the projector installation.

The Selsyn automatically slowed down or sped up the out-of-phase motor's speed until perfect synchronism was achieved. All of that was accomplished in less than two seconds without causing the out of phase image to "bounce".

If the film should break in any of the projectors, the projector was stopped instantly and a warning light would flash at the master control panel to signal the attendant to replace the broken reel with one of the stand-by prints. That screen would be black until a replacement reel was installed.

Whenever a bulb burned out, an automatic bulb-changing mechanism on the projector swung the bulb out of position and replaced it with a fresh one, so that the picture reappeared in less than two seconds. As with a broken strip of film, a warning light would flash on the master control panel to alert the attendant that he had to put a fresh bulb in the stand-by socket.

The sound was recorded on four magnetic channels and fed into a bank of four six-inch speakers mounted beneath each projector. As a result, the theater could be flooded with sound from all the speakers or the sound could be distributed in a directional pattern in just one section. Both formats were used during the screening.

The Ralke Company of Los Angeles installed and maintained the Ciracarama unit, and the Urbran Engineering Company of Hollywood perfected the synchronization of the projectors and the sound system. Kinevox Inc. of Hollywood engineered the audio portion of the presentation. Disney Legend Bill Anderson (credited as William H. Anderson) supervised the entire film.

As the show opens, a narrator explains the projection medium and introduces the line of Kelvinator appliances. James Algar wrote the narration:

> In a few moments you will see the most unique motion picture presentation ever developed. You will be completely surrounded by the picture that you see. We hope that you will enjoy ... Circarama.

Full-color slides of these modern AMC/Kelvinator marvels were projected in quick succession on each of the eleven screens, and done in such a way that the audience follows the progression of images until all the screens are filled and the audience conditioned to expect something on every screen.

Then the screens went black and a title appeared on one of the "forward" screens proclaiming *A Tour of the West*. From there, the real show began, with all eleven screens filled with continuous images of scenery observed from an automobile cruising through Beverly Hills onto Wilshire Boulevard and then onto the Los Angeles freeway system en route to the Grand Canyon, Monument Valley, and finally Las Vegas.

When the film began, the audience had a tendency to look straight ahead at the forward motion but, as the ride continued, people became accustomed to being in a "car" and started to look out the side and rear windows as interesting roadside objects passed by, an illusion reinforced by those black strips which seemed like the window separations in a car.

Probably the most memorable segment in the film was the "race" down Wilshire Boulevard. In reality, the car was driven at fifteen to twenty miles per hour. The effect of a "high-speed" chase was achieved with an old Hollywood trick of slowing the speed of the film as it traveled through the camera, resulting in fewer frames shot, so that when the film was played back at normal speed, it looked like the car was racing. Basically, they shot at about eight frames-per-second and then projected the final film at twenty-four frames-per-second.

Ellenshaw said:

The effect was astonishing. Suddenly we were hot rodders, racing down Wilshire at a hundred miles per hours, jumping out at green lights, and crashing to a stop only inches from the cars in front.

During the whizzing down Wilshire, a police car with wailing siren is in pursuit. The camera car weaves in and out of traffic, swinging to the right and then to the left, alternately slowing down and speeding up, avoiding accidents by split-second maneuvers.

It really was a virtual thrill ride for guests of the mid-1950s, and one they talked about when they left the theater. The wail of the police siren was added to the sound track in post-production to reinforce the illusion of danger.

After Wilshire, the scene shifts to the desert, with the effect upon the audience that it is not just watching this beautiful tableau but actually being in it.

To ensure that audiences would scan all the screens, Disney used subtle manipulation. In the Las Vegas scenes, set at poolside at one of the resorts, the camera films two charming young ladies in delightfully form-fitting swimsuits. With the cameras fixed forward, the bathing beauties walk separately with poise and confidence along paths on either side of the circle of cameras, meeting each other again at the rear screen. Much, if not all, of the male audience frantically tried to follow the action around the screen.

In a little more than eleven minutes, Disneyland guests journeyed through the West, beginning on Sunset Boulevard in front of the Beverly Hills Hotel, then down Wilshire Boulevard at breakneck speed, and then along the Los Angeles freeways to Monument Valley, Arizona. The adventure continued through Newport Harbor in California (with the cameras mounted on a speedboat instead of the car) and then off to Las Vegas and the Grand Canyon.

A review in a 1955 issue of *Popular Photography* magazine speculated:

> Has Circarama a future? It doesn't seem likely as a story-telling entertainment medium. On the other hand, it has infinite possibilities in the form in which it made its appearance at Disneyland — as a travelogue device, to

subject an audience to an unusual visual and emotional experience.

In 1958, Walt created *America the Beautiful*, a brand-new Circarama film for the Brussels World's Fair. The new film showcased the entire United States. In June 1960, the new film debuted at Disneyland, sponsored by Bell Telephone.

In 1967, the film process changed with the opening of the New Tomorrowland: now there was a 35mm print enlarged from the film of nine (rather than eleven) 16mm cameras. A few Bicentennial scenes were added in 1975. The film ran until January 1984.

Other films, including *Wonders of China* and *American Journeys*, were shown in the theater until 1996. *America the Beautiful* returned for a run lasting from July 1996 through September 1997, and then the theater was closed for good.

It all started, however, with the first Circarama presentation on July 17, 1955, of *A Tour of the West*. When William McGaughey Sr. was asked in 1998 about the innovative attraction of which he had sponsorship control in 1955, he said:

> When the Circarama presentation was completed, Sinatra gave his verdict. He turned to Mr. Davis and said, "This is the wave of the future. The motion picture single screen is obsolete and future movies will use this exciting new technology." He was wrong, of course. Nevertheless, his words were encouraging and I felt somewhat redeemed that my Big Boss Romney had accepted my recommendation to pay the heavy rental cost for Disneyland exhibitions.

Liberty Street 1959

*Disneyland is dedicated to the ideals, the dreams,
and the hard facts that have created America*

— Walt Disney, Disneyland Dedication Speech, July 17, 1955

In a 1957 interview with newspaper columnist Hedda Hopper, Walt stated

> There's an American theme behind the whole park. I believe in emphasizing the story of what made America great and what will keep it great.

Even around the dinner table at his home, Walt would engage his family in discussions about the Constitution. So it is not surprising that Walt wanted a section of Disneyland devoted to the founding of America.

To the left of the Disneyland Opera House, Walt wanted a street running parallel to Main Street called Liberty Street. He didn't want guests to follow it to the Hub, so he envisioned it as a cul-de-sac, with Main Street the only path to other lands.

Publicity and signage at Disneyland announced that Liberty Street would open in 1959, and the area remained on Disneyland park maps for several years as a "future development". Originally, the street was to be called International Street, with a variety of buildings representing different countries. That project was announced for 1958. However, by 1957, Walt had decided to use the land to showcase the founding fathers.

The 1957 release of the live-action Disney feature film *Johnny Tremain* (first planned as a two-part episode for the

Disneyland television show) may have influenced Walt to develop an area of the park to capture that time period, especially since planning for Liberty Square officially began during that same year.

Liberty Street was to be an architectural mix of several American cities as they existed during the Revolutionary Era. At one point, there were to be thirteen buildings, one for each of the original thirteen colonies.

Cobblestones would pave the way down Liberty Street and into Liberty Square, where guests would find a blacksmith shop, apothecary, glassmaker, weaver, print shop, insurance office, silversmith, and cabinetmaker. All the shops and exhibits would represent the types of enterprises found in late Colonial America. The shops would showcase people not only selling their wares but also practicing their crafts for guests to enjoy.

On an early Disneyland map, some areas in Liberty Square were identified by name, including Griffin's Wharf (supposedly the site of the infamous Boston Tea Party), with tri-masted schooners in the harbor; Paul Revere's Silver Shop; Boston Observer Print Shoppe; and a Liberty Tree in the town square.

The original outline for the project stated that:

> ... [T]he audience will walk around the street toward Independence Hall where the Liberty Bell would be constantly tolling.

(Fortunately, in Florida, wiser heads realized a constantly tolling Liberty Bell would be more of an irritant than a joy when they installed their own replica of the Liberty Bell.)

One of the exhibits in Liberty Square would have been a scale model of the Capitol building. Long-time Disneyland visitors might remember the model on display for many years at the pre-show area for the Walt Disney Story film. That model was purchased by Walt Disney himself from an artisan who had devoted twenty-five years of his life to carving it out of stone.

Liberty Hall (called Independence Hall in some versions) was the centerpiece of Liberty Square, and the entrance to the land's two major attractions: Hall of the Declaration of Independence and Hall of Presidents of the United States. A large foyer with dioramas depicting famous scenes of the Revolutionary Era would be the common entrance to the two big auditoriums.

The Hall of the Declaration of Independence would present the dramatic story of the birth of the United States through three scenes based on three famous paintings. These scenes would be three framed settings with three-dimensional, sculpted, life-sized human figures in costume. It was hoped the figures would move realistically but in a limited fashion. Narration (sprinkled with quotes from the Declaration of Independence) would tell the story and historical significance of each tableau, accompanied by dramatic lighting and music. Theatrical curtains would open and close on each scene.

The first scene was inspired by the painting *The Drafting of the Declaration of Independence* by J.L.G. Ferris, and shows Ben Franklin and John Adams in consultation with Thomas Jefferson as he drafts the Declaration of Independence.

The second scene would be based on *Signing of the Declaration of Independence* by John Trumbull, and the third scene on *Ringing of the Liberty Bell* by Henry Mosler.

Of course, the theater would try to capture the feel of the time period, with bench-like pews that could seat up to five hundred guests. Overhead, thirteen stars representing the original thirteen colonies would light the auditorium.

However, the main attraction in Liberty Hall was to be the Hall of Presidents of the United States. In 1963, Imagineer Wathel Rogers, who was working on an Audio-Animatronics figure of President Abraham Lincoln, said:

> Lincoln is part of a Disneyland project called *One Nation Under God*. It will start with a Circarama presentation of great moments in constitutional crises. Circarama is a special motion-picture technique Walt developed for Disneyland and the Brussels World's Fair. The Bell Telephone Circarama now at Disneyland tells the story of the great sights of America. It has a 360-degree screen. The audience is surrounded by the continuous action, as if they were moving with the camera and able to see in all directions.
>
> The Circarama for the *One Nation Under God* showing will have a 200-degree screen. After the Circarama showing, a curtain will close, then open again to reveal the Hall of

Presidents. The visitor will see all the Chief Executives modeled life-size. He'll think it's a waxworks — until Lincoln stands up and begins to talk.

Walt assigned James Algar, who would later compose the final speech for Great Moments With Mr. Lincoln from a variety of Lincoln's speeches, to research information on the United States Presidents, and in particular, the Constitution, which was to be the foundation of the show. The Circarama presentation would primarily feature enlarged paintings spotlighting key moments in early United States history, with the climax a violent Civil War battle.

Imagineer Sam McKim recalled:

> Walt wanted artillery that would fire from one screen across to the enemy on a screen on the other side and you'd see things blow up, and then you smell cordite. It was smell-o-vision!

In the Hall of Presidents of the United States auditorium, the stage lights would brighten and the curtains would partially open to reveal life-sized sculpted and costumed figures of the U.S. presidents. They would all be in silhouette except for the main figure — not Lincoln but George Washington.

The show, *One Nation Under God*, was planned as a theater presentation of "the mighty cavalcade of American History". Imagineer David Mumford wrote:

> Martial music would come up as lights played on the features of Washington, creating a feeling of reality. Narrations of the trials, decisions and formation of America's heritage were to be complemented by excerpts from presidential speeches. At the conclusion, all the nation's presidents [thirty-four by 1957] would be seen on the enormous stage against a rear-projected image of the United States Capitol, as clouds panned across the sky and a musical finale closed the show.

The show would depend heavily on the development of Audio-Animatronics, a technology still in its early stages. WED had begun producing prototypes, including the head of an elderly Chinese man for a figure that Walt had originally intended for a Chinese restaurant in Center Street near the Market House. An elderly Chinese man wearing long flowing robes would have justified and concealed any shaky, slow, awkward movements when the figure came to life.

Walt needed a good deal of money for further development, so in June 1961, he went looking for a company to sponsor *One Nation Under God* for the 1964 New York World's Fair.

Imagineering compiled a presentation that included a small model theater and a thirty-two minute slide presentation to entice potential corporate backers. A press package featured a little, smiling Tinker Bell in a tri-cornered hat sitting on a sign that proclaimed "Liberty Street in Disneyland!"

An excerpt from that proposal, dated June 29, 1961, stated:

> As presently planned, *One Nation Under God* will be a twenty-seven minute live-action film dramatizing significant episodes in U.S. history, linked together with off-screen narration. Starting with the adoption of the Constitution, the film traces the development of our concept of government, through trial and tribulation, right up to the present.
>
> The technique is an extension of the Circarama idea, in that five projectors will be used instead of three — thus spreading the picture over an expanse of 260 degrees, or well beyond the field of human vision. As in Circarama, the audience enjoys the sensation of being right in the middle of everything. This feeling is enhanced by the use of multiple stereophonic sound tracks — and even "smells" (*e.g.*, the odor of gunpowder in battle).
>
> In a space age sequence, an extra dimension is added; the picture spreads up onto a dome overhead. For the finale, a "Hall of Presidents" is unveiled. This consists of life-sized moving and talking figures of thirty-four presidents — something brand new now being developed at Disney Studios.

The proposal went on for a few more paragraphs, but unfortunately, the cost of such an attraction was prohibitive, and even those sponsors who were impressed with the presentation felt that it didn't connect with their product.

Imagineering was working on a prototype of President Lincoln, a particular favorite of Walt's, for the Hall of Presidents of the United States, when in April 1962, Robert Moses (who was promoting the New York World's Fair) dropped by the Disney Studios to check the progress on the other attractions. He also got an impromptu demonstration of the Lincoln figure. Moses arranged for the State of Illinois to help pay for the development of the figure for its state pavilion at the fair.

Although crude by today's standards, the "winking, blinking Lincoln", as one reporter called it, thrilled audiences. Many spectators were convinced Lincoln was a live actor, and suspicious children sometimes shot small ball bearings at the figure to try to disrupt the performer's concentration.

A second version of Great Moments With Mr. Lincoln was installed at Disneyland on July 18, 1965, mere feet away from where the entrance to Liberty Street was planned.

Instead of creating Liberty Street in 1959, Walt Disney used his money and expertise to update Tomorrowland with the Monorail, the Submarine Voyage, and the Matterhorn.

But Imagineering never fully abandoned Walt's dream. Disney World's Liberty Square captures the spirit of Walt's plans for Disneyland's Liberty Street in 1959, including a Hall of Presidents housed in a building inspired by Philadelphia's Independence Hall as well as other Federal-style civic buildings that would have been found in the city during that era.

James Algar, author of the original script, said:

> The show was on and off at various times in the Studio, but when it came time to really firm it up for Florida, when I dug out the original script, it dated back to 1961. And the Hall of Presidents was very much Walt's baby. He had this great desire to present to an audience all of the Presidents of the United States on stage at once. He read into that single idea a feeling that it would have great impact and great audience interest and fascination and, in truth, it does.

In May 1957, Walt Disney stated:

> As you know, Disneyland park is sort of a monument to the American way of life but after reading *Johnny Tremain*, we realized we had overlooked one major item in the blueprint ... a memorial to the freedoms that made it all possible. We're putting it in right here off of Town Square. We're calling it Liberty Street. Everything is still in the planning stages, of course. In effect, Liberty Street will by Johnny Tremain's Boston of about 1775.

While that dream never came true for Disneyland, the spirit of Walt's intentions finally were realized with the opening of Liberty Square in Walt Disney World.

Zorro at Disneyland

For a certain generation, the theme song from Disney's weekly television show *Zorro* still stirs the blood and conjures images of Halloweens past, when children dressed up as their swashbuckling hero. In 1958, Ben Cooper, Inc., one of the largest Halloween costume manufacturers in the country, announced that its Zorro costume was outselling all others by a ratio of 3:1. Today, unfortunately, most children know little of Zorro.

Walt considered many actors for the roles of Zorro/Don Diego and Captain Enrique Sanchez Monastario (Zorro's main antagonist in the first thirteen episodes). Dozens of actors were tested, including Hugh O'Brian, John Lupton, Jack Kelly, Dennis Weaver, David Janssen, and Henry Darrow, until it came down to Guy Williams and Britt Lomond, respectively.

Lomond had more theatrical experience, and Walt reportedly wanted him for the part of Zorro, but writer-director Norman Foster preferred Williams, who showed greater flexibility in the role. Williams got the part, with Lomond cast as the villainous Captain. The actors cast as the other two major characters — Henry Calvin as Sergeant Garcia and Gene Sheldon as the mute servant Bernardo — were nearly as popular with the audience in their roles as were Williams and Lomond in theirs.

Today, the fabled Disney backlot where Zorro fought for justice (and where Walt locked up actor Ken Murray's two daughters in a jail cell for their father to rescue them on Murray's home movies) is a parking garage.

Walt was famous for doing cross-promotions like having the Mousekeeters and Fess Parker (as Davy Crockett) appear at Disneyland. When the half-hour *Zorro* adventure show on ABC became a success, Walt had the cast appear at Disneyland for special appearances dubbed "Zorro Days", which he publicized with large advertisements in local newspapers. Williams, Lomond, Calvin, and Sheldon were announced for the event.

Not announced was the appearance of Buddy Van Horn, who performed stunts dressed as Zorro at Disneyland.

Stuntman Wayne "Buddy" Van Horn was hired primarily as Guy Williams' double. Wisely, at the urging of Britt Lomond, Van Horn practiced with fencing instructor Fred Cavens, who choreographed the fencing scenes (just as he had done with Douglas Fairbanks Sr., Errol Flynn, Tyrone Power, and Basil Rathbone in many classic films) and coached the actors. He was also the stunt coordinator for all other action scenes.

Van Horn often doubled for Williams in the horseback riding scenes, and in any scenes that called for dangerous leaping off of walls, running across rooftops, or swinging on ropes. Williams was athletic and capable of doing much of this action himself, but had he been injured doing it, the Studio would have faced costly filming delays. Ironically, the Studio released publicity stills of Van Horn dressed as Zorro, assuming the audience wouldn't notice the difference between him and Williams. Someone joked to Williams that he had better be careful, since Disney could put anyone in the Zorro costume.

It was Van Horn, attired as Zorro, who did some of the daring stunts at the Disneyland shows like dashing over the rooftops of the Golden Horseshoe Revue. At personal appearances, Van Horn accompanied Williams for fencing demonstrations, taking on the role of the villain, and sometimes Van Horn himself performed as Zorro when Williams was unavailable, for example, at a Disney family night at the Hollywood Bowl in summer 1958.

There were five major Zorro appearances at Disneyland in the park's early years: April 26-27,1958; May 30-June 1, 1958; November 27-30, 1958; November 26-29, 1959; and finally, November 11-13, 1960.

Lomond did not appear at the November 1958 appearance because of a conflict, and Williams appeared by himself for personal appearances at Disneyland during the 1958 Christmas season. The *Zorro* cast appeared on a float for the June 15, 1959, televised special *Kodak Presents Disneyland '59.*

In his colorful, self-published memoir, Chasing After Zorro (2001), Lomond remembered:

> Personal appearances for all the principal actors in the *Zorro* cast were always very important to Walt and to the other executives at the studio. They all felt that it was very important for the cast to always stay in contact with their admiring viewers. This was included in every star's contract and many of the featured player's contracts on the shows as well.

During Zorro Days, the actors appeared in the parades and performed in Frontierland for four shows daily. Three of the shows featured a running battle between Zorro and Monastario over the rooftops of Frontierland, usually capped with a sword-fight aboard the *Mark Twain* and some of Zorro's foes ending up in the Rivers of America.

The fourth show, held in Magnolia Park, generally featured an autograph session or an impromptu fencing match with guest volunteers. Williams and Lomond would again cross swords for the enjoyment of the guests, and Calvin and Sheldon would amuse the crowd with comedy and magic.

Publicist John Ormond said:

> I suggested we invite anyone from the audience the opportunity to fence, or "sword fight" as we called it, with Zorro. We always had two or three "takers" at each show who wanted to take Guy on. This is a piece of audience participation that worked well at Disneyland whenever Zorro appeared. And by the way, we were using real swords. At Disneyland, we had a security and screening process so things couldn't get out of hand.

During an interview, Lomond recalled:

> Disney always liked the casts of his shows to make appearances at Disneyland. It was great for attendance at the park and a lot of Zorro products were sold at the same time. Things like little Zorro costumes, play swords, puzzles, games and dozens of other items relating to the series. Money would pour into the Disney coffers. These personal appearances were

a great moneymaker for the studio and Walt knew it certainly helped in the ratings which made ABC a very happy puppy.

The Disney Studio's Production Coordinator, Lou Debney, set all the details of the appearance. The program Lou had for Guy and I at Disneyland was a very good one. There was a replica of a Mississippi steam boat called the *Mark Twain*. We were to perform in costume one of our spectacular fencing routines on the upper deck of the paddle-wheeler, at the end of which, I would be disarmed and go into my usual Monastario fist clenching and facial grimaces. Guy meanwhile would laugh at the commandant's disgrace and run down the gangplank to his trusty black stallion, leap onto the saddle, wave to the adoring crowd and ride off into the sunset (or the usual California smog). Every one of us would then join in a parade down the Main Street of Disneyland. Henry Calvin and Gene Sheldon would sit in a car behind Guy and I riding on our respective black and white horses. We would wave to the adoring crowds that lined either side of the street, cheering us as we passed by them.

Everything sounded great — both Guy and I were very pleased with the program that Lou had presented. We practiced one of our fencing routines for the series for several days in the large back yard of my house in Studio City. My house was easier to work at because Guy still lived in an apartment in Hollywood.

Finally the day came of our first personal appearance at Disneyland. Everything went perfectly smooth ... almost. Guy and I did our fencing routine on the deck of the *Mark Twain*, ending with my sword sailing into the air, as Guy disarmed me. He then strutted down the gangplank and ran to his black stallion where he was to leap into the saddle, lifting his sword in victory and ride off. Great! However, when we tried this routine for the first time at Disneyland, Guy missed the horse's saddle and sailed completely over him, landing on the pavement and sliding into a pool of muddy water on the other side. A bit humiliating! The audience and I laughed uncontrollably. I'm sorry but we just could not help it. The picture of Guy's expression and the mud still dripping off his nose was too much for everyone. I quickly raised my arm in victory and bowed graciously to the applauding crowd. This was the Commandante's one and only victory over his nemesis, Zorro.

To be fair, others don't remember that incident (or at

least not as colorfully as Lomond did). John Ormond, who handled the *Zorro* show as well as *The Mickey Mouse Club*, was involved with the Disneyland presentations as well as some of Guy Williams's personal appearances. He wrote:

> The *Zorro* show was mostly filmed at the studio, although we did have one lengthy spell down near Oceanside, shooting at an old Spanish mission. Walt came down for that four-parter, and brought his wife with him. Walt liked watercress sandwiches and Mrs. Disney made sure she brought a good supply while they were with us on location.
>
> As the weeks went by, I became close to Guy Williams, and we had a lot in common. He liked to play chess, and I liked gin rummy. So we alternated playing while we were on the set. Later, when we toured together for the *Zorro* feature, we always played (magnetic) chess on the planes. Guy was hard to beat at chess, but I outscored him with the cards.

Guy Williams made a host of other public appearances as Zorro, including the Pasadena Rose Parade in 1958 and 1959, state fairs, shopping centers, and more. He said:

> The show has been a great experience, but Zorro is a role I both love and hate. It wasn't what I prepared for as an actor. I'm not worried about being typed as Zorro because the whole thing has had so many pleasant aspects to it. Besides, such typecasting buys a lot of groceries.

Tom Sawyer Island

Tom Sawyer Island at Disneyland underwent a major transformation in 2007 and became the Pirate's Lair on Tom Sawyer Island, theming into the success of the *Pirates of the Caribbean* movie franchise and replacing the simple charm of Mark Twain's world.

Tom Sawyer Island at Walt Disney World's Frontierland has remained the same for forty years and still showcases some of Walt's original ideas.

When asked about Disneyland's Tom Sawyer Island by a Reader's Digest reporter in 1960, Walt explained:

> I put in all the things I wanted to do as a kid — and couldn't. Including getting into something without a ticket.

Tom Sawyer Island is the only part of Disneyland that Walt single-handedly designed himself. He always planned for an island in the middle of the Rivers of America, but he debated about what that island was going to be.

From Walt's 1953 sales pitch for Disneyland:

> Treasure Island. Mickey Mouse, the best-known personality in the world has his Mickey Mouse Club headquarters at Disneyland located on Treasure Island in the middle of the river, a fantastic hollow tree and treehouse serves as the Club meeting place. The hollow tree is several stories high, with interesting rooms and lookout spots for club members. There is a Pirate cove and buried treasure on the island ... and direct from this location the Club presents The Mickey Mouse Club Television Show.

At one point, designs for the island included miniature reproductions of major American historical landmarks like

Mount Vernon, Monticello, and Independence Hall that would have been visible from the *Mark Twain* steamboat.

While many Disney fans know that Herb Ryman did the artwork for the original map of Disneyland, and Peter Ellenshaw did the artwork for the huge map of Disneyland that Walt often used on the television program, few realize that it was Imagineer Marvin Davis who labored through dozens of map designs trying to find a workable pattern for the actual Disneyland that opened in 1955. He struggled over the contours of Tom Sawyer Island, but his efforts failed to please Walt.

"Give me that thing," Davis remembers Walt saying. That night Walt worked for hours in his red barn workshop in the backyard at his home in the Holmby Hills. The next morning, he laid tracing paper on Davis's desk and said, "Now that's the way it should be." The island was built according to Walt's design.

Davis stated:

> The general shape of the island, the way it curves and so forth, was Walt's idea. The idea for Pirate's Cove on Tom Sawyer Island was also Walt's.

Imagineer Herb Ryman remembered:

> I was originally called upon to name some of the nomen- clature for Tom Sawyer Island. Walt came up to me and he said, "Herbie, would you think up some names?" Obviously you think about Smuggler's Gulch and Robber's Cove and kind of inspiring names that little children would be excited about. And then later one day, Bill Cottrell told me, he and Walt rode around on the *Mark Twain* and Walt had this map in front of him where these names were allocated according to my designation. And Walt said, "Why should we let Herbie have all the fun and name all these names on the island? Why can't I name these?" And Bill said, "Yes, I think you could." So Walt re-named all these names.

In 1960, Imagineer Dick Irvine advised a Reader's Digest reporter:

> When you go to Frontierland, make sure that Walt takes you to Tom Sawyer Island. Walt was brought up in Missouri — Mark Twain country — and that island is all his. He didn't let anybody help him design it.

Actually, Vic Greene, the original art director for Frontierland, worked with Imagineers Herb Ryman and Claude Coats to produce the first designs for the Island based on Walt's ideas, including the barrel bridge that appeared in 1957. Sam McKim did some finished renderings for the Old Mill, Fort Wilderness, and the tree house. Bill Evans did the landscaping. Emile Kuri located some "second-hand" stuffed animals at a museum to put on the remote end of the island.

During the second week of June 1956, advertisements appeared of a raft with a pirate skull-and-crossbones flag making its way to Tom Sawyer Island. The ads proclaimed:

> Now Open at Disneyland! Another NEW attraction! Tom Sawyer Island! Cross the river on A RAFT ... explore INJUN JOE'S CAVE ... with the SUSPENSION BRIDGE ... visit FORT WILDERNESS ... see the BURNING SETTLER'S CABIN. Relive exciting days out of America's lusty past. Explore all the magical mysteries of an island built just for FUN! Whatever you want to do, you will find fun and excitement for the whole family at this newest Disneyland attraction ... Tom Sawyer Island.

During construction ,a billboard announced that the island would open June 1, 1956. It didn't. Opening ceremonies were held at noon on Saturday, June 16, 1956, at the raft landing on the island. Two young guests were on hand in costume as Tom Sawyer and Becky Thatcher, and appeared in many newspaper and magazine photos with Walt.

Perva Lou Smith and Chris Winkler, two children from Hannibal, Missouri, had won the very first of the now-annual Tom Sawyer and Becky Thatcher contests in Hannibal.

Although they did not know it when they competed, an added bonus for Hannibal's 1956 Tom and Becky was a chance to travel to Disneyland, stay at the Disneyland Hotel, and together with Walt Disney himself preside over the dedication ceremonies for Tom Sawyer Island.

Perva Lou and Chris carried with them water from the Mississippi River and earth from Jackson's Island (the model for the island frequented by Tom and Huck in Twain's novels). With Walt's help, the two kids christened the raft with a jug of Mississippi River water and planted a box of soil from Jackson's Island near the foot of the landing pier. The island was "officially" made a part of Missouri.

After the dedication, there was a tour of the island, including Injun Joe's Cave (actually an above-ground building covered with earth and landscaping to give the illusion of descending into a cave), Huckleberry Finn's Fishing Pier (the water off the pier was stocked with 15,000 catfish, perch, and bluegill for guests to catch with a bamboo pole and a worm — Walt caught a fish for the press that day, but it got away before he could land it), Fort Wilderness, and other points of interest.

One of the biggest kids of all was Walt Disney himself who, once the island was officially opened, would often take a pole and fish from the dock with the youngsters. One day, after fishing for some time without so much as a nibble, Disney turned to the dock attendant and said, "There's no fish in the river!"

The attendant replied, "There's fish there, all right, but the water's so muddy, they can't even see the bait."

Walt responded, "Well, I fished the Missouri River and it was a lot muddier than this, but the fish sure saw the bait!"

The fishing was soon eliminated, because it became quite a challenge for guests to walk around Disneyland the rest of the day with their increasingly pungent catch that they often discarded in some unusual locations.

After the dedication, everyone boarded the rafts and returned across the Rivers of America to the Plantation House terrace, where an "old-fashioned fish fry" was served, with thirty-eight pounds of authentic river catfish flown in from the Mark Twain Hotel in Hannibal for the occasion.

The Hannibal Chamber of Commerce made the Tom and Becky contests a regular feature of the local Fourth of July celebration. Those winners lucky enough to fill the roles during a year when the Disney Company dedicated a new theme park, such as the Magic Kingdom in Florida or Tokyo Disneyland, would join the dedication ceremonies for the Tom Sawyer Island in that park.

Perva Lou Smith and Chris Winkler are still alive. They returned to Hannibal in 2005 for the 50th Anniversary celebration, along with other Tom and Beckys chosen over the years. Smith still remembers her long-ago lunch with Walt.

The Indian canoes were introduced on July 4, 1956. In

summer 1957, Castle Rock Ridge, the Pontoon Bridge, and Tom and Huck's Treehouse (for many years "the highest point in Disneyland") were added for guests to enjoy. Originally, there were only two rafts, Tom and Huck, but this expansion brought two new rafts, Becky Thatcher and Injun Joe. Each of these free-floating rafts carried up to forty-five guests. The island had two landings, and when the *Mark Twain* was being refurbished, the rafts would carry guests all the way around the island.

Fort Wilderness was built entirely backstage, then disassembled, trucked to Frontierland, and floated across the river, log by log, for reassembly on the island. A mocked up, full-size wood skeleton framework was erected on the island first so Walt and his Imagineers could determine whether the fort would look good in its proposed location, and whether it would be visible from places it shouldn't be.

What was it like in those early years? While Cast Members were scattered about the island to keep an eye on the youngsters, Walt had given strict orders to let the kids enjoy themselves. One security officer took his job too seriously and tried to keep the kids quiet and orderly. Within a week, he was transferred to a gate-watching job on the night shift.

The Saturday Evening Post (June 28, 1958) and other magazines, including *Parade* (April 7, 1957), spotlighted a teenage boy named Tom Nabbe who waylaid Walt in 1956. Nabbe had been selling the *Disneyland News* newspaper in the park since the day Disneyland opened.

Nabbe remembered:

> I found Walt and told him I looked just like Tom Sawyer and he should hire me to be Tom Sawyer on the island. He didn't hire me on the spot like I had hoped. But the key thing is he didn't say "no". So that left the door open. He said that he'd think about it. Anytime I could find Walt in the park, I would ask him if he were still thinking about it. He finally said, "You know, I could put a mannequin ... or was it a dummy? ... I could put a mannequin, I think it was, that wouldn't be leaving every five minutes for a hot dog and a coke.

Referred to in articles as "the luckiest boy in the world", Nabbe was hired to lead other kids through Injun Joe's dark and scary cave, bait guests' fishhooks, and answer questions.

During the summer and weekends, Nabbe worked full-time, but during the week, he had to attend school and maintain a "C" average.

In its June 29, 1958, issue, *The Saturday Evening Post* ran a story about Disneyland that featured Nabbe's role in the park:

> "Mr. Disney comes to me for advice now," brags Tom Nabbe as he sits barefoot on the dock at the island, clad in dungarees and faded green shirt. "Why, when he wanted to put in a slide, I told him it would be bad because a lot of the kids who come here are dressed in their best clothes. So he didn't put the slide in."

Tom Nabbe lived near Disneyland, and he and his mother, an autograph collector, were outside the gates on opening day, July 17, 1955. When Danny Thomas exited the park early, he gave two of his complimentary passes to Tom and his mother, and they went in and enjoyed themselves.

On the next day, twelve-year-old Tom got a job as a newspaper boy hawking the *Disneyland News* to guests coming to the park. If he sold a certain number of issues, he was allowed into Disneyland for free.

Hearing that Tom Sawyer Island was going to open, Nabbe kept approaching Walt about playing the part of Tom Sawyer. Walt believed that children visiting the island should imagine themselves as Tom Sawyer, but eventually, he gave in to Nabbe's persistent pleas.

A Disneyland press release stated:

> It wasn't an easy task, working all day long in the hot sun, but it had many rewards, including the envy of all the other youngsters who came to visit and the attention of national magazines and news writers.

One important job requirement was that Nabbe had to keep a "C" grade average in school. So, every quarter, the boy brought his report card directly to Walt for inspection.

After outgrowing the role of Tom Sawyer, Nabbe managed other attractions. In 1964, he met his wife, Janice, who was working at a concession stand in the park, and they married in June 1968. He continued working for the Disney Company for nearly fifty years (mostly at Walt Disney World) and was made a Disney Legend in 2005.

Tom Nabbe recalled:

Unfortunately, that opening was all scheduled around the winners of the Tom Sawyer and Becky Thatcher contest from Hannibal, Missouri. But from that point forward, I was the one and only Tom Sawyer. They gave me a title as "guest aide". That was my occupational title. I started working in Entertainment, but they didn't know what to do with me, so they gave me over to Operations. They had stocked the Rivers of America will blue gill and catfish, and we had 25 fishing poles on each of the two piers, so a total of 50 fishing poles. I had to ensure the fishing poles were put out each morning and had hooks and sinkers and corks on them. And worms. I had to make sure worms were out in the cans and available for people to bait their hooks, and if they didn't want to bait their hooks, I had to bait the hooks for them.

And I would pose for pictures with them. When you get down to it, I really looked more like Huck Finn, who had the fire red hair and freckles, and some guests thought I was Huck Finn. Tom Sawyer didn't have red hair. The guests fished on the island through about mid-1960. The only change was, when the Tom Sawyer Island opened, it was catch-and-clean the fish, but the dead ones that the guests left behind didn't smell too good, so we went to catch-and-release for the end of the first summer, and I was happy about that decision because I was the one who cleaned the fish.

I worked through junior high and high school as Tom Sawyer. When I was seventeen or so, they didn't know what to do with me. I was a little too old to be Tom Sawyer but not old enough to be a ride operator. When I turned eighteen, I became a ride operator. Very little training. I had already operated the rafts and things early in the morning when guests weren't in the park. So I stepped into that role.

Over the years, Tom Sawyer Island has seen not only changes but tragedy and turmoil, including the drowning death of a young boy who hid out on the island past its closing time and then tried to swim back to shore with his brother on his back. A six-year-old girl lost part of her index finger when she caught it in a rifle trigger in one of the guns at Fort Wilderness. As a result of those incidents, security for the island was increased, and the rifles eliminated.

After a refurbishment of Disneyland's Tom Sawyer Island

in 2003, Fort Wilderness was closed, and then in 2007, Disney demolished the fort due to long-neglected termite and weather damage. A new Fort Wilderness facade not accessible to guests was constructed from standard milled lumber. It's used as a break area for Cast Members and performers.

Today, Tom Sawyer Island bears minimal resemblance to Walt Disney's original vision, partly because times have changed and some of its original activities are now deemed hazardous. Still, parts of the island continue to evoke Tom and Huck, and the rustic playground designed by Walt Disney himself that delighted children for decades.

Mickey Mouse Revue

In the December 31, 1962, issue of *Newsweek* magazine, Walt Disney talked about his plans to create an attraction at Disneyland for "all of the Disney characters, so everyone can see them. I have in mind a theater, and the figures will not only put on the show but be sitting in the boxes with the visitors, heckling. I don't know just when I'll do that."

Almost a decade later, the Mickey Mouse Revue opened on October 1, 1971, at Walt Disney World as an "E" Ticket attraction in Fantasyland.

The Revue began with an eight-minute pre-show of Mickey's career and the use of sound in animated films. At the end of the pre-show, Mickey and the narrator have this exchange:

> Narrator: Join us now in a presentation of the latest colossal achievement in Mickey's illustrious career. Mickey Mouse, bigger and better than ever, appears in a completely new dimension, leading his friends in a medley of Walt Disney musical highlights.

> Mickey: Come along folks! It's time for the Mickey Mouse Musical Revue! [Theater doors open]

Originally, the show — which ran nearly ten minutes — was going to be called the Mickey Mouse Musical Revue, and that was the name used on some early posters as well as in the pre-show. In the show itself, an Audio-Animatronics Mickey Mouse conducts an "all-toon" orchestra of twenty-three characters to showcase scenes and songs from memorable Disney animated films that were staged around the orchestra.

Seventy-three different Disney animated characters performed in the show, including the Fab Five, Humphrey the Bear, Timothy Mouse, Winnie the Pooh, Baloo, Scrooge McDuck, and many others who filled the eighty-six-foot-long stage. (To be precise, a total of eighty-one figures were in the show, since some characters like the Three Caballeros appeared in different places on the stage, while others appeared in different costumes.) Several characters planned for the show, including Horace Horsecollar, Clara Cluck, and the Big Bad Wolf, didn't end up in the final production. However, a shadow of the Big Bad Wolf did appear during the song "Who's Afraid of the Big Bad Wolf?"

Songs performed during the show included:

- "Heigh Ho"
- "Whistle While You Work"
- "When You Wish Upon A Star"
- "Hi Diddle Dee Dee"
- "Who's Afraid of The Big Bad Wolf"
- "I'm Wishing"
- "The Silly Song"
- "All In The Golden Afternoon"
- "Bibbidi-Bobbidi-Boo"
- "So This Is Love"
- "Zip-a-Dee-Doo-Dah"
- "Mickey Mouse Club March"

The artists who sang these songs in the Revue were not the same artists who had sung them on the film soundtracks, perhaps for legal reasons or because Disney found it cheaper to use new artists rather than compensate the original artists.

Imagineer Bill Justice had a long and illustrious career with the Disney Company. Among his many achievements, he was the primary animator of Chip 'n' Dale, he experimented with stop-motion animation for *Babes in Toyland*, he created the opening credits for Disney live-action films, he designed character costumes at Disneyland, he was one of the original Audio-Animatronics programmers for attractions like Pirates of the Caribbean, and he directed the animated opening sequence for the original *Mickey Mouse Club* television show.

Justice came up with the idea for the Mickey Mouse

Revue around the same time work began on the Magic Kingdom in Florida, though of course, others were involved in the process, including John Hench and Blaine Gibson. In his limited edition memoir, *Justice for Disney* (1992), Justice first revealed his role in the creation of the Revue. I conducted two lengthy interviews with him, the first when he visited the Disney Institute and the second when he performed with me at Give Kids the World (a non-profit resort facility for terminally ill children in Central Florida).

During those interviews, Justice told me, in part:

> WED had designed some imaginative shows for the parks, but we seemed to be getting away from our heritage. Pirates of the Caribbean was a big hit, but what did it have to do with Disney? What we needed was a reminder of what Walt had accomplished. I pulled out a sheet of paper and got to work.
>
> Mickey Mouse would have to be the main figure. Yet some mention must be made of our great animated classics. I made sketches of all the characters I thought should appear. Then, I called upon my modeling skills to build a 1/16 scale paper cut-out model of what I wanted. This was before photo-copying machines with reducing capabilities, so I had to make all the drawings in scale. Many of the figures had to be drawn, a quarter-inch high. The entire set was about 18 inches long by 3.5 inches high. But this model was a good tool for planning the show sequence and experimenting with different scenes.
>
> Once I thought I had a winner, it was time for a bigger model. I recruited some craftsmen and we built a room size miniature theater with a stage about twelve feet wide. Blaine Gibson and his assistants sculpted all the figures to 1/4 inch scale from my drawings. Everything worked except the figures themselves — lighting, turntables, curtains, sound tracks. When we were done, I notified my bosses. They invited Roy O. Disney to see the results of our work. The show we had in mind was this:
>
> Mickey Mouse would lead an orchestra of Studio characters through a medley of Disney tunes. Then on the sides of the stage and behind the orchestra, scenes from our most popular animated features would appear one by one. Mickey and his orchestra would close the performance. Roy looked the model over, then paid me the best compliment I ever had in my career: "This is the kind of show we should

spend our money on." That's how The Mickey Mouse Revue was born.

I monitored the show's progress until it opened. Blaine and his sculptors made full-size characters to serve as models for the Audio-Animatronics figures. The figures were built and a theater was designed. One problem surfaced: Mickey. With thirty-three functions crammed into a 42-inch body, he was the most complex figure to date. He also became my biggest programming challenge because he was supposed to lead the orchestra.

I finally discovered I should program Mickey's arms to raise as high as possible, then immediately drop as low as possible. Same thing with his wrists and elbows — bend back and forth as quickly as he could to the extremes. This is the only way Mickey could appear to keep up with the tempo.

As the show's theater in the Magic Kingdom of Walt Disney World was being constructed, someone came up with the idea of having a pre-show. They designed an area just outside the main theater where guests could watch a film on Mickey while they were waiting to enter. Good idea, except there was a glitch. The theater seated 504 people, but the space available for the pre-show could only accommodate 300. Unfortunately, there was no time left to make further changes. It came as a shock when I was told my pride and joy was being moved to Tokyo Disneyland. "Because it never played to full capacity." Of course not! How can you fill 504 seats with 300 people?

The Mickey Mouse Revue never became a signature attraction for the Magic Kingdom. Its ticket level was downgraded from "E" to "D", then on September 14, 1980, it was closed, the first attraction to be removed from the Magic Kingdom since opening day

The theater that once housed the Revue was renamed the Fantasyland Theater and became home to several other shows over the years, including The Legend of the Lion King and Mickey's PhilharMagic.

Upon its closure, the Mickey Mouse Revue was dismantled and sent to Tokyo Disneyland as an opening day attraction for that park in April 1983. The entire show, including the pre-show, was re-recorded in Japanese, and a few small cosmetic enhancements were made to some of the characters.

The Japanese love of "cute things" was why the Oriental

Land Company, which owns and operates Tokyo Disneyland, put the Mickey Mouse Revue on the list of attractions it wanted for the new park. Another reason, however, was that shipping the Revue to Japan was far cheaper for the Disney Company than replicating the attraction in Japan.

Bob Mathieson, whose many positions with Disney included Vice President of Operations at the Magic Kingdom, recalled in an interview with David Koenig:

> It was a very big fight. We screamed like crazy on that one. It [the Revue] was a very popular attraction, and it was so much of our culture. It was what people really loved. But they didn't have time to build their own. They had to take it.

On May 25, 2009, the Mickey Mouse Revue closed at Tokyo Disneyland after nearly twenty-six years of delighting Japanese guests, and was replaced by Mickey's PhilharMagic.

When the original Revue ended its Magic Kingdom run in 1980, some of the figures used in the show were recycled for other attractions.

Imagineer Tony Baxter took the mold for Alice (from *Alice in Wonderland*) and made a lightweight fiberglass model that he painted to look like Tinker Bell. He installed equipment inside so that it would operate like a radio-controlled, model helicopter and fly down Main Street during the parade. A successful test was done in the Imagineering parking lot, but the project was abandoned over fears that that the twelve-pound figure might malfunction and drop on a guest.

Imaginer David Mumford, show designer for the Alice in Wonderland dark ride at Disneyland, claimed in a 1999 interview that the Alice figure added during the 1984 renovation of that ride came from the Mickey Mouse Revue:

> The Alice figure was a last-minute addition, after some debate over showing the character There was a set of Alice figures in storage from the 1971 Mickey Mouse Revue attraction in Florida. Included were some Flower Garden heads, the Mad Hatter, the March Hare, and Alice, so we used them at Disneyland in 1984.

In addition, the Seven Dwarfs figures and their organ were reused in the 1994 renovation of Snow White's Scary Adventures.

The Carousel of Progress

For years, the distinctive drawl of cowboy actor Rex Allen narrated one of Disney's most popular and beloved attractions, the Carousel of Progress. The narration began:

> Welcome to the General Electric Carousel of Progress. Now most carousels just go 'round and 'round without getting anywhere. But on this one, at every turn we'll be making progress. And progress is not just moving ahead. It's dreaming and working and building a better way of life. Progress is people getting release from drudgery, gaining more time to enjoy themselves and live richer lives. And as long as man dreams and works and builds, this progress will go on ... in your life and mine.

Walt Disney was intimately involved with all aspects of the attraction, especially its core messages of the importance of family, in particular the American family, and the prospect of a future global community where people of all ages and from all countries would live and work together, using and enjoying the newest marvels of technology.

It was an optimistic vision, a belief that progress was not to be feared but embraced. The Carousel of Progress was a physical representation of Walt's personal philosophy that people, despite their foibles, were basically decent, and that life was good in any era and would only keep getting better.

In 1958, the attraction was first envisioned as part of an extension of Disneyland's Main Street, USA, with sponsorship from General Electric.

Edison Square was to be a cul-de-sac off the right side at the end of Main Street. It would include a paved brick street, electrical horseless carriages, and brand-new electric street lights, with turn-of-the-century facades representing San Francisco, Philadelphia, New York, Boston, and Chicago. A life-size statue of Thomas Edison, the founder of General Electric, would be in the center.

The main attraction would have been a 40,000 square foot horseshoe structure with four theater spaces and an exhibit area. A four-act, fifteen-minute show, Harnessing the Lightning: A Story of Yesterday, Today and Tomorrow, would have featured Mr. Wilbur K. (for "Kilo") Watt and his family demonstrating how electricity had improved their domestic lifestyles in 1898, 1918, 1958, and finally "19?8". The question mark was intentional, since the final scene was an Electronic Island in the Sky set in a future New York.

Watt and his family would have been portrayed by "electro-mechanicals", the same type of simple mechanical figures with limited repetitive movements as the friendly Indian chief waving on the shores of the Rivers of America or the unfriendly natives at the end of the Jungle Cruise.

The audience would have stood on a three-tiered viewing area with continuous railings (similar to the ones at the pre-show area of the Stitch's Great Escape attraction), and automatic doors would open and close to move the audience through the various stages and into the General Electric product area.

The project was sidetracked when G.E. approached Walt Disney in early 1959 to design and build an attraction for the upcoming 1964 New York World's Fair.

The Disney Company eventually created four popular attractions for the Fair: The Carousel of Progress for General Electric, The Ford Motor Skyway for Ford Motor Company, it's a small world for Pepsi/UNICEF, and Great Moments with Mr. Lincoln for the state of Illinois.

The Edison Square show was re-designed into the Carousel of Progress and the General Electric pavilion (Progressland), because the marketing slogan of G.E. in the 1950s and 1960s was "Progress is our most important product".

The Disney Company has always been vague as to whether the Carousel of Progress story represents one family living through several decades, or whether it showcases different but similar families. There is no indication in any of the scripts or in any of the supplemental material to confirm either assumption.

Singing cowboy actor Rex Allen provided the comforting voice of the father for the first two versions of the attraction, and for the grandfather in the current version of the show. Allen also provided narration for several Disney live-action animal films, including *The Incredible Journey*. When the Carousel of Progress moved to Walt Disney World in 1975, actor Andrew Duggan was the voice of the father until 1988, when he passed away. In 1994, author Jean Shepherd not only helped with the new script, but took over the role of the father as well. The original live-action reference model for the character was actor Preston Hanson.

In the earlier versions of the show, the mother was more deferential to her husband (sighing "Yes, dear", in response to his blunt remarks), but in the Walt Disney World version, she became more assertive, especially in the rumpus room scene where she asks about the right of women to equal pay for equal work. The revised final scene also saw the mother involved in several organizations and eventually running the household through a computer. The original arms of the character were cast from those of Imagineer Harriet Burns.

Originally called Jane, the daughter is now known as Patricia. Like her mother, she became more assertive in the WDW attraction, pointing out that it wouldn't always be a "man's world".

In the earlier versions, the son was unnamed, but since 1994 he has been James or Jimmy. He had been unnamed because he had no dialog, and was just a mute observer in his scenes. It was only in the 1975 WDW version that he first spoke and became a teenager in the final scene.

Also in the first versions, the dog was known as Rover in the first scene, Buster in the second scene, and then Sport in both the third scene and in the voice-over narration for Progress City. In the original version, a different breed of dog was used in each scene.

When Carousel of Progress moved to WDW in 1975, the dog was called Queenie in the second scene and Sport in the third scene. Today, he is just called Rover in all scenes, and resembles the same key-carrying dog from Pirates of the Caribbean. Special nylon fur was created for the dog in place of a real animal pelt. It was Walt's idea to include the dog in every scene.

Mel Blanc, well-known for voicing such animated characters as Bugs Bunny and Daffy Duck, has always supplied Cousin Orville's single line of dialog while in the bathtub: "No privacy at all around this place!" He also voiced the parrot in the first scene.

Neither Grandpa, Grandma, the son, nor the daughter appeared in the original two versions of the final scene. The script explained their absences:

> You're probably wondering what happened to Grandma and Grandpa. Well, they're no longer with us. They have their own home now in a community for senior citizens. Grandpa's in his eighties ... his golf score, that is. The children are meeting Grandma and Grandpa right now at our new jet airport.

The entire family did not appear together in the final scene until the third version of the attraction at Walt Disney World.

While the Audio-Animatronics characters were simpler in movement than President Lincoln, there were roughly thirty-two of them that had to be coordinated, each on its own separate recording track.

The Oscar-winning songwriting team of Robert and Richard Sherman wrote the theme song "There's A Great Big Beautiful Tomorrow", with Buddy Baker doing orchestration, as he did for many Disney attractions. The song not only provided a transition to each new scene, but linked together the entire show:

> There's a great big beautiful tomorrow
> Shining at the end of every day!
> There's a great big beautiful tomorrow
> And tomorrow's just a dream away!

Richard Sherman recalled:

> There were all these directions being fed to us — "You have thirteen and a half seconds to get from the first stage to the second stage" — and so on. The song had to be able to change eras so we could play it convincingly as a turn-of-the-century rag, as a jazz piece, as a swing tune, and as a sweet

mellow piece. It was like being told "Come and design me a foot to fit this shoe." This is really a song about Walt. This is really the way he thought — his vision of the future was great, big and beautiful. We actually began by writing, "Walt had a dream and that's the start." We followed that dream.

The show included four scenes and a prologue. At the World's Fair, and later at Disneyland, the prologue featured a sixty-foot-long "Kaleidophonic" display of colored G.E. lights synchronized to the music and sound effects as the narrator talked. In the center was the huge circular logo of General Electric.

In the first scene, "The Gay Nineties", set at the end of the 19th century, audiences were to be amused at the supposed luxuries enjoyed by the family, including hand-operated washing machines that reduced clothes washing to a mere five hours, ice boxes holding fifty pounds of ice to further preserve and store foods, water pumps bringing water right into the kitchen, coal-burning kitchen ranges, and other examples of progress.

In scene two, "The Roaring Twenties", set just before the Great Depression, tangles of wire cords are in every room to power fascinating new "household servants": the refrigerator that has replaced the messy, dripping ice box; an electric fan that circulates fresh air throughout the house; an electric sewing machine, coffee percolator, toaster, waffle iron, and vacuum. At the flick of a switch, all go to work ... and then blow a fuse.

In scene three, "The Frantic Forties", set after World War II, the General Electric refrigerator is bigger and better than ever, with meat compartments, large ice trays, and improved freezers. Electric washing machines do just about everything but hang up the clothes. A food mixer has eliminated tiresome beating and mixing. There is even a small black-and-white television to watch wrestling and Westerns.

The final scene, "On the Verge of Tomorrow", took place just a few years into the future from today.

Imagineer Marty Sklar wrote:

> The last act would remain entirely flexible, so that General Electric products of today and tomorrow could be brought up to date from year to year.

At the World's Fair, mother and father sat comfortably by themselves in a General Electric Medallion Home amid such wonders as translucent plastic walls with Coloramic lights to change the mood and a glass-enclosed, electrically heated patio.

At Disneyland, mother and father sat comfortably in the living room at Christmas, where they could see Walt's version of E.P.C.O.T. out their picture window.

The theater itself has been described as a huge doughnut on railroad wheels where the stage remains stationary and the audience sits on the circular exterior that moves around to each new scene. Under the audience are huge metal trucks, each with thirty-six railroad car-type steel wheels able to carry over three-quarter-million pounds. More important, the set-up allowed almost four thousand guests per hour to view the show.

At the World's Fair, an average of 41,000 visitors saw the show every day. By the end of the first year, over seven million people had seen it. Surveys conducted by General Electric revealed that 87% of the audience rated the show as "excellent" and 12% as "good". People gladly waited in line (under blue-and-white canopies) for up to an hour-and-a-half.

Marty Sklar put together a colorful, twenty-eight page brochure with text, photos, and artwork resembling a Disneyland guide book entitled "Progressland at Disneyland" to convince General Electric to sponsor the pavilion at the theme park when the Fair ended. Walt planned to update all of Tomorrowland and re-open it in 1967 with three new attractions: PeopleMover, Adventure Thru Inner Space, and the Carousel of Progress.

Inside the new, two-story building for the Carousel of Progress, designed by John Hench, were two major changes to the show.

First, the final scene was updated, eliminating references to dated products like color kitchen lighting and adding new miracles like videotape recording of color television programs. In the background, the Christmas-time night showed the E.P.C.O.T. skyline, as Walt had envisioned it, with the Cosmopolitan Hotel towering in the center.

Second, as guests exited up the speed ramp to the second floor, they saw an amazingly detailed miniature of Walt's dream for E.P.C.O.T. However, since the Disney Company was still debating whether to pursue making that dream a reality, the city was re-dubbed Progress City to tie in with all the Carousel references to progress. The narrator explained:

> The overall design of General Electric's Progress City is based on a concept developed by Walt Disney for the Experimental Prototype Community of Tomorrow, E.P.C.O.T., which he had planned for Disney World in Florida.

Built to 1/8 scale, the miniature city measured 115 feet wide and 60 deep, with a total area of 6,900 square feet. It had 2,500 moving vehicles (monorails, peoplemovers, moving sidewalks, and electric trains), 20,000 trees, 4,500 structures (Walt insisted that the interior of the buildings be finished, furnished, and lit), and 1,400 working street lights, and it all came alive as audiences moved from one side of the room to the other on a three-tiered viewing area.

Over thirty-one million guests experienced this version of the attraction from July 2, 1967, to September 9, 1973.

When Florida's Magic Kingdom opened in October 1971, General Electric saw the opportunity to reach a new audience. Surveys had shown that only 8% of guests visiting Disneyland came from east of the Mississippi. So, the still popular Carousel of Progress was closed and relocated to Walt Disney World.

On January 15, 1975, the Carousel of Progress opened in Tomorrowland in Walt Disney World — the same day as another attraction, Space Mountain.

Extensive changes were made, such as the removal of the Kaleidophonic screens in the prologue and the second-floor model of Progress City. The theater no longer rotated clockwise, since there was no reason to position guests to go up a speed ramp. The theater now rotated counter-clockwise, with the exit next to the entrance.

The new leadership at General Electric felt that the song "There's A Great Big Beautiful Tomorrow" implied that G.E. customers should wait to purchase products, because new and better things were coming soon in a beautiful tomorrow. The Sherman Brothers composed a new song, "The Best Time of Your Life", often mistakenly referred to by its opening lyric: "Now is the Best Time". In other words, *now* was the best time to buy products from General Electric. Not only was there a new theme song repeated throughout the show, but the final scene was updated to showcase the 1970s, with a new cast providing dialog for the entire show.

Over the decades, the Carousel of Progress has changed more than any other Disney attraction. In 1981, the final scene was again updated to showcase the 1980s. Early in 1985, General Electric decided not to renew its contract for the show, especially since it was sponsoring a similar attraction at the newly opened Epcot Center called Horizons. So the Disney Company again updated the show, removing General Electric references. Finally, in 1993, the entire attraction was rewritten and re-recorded with another new voice cast, and re-named Walt Disney's Carousel of Progress.

The current attraction remains an homage to Walt Disney and his dream of a better future for everyone, as it continues to spin daily at the Magic Kingdom in Walt Disney World.

Part Four

The Other Worlds
of Disney Stories

There are some wonderful untold stories about Disney history that don't fit comfortably into the other three sections of this book but still deserve to be shared.

Disney has been involved in so many different areas over the decades — from merchandise to music to projects for other companies — that the list seems endless. Many of the people involved in these activities never received proper credit, or even any credit at all. Their stories reveal insights into Disney history.

In 1999, animation historian John Culhane wrote the book *Walt Disney's Fantasia* about the making of the animated feature *Fantasia* (1940). Several extensive documentaries about that film have also been shot and included with its various DVD releases. However, the following story, which originally appeared in the *Philadelphia Inquirer* newspaper, was not recounted in either Culhane's book or the documentaries.

When Leopold Stokowski was recording the music for *Fantasia* with the Philadelphia Symphony Orchestra, the complex recording system set up in the basement of the Academy of Music (also known as the American Academy of Music, and the oldest opera house in the United States still used for its original purpose) was declared a fire hazard and work was ordered to stop.

On the advice of friends, Stokowski called Joe Sharfain, then city solicitor for Philadelphia, and an ardent music fan. Sharfain withdrew the stop order so recording could proceed. Later, Stokowski expressed his gratitude and asked, "Now, what can I do for you?" Sharfain joked that one of his greatest wishes was to be rich enough to engage Stokowski and the orchestra for a single performance at which he would be the sole audience. (Such a performance would have cost at least $10,000.) Stokowski asked, "When did you have in mind?" Sharfain answered, "Oh, that's a long time away." Stokowski countered, "How about tomorrow at two o'clock?"

The incredulous Sharfain appeared at the side door of the Academy of Music the next afternoon and was escorted by a deputy of the maestro into the hall empty except for Stokowski and the orchestra. The maestro turned to make sure Sharfain was there, raised his arms, and conducted for four hours — all the music of *Fantasia* — just for Joe Sharfain.

An amusing anecdote but never included in either the book or the documentaries, because there was so much more important information to cover about *Fantasia*, including all the sequences that had been planned for future versions.

This section of *Vault of Walt* covers some personalities and projects that never get discussed in the bigger picture of Disney history, but are still highly entertaining and offer a rich perspective into the wonderful wide world of Disney.

Khrushchev and Disneyland

For those who grew up during the Cold War, Nikita Khrushchev was the boogeyman who was going to bury the United States. Following the death of Joseph Stalin, Khrushchev served as First Secretary of the Communist Party of the Soviet Union from 1953 to 1964, and as Premier from 1958 to 1964. Khrushchev's party colleagues removed him from power in 1964, with Leonid Brezhnev replacing him as First Secretary and Alexei Kosygin as Premier.

Khrushchev was removed from power partly because conservatives in the Communist Party found his flamboyant and dramatic gestures embarrassing on the world stage. At the United Nations, Khrushchev once pulled off his shoe and pounded it on a desk to make his point. He threatened America, vowing "we will bury you", at the time when nuclear war was a real possibility.

Other than the total destruction of capitalism and the triumph of communism, what did Khrushchev really want? He wanted to go to Disneyland.

Nikita Khrushchev, fiery opponent of American capitalism, arrived in the United States on September 16, 1959, for an eleven-day visit, culminated by a long summit with President Dwight D. Eisenhower. During his trip, he visited such American cities as New York and San Francisco.

The Russian leader had indicated his desire to see Hollywood, and so a visit was arranged. Khrushchev had also indicated that he and his family wanted to visit Disneyland during his time in Los Angeles. He was not informed until his plane was en route to the Los Angeles airport that, while his wife and children might be able to visit Disneyland, other plans had been arranged for him.

Major General Nikolai S. Zakharov of the Soviet Security Police had come to Los Angeles three weeks before Khrushchev's visit to review security arrangements with Los Angeles Police Chief William H. Parker.

Parker was adamant that his department could not guarantee security, because Khrushchev's motorcade would have to travel more than thirty miles to Disneyland, and also because Anaheim was in Orange County, outside Parker's jurisdiction.

Other Los Angeles police escorts to Disneyland had been provided for former President Harry Truman and for other visiting Soviet dignitaries. Kings and queens, princes and princesses, presidents, heads of state, and a host of other dignitaries had already visited Disneyland without incident.

Parker was probably aware that there were heated feelings about Khrushchev's visit to the Los Angeles area. Even before the Soviet leader arrived, there was a huge anti-Soviet rally at the Rose Bowl, and President Eisenhower had to personally urge calm. When Khrushchev arrived in Los Angeles, his motorcade was bombarded with tomatoes on the ride from the airport to the 20th Century Fox studios.

Parker advocated dropping a Disneyland visit from the schedule. However, since the Khrushchevs wanted to see the park, two different alternate security plans were prepared. One plan was to be used if just Mrs. Khrushchev and her children decided to visit the park, and the other was to be used in case Mr. Khrushchev chose at the last minute to join them.

On September 19th, the Khrushchevs arrived in Los Angeles. The day began with a tour of the sound stage at 20th Century Fox, where the movie *Can Can* was being filmed.

At Fox, Khrushchev saw the cast members perform a musical number from the film. Superstar performer Frank Sinatra was an unofficial master of ceremonies for the visit, and the Soviet premier lunched with dozens of Hollywood celebrities, including Marilyn Monroe, Shirley MacLaine, and Maurice Chevalier, before his arranged housing tour that afternoon.

Supposedly, at lunch, comedian Bob Hope was seated near

Mrs. Khrushchev and, in trying to make polite conversation, told her something along the lines of, "You should really try to go to Disneyland. It's wonderful."

Hollywood columnist James Bacon remembered:

> Mrs. Khrushchev was lamenting to Frank [Sinatra] that their trip to Disneyland had been nixed because of security reasons. "It's the only place I really wanted to see here," she told Sinatra in accented but good English. Frank told her: "Why Disneyland is the safest place in the world. I'll take you there myself if you want to go." David Niven, who was sitting nearby, chimed in and said the same thing.

(Another report from that luncheon has Sinatra leaning over to Niven and saying, "Tell the old broad you and I will take her there this afternoon if she wants to go that badly.")

At that point, Mrs. Khrushchev wrote a note in Russian and had it delivered to her husband on the podium. In the note, she wrote about how disappointed she was that the Khrushchevs, for security reasons, would not be allowed to visit Disneyland. Khrushchev confirmed this with the Secret Service near him.

On September 22, 1959, the *New York Times* reported that the Moscow newspaper *Izvestia* wrote that Khrushchev felt during the trip like he was under arrest because of the strict security measures. *Izvestia* informed the Soviet citizens that the real reason Mr. Khrushchev was not allowed to go to Disneyland was that it was a Saturday, a day on which tens of thousands of ordinary American citizens and their children would have filled the park, and that U.S. authorities did not want them interacting with the Soviet premier.

Khrushchev's son-in-law, a writer for *Izvestia*, later wrote a 700-page book about Khrushchev's trip entitled *Litsom k litsu s Amerikoi (Face to Face with America)*.

Still fuming from an earlier comment by 20th Century Fox President (and strong anti-Communist) Spyros P. Skouras, who tried to goad the Soviet premier with a reference to a previous speech about burying American capitalism, Khrushchev's famous temper probably got the better of him. He stood up and, in a voice shaking with emotion, complained about the level of security that prevented him from visiting Disneyland.

We have come to this town where lives the cream of American art. And just imagine. I, a premier, a Soviet representative, when I came here to this city, I was given a plan. A program of what I was to be shown and whom I was to meet here.

But just now I was told that I could not go to Disneyland. I asked, "Why not? What is it? Do you have rocket-launching pads there?" I do not know.

And just listen — just listen to what I was told — to what reason I was told. "We, which means the American authorities, cannot guarantee your security if you go there."

What is it? Is there an epidemic of cholera there or something? Or have gangsters taken over the place that can destroy me? Then what must I do? Commit suicide?

This is the situation I am in. Your guest. For me, this situation is inconceivable. I can not find words to explain this to my people.

The State Department later said that Mrs. Khrushchev and her daughters were free to attend Disneyland, but that Mrs. Khrushchev decided "at the last minute" to remain with her husband. Supposedly, Mr. Khrushchev had said that if Disneyland wasn't safe for him to visit, then it wasn't safe for his family, either.

Imagineer Marty Sklar recalled everyone at Disneyland waiting in case any of the Khrushchevs decided to come:

We were all set. We were ready. We had, I would guess, over a hundred Highway Patrol motorcycle cops and Anaheim police. So we invited them all in [to the park] and fed them all.

Walt Disney was eager for the Khrushchevs to visit, especially because of the worldwide publicity it would generate for Disneyland (then barely four years old). Walt had no sympathy for Communists, but his wife wanted to meet Mr. Khrushchev.

Later, after lunch at 20th Century Fox, an apologetic Khrushchev supposedly told some of the performers in *Can Can* that the studio commissary had been too hot and had put him in an ill humor. He later denounced in the press the *Can Can* dance he had seen in rehearsal as "decadent".

Instead of visiting Disneyland, Khrushchev was driven behind a large police escort through shopping centers, housing developments, and the UCLA campus. Sirens howled. Helicopters hovered overhead. Shouting people lined the streets.

Khrushchev was told he could stop anywhere to get out and visit, but the Russian leader chose not to stop, and reportedly, in a petulant mood, hardly looked out the window of his limousine. He said:

> Putting me in a closed car and stewing me in the sun is not the right way to guarantee my safety. This [not being allowed to go to Disneyland] development causes me bitter regret. I thought I could come here as a free man.

Ironically, four Russian newsmen who were covering Khrushchev's trip did slip away to visit Disneyland, and spent four hours enjoying the experience. They told American reporters they believed that Khrushchev and his family would have really enjoyed the park.

The newspaper reports focused on Khrushchev's outburst at not being allowed to visit Disneyland instead of the prepared speech he gave later that evening. Soon, even political cartoons were commenting on the tantrum.

The following morning, many people saw Khrushchev's train depart the Glendale train station and pass through the San Fernando Valley on its way to Santa Barbara and San Francisco. The Soviet leader continued his trip through California without further incident, and returned to Washington for his meeting with Eisenhower.

Author Herman Wouk (*The Winds of War*) commented:

> I don't blame Khrushchev for jumping up and down in rage over missing Disneyland. There are few things more worth seeing in the United States, or indeed anywhere else in the world.

Later that year, Bob Hope used the incident for a gag when he was entertaining troops in Alaska during one of his Christmas tours. Hope joked:

> Here we are in America's 49th state, Alaska. That's halfway between Khrushchev and Disneyland.

In 1963, Walt reminisced:

> We didn't refuse him [Khrushchev] permission. No, we were all set. You see, we work according to what the State Department wants to do when they come in and they have guests. Khrushchev was a guest of the government. So, I

mean we were ready to receive Khrushchev. But it so happened that the security problem here in Los Angeles ... because, actually, Disneyland is in another county, you see ... and the chief of police, we can't blame him. He had quite a chore there to carry out. He just was a little worried about somebody maybe walking in Disneyland with a shopping bag and what they might have in it. You'd never be able to know, you know.

Although anti-Communist, Walt did see the potential for publicity and fun in Khrushchev coming to Disneyland:

But we were ready for him. The press was ready. Both the State Department security and the Soviet security had come and cased Disneyland and they were all set. And I was all ready. In fact, we've had a lot of dignitaries down there and he was one that Mrs. Disney wanted to go down and meet. So, she was disappointed he didn't come.

I had ... we had different shots, places where we'd take pictures with Khrushchev and I had one that was my favorite. We'd be lined up in front of my eight submarines, you see, and I thought, well, it'd be nice. I'd be pointing to Mr. Khrushchev and saying, "Well, now, Mr. Khrushchev, here's my Disneyland submarine fleet." It's the eighth-largest submarine fleet in the world.

Robert Wormhoudt, Disneyland's chief protocol official at the time, stated:

Our job is to receive heads of state and royalty in accordance with their official stature. We always grant protocol admissions to individuals who are guests of the American President. Actually, Disneyland was not on Chairman Khrushchev's official itinerary. It was Ambassador Henry Cabot Lodge who accepted the responsibility for deciding against the Chairman's impetuous decision to come. After the incident, Disneyland had an unusual number of Soviet visitors. I guess they are all trying to outdo the boss.

Walt got a kick out of the situation and the publicity it generated. Years later, he talked with Bill Walsh about writing a screenplay for a live-action comedy about the incident. Disney Legend Walsh's successful career at the Studio included writing and producing such top films as *Mary Poppins*.

Walsh teamed with another top storyman, Don DaGradi, to write *Khrushchev at Disneyland*. In the screenplay, an excited Khrushchev comes to the United States to visit Disneyland under the pretext of meeting with the President for high-level talks about the Cold War. When Khrushchev discovers that, due to safety concerns, he won't be able to visit the Happiest Place on Earth, he comes up with a wacky scheme to get there.

At his Los Angeles hotel, Khrushchev disguises himself, slips by his own Russian security detail and the U.S. Secret Service, and sneaks off to Disneyland, with security officers soon in hot pursuit. Walsh recalled:

> He gets mixed up with the animals down there and dresses up as a bear or as a wolf or something as I remember. ...
>
> Walt liked Peter Ustinov. He also liked the idea of Ustinov playing Khrushchev going to Disneyland. It was somebody's idea who sold it to Card Walker and Card thought maybe we'd better just take it out of circulation because somebody would do something with it or would do something wrong. So, I said, "Yeah, I'll do it." I like stories where there's a gimmick like that. I immediately knew that that would be fun, doing that with Ustinov playing it.

Khrushchev at Disneyland would have been the second theatrical film to use Disneyland as a setting. The first film, *40 Pounds of Trouble*, was released in 1962 by Universal, and starred Tony Curtis as a Lake Tahoe casino manager who inherits a five-year-old girl abandoned by her debt-ridden father. The film was based on the Damon Runyon story that inspired such previous films as *Little Miss Marker* (1934) and *Sorrowful Jones* (1949). Curtis ends up taking the girl and his love interest (played by Suzanne Pleshette) to Disneyland, where a detective hired by his ex-wife chases Curtis through the park. The Disneyland segment of the film lasts about twenty minutes.

Peter Ustinov was to play the title role part in *Khrushchev at Disneyland*. He was then filming his first Disney live-action film, *Blackbeard's Ghost*, with producer Walsh and director Robert Stevenson, both of whom were also connected to the *Khrushchev at Disneyland* project. In fact, the last Disney live-action film Walt saw in production was *Blackbeard's Ghost*. On his final visit to the set before he returned to St. Joseph's hospital for the last time, Walt joked with Ustinov and Stevenson about the upcoming project.

An excited Ustinov told Walt that he intended to shave his head to look more like Khrushchev, and that his mother resembled Khrushchev.

Walt quipped, "I didn't know your mother was bald."

The Disney Studios wasn't as confident as Walt had been about *Khrushchev at Disneyland*.

When Walt died in late 1966, the initial work was shelved. It still gathers dust, somewhere.

A/K/A The Gray Seal

Artist and storyman Floyd Norman once mentioned that, during an early storyboard meeting about *The Jungle Book*, Walt summed up his dissatisfaction with the storyline by saying it was "too dark, like Batman." What did Walt know about masked mystery men?

Ah, that is one mystery that has been solved!

When Superman, Flash Gordon, Buck Rogers, Batman, and their fellow heroes first appeared, Walt was in his thirties and struggling with the adult responsibilities of his animation studio, so these characters didn't capture his boyhood "sense of wonder". It is interesting to speculate on their effect upon Walt had he encountered them as a child.

As a young boy, Walt read all the works of Mark Twain, as he told at least two interviewers, and he also claimed to have read books by Charles Dickens and Robert Louis Stevenson — all standard reading for most youngsters in those days. He told author Bob Thomas that he also liked reading Shakespeare as a boy, but only the "fighting parts".

Walt Disney's brother-in-law Bill Cottrell mentioned in an interview that Walt loved the fictional character Jimmie Dale, Alias the Gray Seal, and that as a boy, Walt would reenact those adventures with his friend Walt Pfieffer.

In the 1950s, Walt purchased the rights to all the Jimmie Dale books in hopes of developing a television series based on the character. A document filed with the Copyright Office of the United States located by animation historian Michael Barrier helps provide another piece of the story.

Originally signed on April 2, 1952, and filed for record on

May 19, 1952, the document states that Marguerite Pearl Packard, acting on behalf of the late author Frank Packard, freely gave "for valuable consideration paid to the under-signed by Walt Disney Productions" the "sole and exclusive" rights to make motion picture, photoplay, television, radio and/or any other adaptations of every kind and character" as well as the right to "obtain copyright in all countries upon said work and upon any and all adaptations".

This document gave Disney the rights to "All stories which were written by Frank L. Packard, deceased, utilizing the fictional character, JIMMIE DALE." Want to look it up? It is in volume 832, pages 120–123, at the Copyright Office.

So who was Jimmie Dale?

Jimmie Dale, the infamous "Gray Seal," was created by Frank Lucius Packard (February 2, 1877 – February 17, 1942), a Canadian novelist born in Montreal, Quebec, and who worked as a civil engineer on the Canadian Pacific Railway. His first stories were railroad stories, but he earned a living by writing other "pulp-ish" tales, including several Westerns. If he is remembered at all today, it is for his work on Jimmie Dale.

Those adventures first appeared in 1914 as serials in *People's Magazine* (and later in magazines like *Short Stories* and *Detective Fiction Weekly*) before they were compiled and published as novels:

- *The Adventures of Jimmie Dale* (1917)
- *The Further Adventures of Jimmie Dale* (1919)
- *Jimmie Dale and the Phantom Clue* (1922)
- *Jimmie Dale and the Blue Envelope Murder* (1930)
- *Jimmie Dale and the Missing Hour* (1935).

When the Jimmie Dale stories first appeared, the *Saturday Review* called them: "Stories of excitement, intrigue, etc., which have no equal." The *New York World* agreed: "These tales are abounding in 'pep'! Beyond doubt the most polished narratives of the underworld yet published."

The Dale character was so popular that Broadway actor E.K. Lincoln (not to be confused with actor Elmo Lincoln) starred in a sixteen-chapter silent movie serial, *Jimmie Dale Alias the Gray Seal*, produced by the Monmouth Film Company and distributed through the Mutual exchanges.

Directed by Harry McRae Webster and written by Mildred Considine (based on Packard's stories), the film was released on March 23, 1917, and closely followed Packard's concepts, including his use of the "mystery woman".

But who was Jimmie Dale? Writer Walter Gibson, who created The Shadow, claims that he "borrowed" elements for his famous character from Jimmie Dale.

In an interview on May 24, 1973, Disney Legend Donn Tatum told author Bob Thomas:

> He [Walt] also used to talk about ... He loved The Gray Seal stories. Do you ever remember that? Jimmie Dale Alias the Gray Seal? He used to propose that as a television show. The "Gray Seal" was really an amateur private eye who lived in Boston. His name was Jimmie Dale and Walt used to act them out all the time. Jimmy Dale was a disguise artist. In every story he'd put on a different disguise and find the criminal. And if he didn't find the criminal he prevented someone from committing a crime. And his trademark was a gray seal pasted somewhere. Walt had bought all the books. There were a number of them and he owned all the rights to them.

According to the Disney Archives, there was a story number (1764) assigned to the "Jimmie Dale project" on December 26, 1951, with John Lucas as head of the story crew. This was several months before Walt actually got the rights to the character. No other information — at least none that has been found — about the project exists at the Disney Archives other than that it was eventually abandoned within the following decade.

Part of Walt's agreement with ABC and later NBC was that the networks had the right of first refusal on any new television series that Walt wanted to produce. For ABC, of course, those series included the original *Mickey Mouse Club* and *Zorro*.

One of the projects that Walt proposed to NBC was a series called *Jimmie Dale, Alias the Gray Seal*, but the network felt the concept was not what the public expected from Disney, and rejected the proposal.

Jimmie Dale was the son of a wealthy New York City family. He spent his teenage years working at his father's safe manufacturing factory, and later entered Harvard University, where he spent a lot of time reading detective fiction and amusing himself with amateur theatrics.

After graduation, he joined the exclusive St. James Club and lived the life of leisure that only a gentleman could. To amuse himself, he created the identity of the Gray Seal, a two-fisted, masked, mystery man who broke into homes, stores, and public buildings, and who opened even the most tightly guarded safes just to prove that no safe was safe. He always left his calling card, a gray-diamond paper seal, and never took anything.

He lived alone in his mansion, except for his faithful older butler, Jason, and his devoted but rough chauffeur, Benson. In addition to being the Gray Seal, he also adopted another secret identity, Larry the Bat, a disreputable dope fiend who could more easily maneuver through the underworld of crime to obtain information. Later in the series, he creates yet another persona, Smarlinghue, a junkie-artist.

Jimmie kept all his equipment, including a disguise kit, at a secret hideout on the third floor of a tenement in the worst part of New York, the Bowery. This fortress of solitude, called the Sanctuary, also served as a refuge for the foppish playboy. As the Gray Seal, Jimmie's attire includes a "wide leather belt filled with small pockets," each with the tools of his trade.

Unfortunately, Jimmie made a mistake on one of his playful capers, and ended up being blackmailed by a mystery woman known only as the Tocsin. She later turns out to be Marie LaSalle, a young and beautiful woman who uses Jimmie's skills to put an end to the bosses controlling New York City's criminal organization, the Crime Club. After many years of flirtations, Jimmie and Marie walk off into the sunset together once the Crime Club is destroyed.

During these adventures, the Gray Seal developed an adversarial relationship with Herman Carruthers, a former Harvard classmate of Jimmie Dale and editor of the *Morning News-Argus* newspaper.

Packard describes Jimmie's physical appearance as:

> Six feet he stood, muscular in every line of his body, like a well-trained athlete with no single ounce of superfluous fat

about him — the grace and ease of power in his poise. His strong, clean-shaven face, as the light fell upon it now, was serious — a mood that became him well — the firm lips closed, the dark, reliant eyes a little narrowed, a frown on the broad forehead, the square jaw clamped.

Jimmie had an unusual aptitude for all things mechanical, and his memory is phenomenal. He is also an accomplished painter, disguise artist, and mimic, among other talents.

A thief who uses his talents for good? Well, that was the Saint. A gentleman safe-cracker? Well, that is probably Raffles. A special utility belt with the tools of the trade? Well, that was Batman. Multiple secret identities? Well, that's the Shadow. A secret lair? Well, that was Doc Savage. Leaving behind a signature icon? Well, that could be the Spider or the Scarlet Pimpernel (who in the novel never left behind flowers but did in his first film outing, made long after Jimmie Dale's success) or maybe even Zorro, who left the famous "Z".

However, the Gray Seal stories first appeared in 1914, when Walt Disney was about thirteen years old, and almost two decades before the era of the pulp hero. Probably the only pulp-like hero to precede the Gray Seal was created by Baroness Orczy in *The Scarlet Pimpernel* (1903).

Jimmie was a model for later classic heroic characters and their secret identities (especially the ineffectual wealthy playboy who becomes a masked, two-fisted man of action), secret hideouts, special gadgets, beautiful mystery women who helped them in their endeavors, costumes and disguises, battles with local newspaper editors, and so many other iconic elements. The Jimmie Dale stories captured Walt's sense of wonder.

There is a picture of Walt sitting behind his desk at the Hyperion Studio in the mid-1930s with stacks of books, some in foreign languages, including four written by Brüder Grimm. One of the few American books in the stacks, at the very top of a stack under a revolver that was probably a cigarette lighter, is *Jimmie Dale and the Blue Envelope Murder*.

Donn Tatum recalled:

> Walt never got around to doing it. Every time he'd see Leonard Goldenson [founder and chairman of ABC, the

network that presented the first Disney television programs]
he'd tell Leonard the story of the Gray Seal. Leonard wasn't
interested. Walt was very disappointed about that.

Unfortunately, except in his vivid imagination, Walt never
brought to life the adventures of his boyhood hero, the man
of mystery, Jimmie Dale Alias The Gray Seal.

Tinker Bell Tales

The little fairy Tinker Bell is one of the most popular Disney characters. She stars in her own straight-to-DVD feature films (voiced by Mae Whitman) and appears at the Disney parks, often in an area dubbed Pixie Hollow. For over fifty years, she has brought her special magic to the Disney Company.

In the first draft of James Barrie's famous story about Peter Pan, the magical boy who never grew up, he christened the world's most famous female fairy as Tippy-Toe. Fortunately, by the time the play based on the novel was performed, he had renamed her Tinker Bell, and so she has remained ever since. She appeared on stage as a spot of light reflected from an offstage, hand-held mirror, and her "voice" was a tinkling sound created offstage by a collar of bells, including two special ones that Barrie had purchased in Switzerland to create just the right tone.

Over the years, the fairy's name has been spelled a variety of ways, for example, Tinkerbelle, but Disney Archivist Dave Smith has determined the official name is Tinker Bell, because in the film Captain Hook refers to her as "Miss Bell", indicating that Bell is her last name. A tinker was an itinerant tradesman who mended pots and pans. He rang his distinctively high pitched "tinker's bell" to announce he was in the neighborhood.

Barrie pictured the fairy with fiery red hair, because she was so small she could have only one emotion at a time, and the red hair seemed to reflect her most common emotions: anger, passion, and embarrassment.

In 1924, Barrie wrote a screenplay for a proposed film about

Peter Pan, but it was never used. His screenplay describes the first appearance of Tinker Bell:

> The fairy, Tinker Bell. Now we have the outside of the window, with swallows still there. The fairy music comes now. The fairy, Tink, flies on and alights on the window sill. The swallows remain. She should be about five inches in height and, if the effect can be got, this should be one of the quaintest pictures of the film, the appearance of a real fairy. She is a vain little thing, and arranges her clothes to her satisfaction. She also keeps shoving the birds about so as to get the best place for herself. There should never be any close-up pictures of Tink or the other fairies; we should always just see them as not more than five inches high. Finally, she shoves the swallows off the sill.

When Disney released its animated version of *Peter Pan* in 1954, the company's publicity department insisted it was the first time Tinker Bell had appeared as more than the little spot of light flitting around the scenery so familiar to audiences from the stage productions of the play.

In actuality, Paramount's silent movie version of *Peter Pan*, released in 1924, featured actress Virginia Brown Faire appearing briefly in some close-ups as Tinker Bell. Faire had acted in silent films for over three years before she won the role of Tink.

Through the special effects of Roy Pomeroy, using "in-the-camera matte photography", Tink was seen in the Paramount film as a real person for the first time.

The director wanted audience members to believe she was real so they would understand why it was necessary for them to clap their hands to save Tink's life near the end of the film. For most of the film, however, she remains the familiar ball of light.

Film magazine *Exceptional Photoplays*, in its December 1924/January 1925 issue, was delighted by the final effect:

> What could be more delightful than the picturing of Tinker Bell as a brilliant ball of light, flitting swiftly through the air and which, when alighting, is disclosed to the wondering audience as a tiny creature in the wind-blown draperies — all flame and unreality and beauty?

Herbert Brenon, who directed the 1924 film, was still alive when Disney released its animated version in 1954. He was complimentary about Disney's interpretation:

Tinker Bell is absolutely magnificent. That was something we had to do most of the time with just a light on the end of a wire. Cartoon is the ideal medium for portraying the role.

For the Disney film, actress Margaret Kerry (who also modeled and provided a voice for one of Neverland's mermaids) was the model for Tinker Bell. Kerry had to audition in pantomime for the film's directors. She had previously played a fairy in the Warner Bros' film adaptation of *A Midsummer Night's Dream,* and had a host of other professional acting credits from the time when she was only four years old.

Animator Marc Davis, responsible for designing and bringing Tinker Bell to life, stated:

One of the greatest misconceptions about Tinker Bell is that she was modeled after Marilyn Monroe. There is no truth whatsoever to this. Margaret Kerry was our only live-action reference and she was a tremendous help in allowing us to rough out the action.

Kerry recalled:

I had an agent who sent me over for the Disney audition for *Peter Pan.* How do you audition for animation and for a character who doesn't speak? At home I had a room set up ... my dance room ... with all these mirrors and a bar, etc. ... so I got this little record player and put on an instrumental record and I worked up a pantomime to the beat of the record of making breakfast. You know, carrying eggs and maybe dropping one, etc. So the next day I went to the Studio and took the record player and put on the record and did this mime I had created. I believe there were three people there ... probably Marc Davis and Gerry Geronomi and somebody else I can't remember right now. Anyway, they gave me some direction of "look up as if you see such and such", etc.

The sessions were very exciting. There were all kinds of props for me to interact with including an oversized keyhole which I had to pretend to squeeze through. They also had a pair of twelve-foot scissors which I had to move. It's difficult to do a pantomime if you don't have a rhythm so I did a lot of action with songs like "The Donkey Serenade" going through my mind.

They called me Two Take Tink because I would get it right the first time and then they would have me do it a second time for "safety". I was so young and foolish. I could have made a lot more money messing things up so they would have to do it over and over. When I showed up that first day, I was in a bathing suit ... and tennis shoes! You can see it in a publicity photo or two and they offered to get me ballet slippers and I told them I had those at home and I would bring them in the next day and I did.

Disney publicists took great pains to point out that Tinker Bell's personality — characterized by traits like jealousy, anger, and vanity — was entirely different from Margaret Kerry's personality. Marc Davis recalled:

> Our intention was always to make [Tinker Bell] attractive. She is basically a jealous woman and that is what motivates all her actions. The pouting aspect of her personality was suggested by Barrie.

More time and money were spent on the development of Tinker Bell than on any other animated character in the film, including Captain Hook. A press release claimed that Tinker Bell was on the drawing board for twelve years, and during that time her hair changed from blonde to red to dark brown and finally back to blonde. One interpretation had her as a cool, sophisticated, ballerina-like fairy. In the final film, her wings were animated on a separate cel level to give them a more translucent appearance.

Disney Legend Ollie Johnston said:

> [Tinker Bell is] a prime example of how much an artist can do with a character that doesn't talk by simply using pantomime. Marc made the character much more memorable than if she had some kind of voice.

When the film was released, critics were not kind to little Tink. Bosley Crowther, in his review for the *New York Times*, described her as "a bit of vulgarity, with her bathing beauty form and attitude", and Francis Clarke Sayers called her "a vulgar little thing, who has been too long at the sugar bowls."

The official Disney coloring instructions for the original animated Tinker Bell list the color of her outfit as "dreiss".

That term may puzzle art students, because it only existed at Disney. Legendary Disney ink and painter Phyllis Craig, who started work at the Disney Studios during the production of *Peter Pan*, stated that dreiss was "a color named after a lovely woman who worked there who always wore this distinctive chartreuse green". It was the color selected for the famous pixie.

Audiences immediately fell in love with Tinker Bell, and she was featured on a variety of products, such as clothes, jewelry, comic books (including two issues in the Dell *Four Color* series illustrated by Al Hubbard), dolls, games, night lights, sunglasses, and many more items like souvenir bells sold at Disneyland.

One of the first Disneyland-specific products sold at Walt's new theme park (for twenty-five cents) was a glow-in-the-dark toy called Tinker Bell's Enchanted Wand. After holding it under a light bulb for several minutes and then going to a darkened location, the star mounted on the top of the wand would glow faintly and mysteriously.

There was even a series of commercials produced by the Disney Studios in the mid-1950s with Tinker Bell as the "spokes-pixie" for Peter Pan Peanut Butter, one of the major sponsors of the weekly Disneyland television series.

The primary director for these commercials was Charles Augustus "Nick" Nichols, who began his Disney career as an animator on the Disney shorts, and then became a director for the Pluto cartoons from 1944-1951.

The commercials provided work for some of the Disney animators, such as Phil Duncan, Volus Jones, Bob Carlson, Bill Justice, Paul Carlson, who had been employed on the short cartoons that were being phased out of the theatrical schedule.

One of the greatest Disney storymen, Bill Peet, remembered butting heads with Walt Disney on a segment of *Sleeping Beauty*:

> [The] next day, I was sent down to the main floor to work on Peter Pan Peanut Butter TV commercials, which was without a doubt my punishment for what Walt considered my stubbornness. I toughed it out for about two months on peanut butter commercials, then stubbornly decided to return to my room on the third floor whether Walt liked it or not.

The commercial work also provided jobs for other talent at the Disney lot.

Sterling "Winnie the Pooh" Holloway and Cliff "Jiminy

Cricket" Edwards narrated the Peter Pan Peanut Butter commercials. Tinker Bell was mute in those days, and had to pantomime her delight at the peanut butter that could be put on hot toast because it melted like butter and was so smooth that it could even be spread on "crispy potato chips".

Tinker Bell would fly around huge jars of Peter Pan Peanut Butter while the theme song reminded audiences:

> [Y]our eyes know and your tummy knows ... best of all, your taster knows ... Peter Pan Peanut Butter is so grand — the smoothest peanut butter in the land.

These commercials often appeared on the weekly Disneyland television show, which opened with Tinker Bell introducing audiences to the four lands of Disneyland. The memorable animation of Tink was done by Disney Legend Les Clark.

Tink became so associated with the new theme park that guests often asked Cast Members, "Where is Tinker Bell?" Walt came up with a solution to that problem in summer 1961 by having a real-life Tinker Bell fly over Sleeping Beauty Castle during the nightly fireworks display.

The first person to portray Tinker Bell in Disneyland was Tiny Kline, a Hungarian immigrant who had come to America at age fourteen as part of a dance troupe. She caught the attention of a renowned Wild West trick rider, and soon married him. Five weeks after the wedding, he fell off his horse and died, leaving Kline to begin her own career in the circus.

Her trademark performance with the Ringling Brothers Circus was an aerial iron jaw act where she was suspended in the air from a metal bit in her mouth on a long glide wire, down which she slid from the top of the tent to the ground.

On August 1, 1958, at a special Disney Night at the Hollywood Bowl, Walt was impressed with Kline's spectacular, one-thousand-foot glide from the top of the amphitheater, over the audience, and onto the stage. Kline was dressed as Tinker Bell.

In 1961, at age seventy, standing just four feet ten inches tall and weighing ninety-eight pounds, Kline became Disneyland's first Tinker Bell. Suspended nearly one-hundred-and-fifty feet up in the air, she glided down a long wire from the Matterhorn to Sleeping Beauty's Castle to signal the start of the fireworks.

William Sullivan, then a supervisor at Disneyland, recalled:

> Tiny Kline wanted to fly as Tinker Bell with the "jaws of life" device where she would use her teeth to hold on to a harness because she didn't want to look down. She'd hit two mattresses. The harder she hit the better she liked it. She took the bus in each night and had to run to catch the last bus going back to Los Angeles.

Gushed Kline:

> I have become a part of the most joyous experiment the world has ever known. It's like the frosting on the cake.

Kline performed for three summers, but in 1964, health problems required her to hand over the wand (and harness) to nineteen-year-old Algerian circus acrobat Mimi Zerbini, also a circus family veteran. Zerbini performed as Tinker Bell only during summer 1964. Kline passed away later that year.

In 1965, Judy Kaye began a career of more than a decade flying across the night sky at Disneyland. Kaye, who stood five-feet-one-and-seven-eighth inches tall, was born into a circus family and first visited a circus arena when she was barely three weeks old. She said:

> I love doing Tink because of the flying. I'm partially a ham anyway. I enjoy my work ... I wouldn't otherwise do it. In show business I can put forth what I've been observing and learning all my life. I like satisfying people. Show people stay young — Tiny Kline was a classic example of that.

Kaye's father, Terrell Jacobs, worked with lions and tigers for the Ringling Brothers Circus. Her mother, Dolly, was a dancer and an aerialist, who also began working with circus animals after she was grounded due to a series of falls.

When Walt Disney began making films that featured live animals, many of the animals were owned and trained by Judy's mother. Walt even included some of these animals in the old Disneyland Mickey Mouse Club Circus, which ran only from November 1955 to January 1956.

Judy remembered that, in those days, they had a young Indian elephant owned by her mom. Walt walked up to the baby pachyderm and exclaimed: "That's Dumbo!" Judy's mom corrected Walt, "But her name's Dolly." "From now on," proclaimed Walt, "she's Dumbo."

When not performing as Tinker Bell, Judy still trained and worked with animals, and designed and made circus costumes as well. Her husband, Paul V. Kaye, had his own circus that toured internationally. Judy and her husband also were co-partners in a talent agency, and booked some of the talent that toured the U.S. and Europe as part of the *Disney on Parade* show.

Shortly before nine o'clock each night during the summer, Judy Kaye would go into the Entertainment Office (then located above the America Sings attraction) dressed in her street clothes. With some assistance, she was transformed into Tinker Bell. Wearing a long coat and her head covered, she was moved through the park to the Matterhorn where, through a series of stairs, elevators, and ladders, she was taken up to her position.

She was helped into a harness resembling a parachute-like contraption, her wings attached, and then she was hooked up to the cable. Her "launcher" would hold her ankles in position as she awaited the signal. Her "catchers" stood behind the Fantasyland break area with a large mattress or two.

At the end of the night parade, the park announcer directed guests to look into the skies over Sleeping Beauty's Castle where Tinker Bell would light up the night with Fantasy in the Sky.

A recorded "click track tape" counted down the seconds before take-off. At the highest point of her journey, Tinker Bell is on a wire about one-hundred-and-fifty feet in the air — most circus high-wire acts are no more than fifty feet above the ground.

Approximately thirty seconds from the time she leaves the mountain top, Tinker Bell lands at the tower, sometimes slowly, sometimes rapidly, and packing a real wallop, depending on such factors as weather, weight, and flight speed. The other half of her crew catches her in a large, padded body mitt, calls the mountain to let them know she made it and how, unhooks her from the cable, de-wings her, and then she's down and off in a waiting van, back to the Entertainment Office, where she becomes Judy Kaye once again.

Tinker Bell's nightly flight was sidelined when her landing tower was torn down in the 1980s to build the new Fantasyland. When Fantasyland re-opened in 1983, twenty-seven-year-old Gina Rock was hired to replace Kaye.

Rock had performed with Ringling Brothers Circus for two years, and then spent another three years on the flying trapeze at the Circus-Circus casino in Reno, Nevada. Eventually, Rock returned to her home in the San Fernando Valley, where she married a trapeze artist. In need of work, she recalled her Grad Night at Disneyland, when she first saw Tinker Bell fly, and thought: "I want that job!"

The only stipulation from the Disney Company was that she not get pregnant. "Two weeks after they put that wand in my hand … ," Rock laughed. She flew through the first summer in the early stages of pregnancy, with no one the wiser. (In fact, she flew two summers as Tink while she was pregnant.) Rock recalled:

> It was like launching a rocket, What I would do is close my eyes right before I flew. On top of the Matterhorn, especially on a full-moon night, it was so beautiful. I would listen to the story, and become the character.

With a spotlight on her, Rock traveled thirteen miles per hour, as high as one-hundred-and-fifty feet above the park for the length of two football fields. Her actual flight lasted about twenty-three seconds, depending on the wind. At age forty-eight, after twenty-one years (the last eight shared with another Tink), Rock retired from the role.

Shortly before his death, animator Marc Davis said of the Tinker Bell character:

> She's a pure pantomime character. She had to be a visual character, not just a spot of light, in our medium. For the most part, everybody has liked the character and the Disney Company has used her in so many different ways. I feel really good about that.

FBI's Most Wanted:
The Mickey Mouse Club

Indeed sorry to learn of passing of your husband and want to extend my heartfelt sympathy. I know words are most inadequate to ease your grief, but it is my hope that you will derive consolation from knowing that his outstanding contributions will be a lasting memorial to him. His dedication to the highest standards of moral values and his achievements will always stand as an inspiration to those who were privileged to know him.
John Edgar Hoover,
Director of Federal Bureau of Investigation.

— Western Union telegram sent to
Lillian Disney, December 15, 1966

At the same moment as that telegram was sent, Walt Disney was also officially deleted as an FBI SAC contact.

In an official memo to J. Edgar Hoover, dated December 16, 1954, agent John Malone of the Los Angeles Field Division of the FBI recommended that Walt Disney be made a Special Agent in Charge (SAC) contact. The Bureau approved Walt for that role on January 12, 1955.

According to the FBI's Office of Public Affairs, a SAC designation did not entail undercover cloak-and-dagger spying. It identified for FBI agents reliable, acceptable sources of information about a particular industry or area of expertise. It saved agents from having to locate these sources themselves.

While an honor, Walt's status was not unique. For example, Samuel Engel, then a producer at 20th Century Fox and head of the Screen Producers' Guild, was also a SAC contact, as were many others. Walt was never paid for this work, nor is there indication in any FBI file what information agents might have requested from Walt, or asked him to confirm, during his decade as a SAC contact — which is a trifle odd, since even the most insignificant things appear in FBI files.

Agent Malone's memo to Hoover in 1954 explained:

> Because of Mr. Disney's position as the foremost producer of cartoon films in the motion picture industry and his prominence and wide acquaintanceship in film production matters, it is believed that he can be of valuable assistance to this office and therefore it is my recommendation that he be approved as a SAC contact. Mr. Disney has volunteered representatives of this office complete access to the facilities of Disneyland for use in connection with official matters and for recreational purposes. No derogatory information concerning this individual appears in the files of this office.

The FBI has on file hundreds of pages about Walt and the Disney Studios. Many of these files are available through the Freedom of Information Act, but certain sections are redacted, or blacked-out, to make them unreadable.

In the case of the telegram Hoover sent to Lillian Disney upon Walt's death, for example, her home address is redacted to protect her privacy. In other cases, a passage may be redacted to protect the identify of a confidential source or for reasons of national security. It has always been curious why so many FBI documents, including the ones on Walt, are so heavily redacted.

Of course, some know that Walt's relationship with the FBI became strained around 1961 with Disney's production of the live-action comedy *Moon Pilot* that Hoover feared would depict inept FBI agents. The FBI protested vehemently, even threatening the Studio with Public Law 670, a Federal statute that prevents the commercial exploitation of the name of the FBI or its use in any way that implies an endorsement by the Bureau.

To further aggravate things, Disney planned to make a film of former FBI agent Gordon Gordon's book *Undercover*

Cat. Gordon had been challenged by the Bureau over the years for his unflattering literary portrayals of FBI agents. Disney released the film adaptation as *That Darn Cat.* (By the way, in the book, the name of the cat — D.C. — stood for Damn Cat.)

Disney reassured the Los Angeles Field Office that "any portrayal of the FBI or its agents in this picture would be done in a dignified and efficient manner", but FBI documents from the period kept emphasizing:

> [J]ust another instance where Gordon Gordon is trading on his former affiliation with the FBI to further his own personal motives. Certainly any production or book authored by Gordon is not going to do the Bureau any good.

Walt had set the pot boiling with the FBI back in 1958 with *The Mickey Mouse Club*, which was then highly popular and televised weekly on ABC at 5:30 PM.

One of the segments on the show was a short documentary-like newsreel segment, sometimes shot by independent companies. These were inexpensive to purchase or make, and were popular with viewers, according to surveys.

In January 1956, a Disney Studios representative in Washington, D.C., Jerry Sims, took a public tour of FBI headquarters and thought it would make an interesting segment for *The Mickey Mouse Club*. Senior FBI agents vetoed that request.

One year later, a new Disney representative in Washington, Hugo Johnson, asked again for permission to film the public tour of FBI headquarters for *The Mickey Mouse Club*. According to a memo dated March 1, 1957, Johnson and show producer Bill Walsh met with Agent Malone in Los Angeles to pitch the idea of an FBI segment for *The Mickey Mouse Club*.

Initial correspondence reveals that the Bureau preferred an hour-long show about the history of science in law enforcement on the more prestigious Disneyland television show on Wednesday night, following the format of previous episodes about atomic energy and aviation that combined animation and live action to tell the history of the subject. Using that same combination of animation and live action, the program would trace law enforcement practices from the

Dark Ages through the establishment of the FBI laboratory in 1932, just in time for its upcoming 25th anniversary in 1957.

Walsh informed the FBI that:

> [Walt] is interested in filming the show on the FBI, but feels that a production on the Laboratory would be impossible at this time because of the amount of work which would be involved, and the limited time available between now and the Laboratory anniversary.

Walsh pointed out that it took more than a year and a half to produce "Our Friend the Atom" and that "this type of film is usually not profitable for the Disney company", but Walt "likes to do films of this type occasionally as a public service".

One month later, Walt brought up the subject again with Malone in Los Angeles, but senior agents once more disapproved the memo that Malone submitted in support of the project. Johnson continued to pursue the request through a friend, FBI Assistant Director Louis Nichols, who recommended to Hoover's protégé, associate director Clyde Tolson, that the Bureau cooperate with the Disney Studios. After some prodding, Tolson finally agreed.

For its part, Disney was eager to work with the FBI, and could produce segments for *The Mickey Mouse Club* quickly. Those were the deciding factors that led Disney to proceed, despite the time constraints, so that the FBI could use the segment to publicize the anniversary of its Lab.

The segment would feature young Dirk Metzger in Washington, D.C. Four parts dealt with the FBI, two with Congress, three with the making of money, and two with the White House. Each part was edited down to a ten-minute short. The segment began with:

> EXTERIOR DAY — Dirk Metzger is against backdrop of Washington, D.C. with Capitol Building in foreground, as seen through window. Desk is in foreground. OPEN Close Up on window, pull back to find Dirk in Medium Shot partially facing backdrop. He speaks before turning. FADE IN.

> "Washington, D.C.! Quite a place! Believe me! I'm Dirk Metzger. Maybe some of you will remember me as a Mickey Mouse Club foreign correspondent from a couple of years ago. Well, Walt Disney has now assigned me to cover Washington ... not from the tourist angle, as we just

saw ... but Washington from the inside. What goes on behind those big doors? As a Mickey Mouse Club reporter I did a little exploring, and for the next two weeks, I'm going to show you what I saw ... where I went ... what I did. Follow me!"

The segment's four episodes were aired in succession:

- Friday, January 24, 1958: Dirk was photographed with J. Edgar Hoover on May 15, 1957, by Hugo Johnson, using a handheld camera and one light in the Director's outer office. After that meeting, Dirk goes right to Quantico, and there is a sequence with firearms training.

- Monday, January 27, 1958: Dirk visits the FBI Identification Division.

- Tuesday, January 28, 1958: Dirk visits Quantico for a crime scene search, followed by a visit to the Laboratory to see the examination of evidence.

- Wednesday, January 29, 1958: Dirk follows up the Tuesday episode with more time in the Laboratory.

In 1958, fourteen-year-old Dirk Metzger was a freshman at Wakefield High School in Arlington, Virginia. After school, he filmed establishing shots for each scene, and then Disney shot the rest of the scene without him.

Three years earlier, Dirk had been attending an American school in England because his father, Marine Colonel Louis Metzger, was stationed in London. From his seventh grade class of twenty-eight boys, Dirk was picked by Disney to make twenty 15-minute travelogues, which aired as newsreels during the first and second seasons of *The Mickey Mouse Club*, with Metzger featured as a correspondent in England. (There were also Italian, Mexican, Danish, and Japanese correspondents.)

For a year and a half, Dirk spent his weekends being filmed in and around London, as he visited the secret tunnels of a pirate's cove, took a lesson in roof thatching, watched wild ponies in the west of England, and talked to what he remembered as a:

> ... grizzly sheepherder with a mouthful of teeth. But the most fun was riding a canal boat from Manchester to London.

When Dirk's family returned to the United States, Disney asked him to stay in England and make more segments, but he declined, saying, "London is an adult town. America is better in every way." Robbie Serpell replaced him.

When Disney decided to do a series based in Washington, D.C., they were delighted to learn that Dirk was living in nearby Arlington. For the new series, Dirk met President Eisenhower, Vice President Nixon, J. Edgar Hoover, and other government officials, as he visited various Washington landmarks. He told a newspaper reporter in 1958:

> I waited a couple of weeks in the President's outer office. Then the President talked to me for eight minutes instead of two. He asked me quite a few questions like what does my family do. The President was really terrific and so nice — nothing but the best. He told me about his Bureau of the Budget. I wasn't too interested in that. He also said two of his grandchildren watched the Mickey Mouse show.

Dirk was flown to Hollywood, where he stayed for two weeks recording his commentary. The FBI liked that Dirk was a Boy Scout. From an FBI memo dated May 15, 1957:

> This young man makes an exceptionally fine appearance and is the son of a Marine Corps Colonel assigned here to the Fiscal Section of U.S. Marine Corps Headquarters. Metzger is not a professional actor and he has greatly impressed the Bureau personnel with whom he has come in contact during the course of films shot at Quantico last week.

In that same memo, it was revealed that the FBI had investigated Dirk's father but found nothing negative.

Dirk told a reporter that his fame led to teasing at school:

> I didn't advertise too much. Sometimes I sort of get it in the face. There's always some Mickey Mouse show viewer at school who yells, "Hey, you forgot your ears!"

The FBI reviewed the initial rough-cut footage, and then set forth in a memo dated October 22, 1957, a list of twenty-two things they wanted changed in the four episodes. Some were as elaborate as:

> ... the scene of the Agent firing two revolvers simultaneously and breaking the clay targets does not show the targets themselves breaking. This footage is available, and it is felt that if the scene is used at all, it should show the Agent's bullets breaking the clay targets.

And some were simple phrase changes like:

... in line 3 of the narration, the word "department" should be deleted and the word "division" inserted.

A follow up memo from October 28, 1957, stated:

> The contents of the memorandum regarding the above captioned program were discussed in detail with Mr. William Park, News Reel Editor, and Mr. Douglas Duitsman, News Reel Staff Writer, who composed the script for the film by Special Agent John Cashel at Disney Productions, on October 25, 1957. The changes suggested were reviewed and made in the film script. Both Disney executives indicated that any subsequent changes which might be desired by the Bureau in connection with this program would be readily undertaken. It was their opinion that no retakes of scenes will be necessary in order to accomplish the suggested changes.

All of this correspondence sounds positive, but problems arose when the Bureau was shown the scripts and rough unedited film, but not the finished film, which they wanted to approve before release. A series of memos to Disney expressed concern that the Bureau had not seen the final cut.

Walt wasn't comfortable with others having final approval, an issue that arose again with P.L. Travers over Disney's film of her novel, *Mary Poppins*.

The situation escalated to the level of Hoover himself, who wanted confirmation (which he received) that the Disney Studios had agreed the Bureau must see the films for clearance before airing them on television.

A memo from January 23, 1958 (one day before the first broadcast), included the statement:

> Obviously, the mishandling on the part of the Disney Studios and failure to live up to their agreement will be taken into consideration when future approaches are made to the Bureau by this outfit.

Disney was to supply the Washington Bureau with the completed films by Monday, January 20, several days before the first air date. The Bureau protested to Disney's Washington representative, Hugo Johnson, who was also upset and urged the Disney Studios in Burbank to send the films. An FBI memo, written Friday morning, January 24 stated:

> Apparently our protest with Disney Studios took effect. Hugo Johnson, local manager Disney Studios, advised at 9:45 a.m. this morning that he was en route to the airport where he would pick up the film and would have it back to us no later than 10:45 a.m. this morning. We have arranged an immediate viewing of the film.

After all that turmoil, the FBI saw nothing objectionable in the films. A letter from Hoover on January 30, 1958 included the statement:

> I thought that the whole series was exceptionally fine in that it gave very young people an excellent concept of the operations of the FBI.

Hoover even sent a note of praise to Dirk Metzger, as did President Eisenhower.

But a bond of unspoken trust had been strained, and some at the Bureau were angry at the perceived snub. In a memo, Clyde Tolson scribbled "no further cooperation".

Nearly two years later, the Bureau, which routinely monitored several publications about current events in Hollywood, discovered in a Hedda Hopper column that Disney was going to make a movie called *Moon Pilot*. Warning flags went up instantly. Early reports that the film would feature an "ineffectual" FBI agent body-guarding an Air Force pilot who, during a space flight, had seen something odd in outer space once again brought a flood of memos and clippings into Walt's FBI files.

Walt had no intention or desire to ridicule the FBI, but was just using his story sense to include the time-honored device of a bumbling authority trying in vain to thwart the hero.

Even though Walt changed the name of the organization in the film to the Federal Security Agency, reviewers weren't fooled. A review of the film in the *Washington Daily News* on April 26, 1962, stated: "Air Force brass are mutton-heads, and the FBI is an ineffectual as the DAR."

Whatever became of the boy wonder Dirk Metzger?

Dirk became an officer in the Marine Corps, then went to law school and is still a practicing attorney. One of his skills, conflict management, could have been put to good use more than half-a-century earlier, when both Hoover and Disney struggled for ultimate control of the final cut, and Walt fell out of favor with the F.B.I.

Chuck Jones:
Four Months at Disney

On Sunday, September 21, 1997, at his 85th birthday celebration, the legendary Chuck Jones spoke to a group of five hundred friends, family, fans, and colleagues. He recalled the many letters he had sent to Walt Disney in his early years, and how Walt had personally replied to each one. Later, when he met Walt, Jones thanked him for those letters, and Walt replied, "Well, of course, you're the only animator who ever wrote to me!"

He told that story many times over the decades, and some have wondered whether it was merely apocryphal. Jones did have much respect for Walt Disney, as he often stated:

> Walt was a strange kind of guy, but he's still by all odds the most important person that animation has ever known. Anybody who knows anything about animation knows that the things that happened at the Disney Studio were the backbone that upheld everything else.

In a 1980 interview with well-respected animation historian Joe Adamson, Jones further stated:

> When Warners shut down the [animation studio], I went to work at Disney's for a while. I couldn't stand it. [Walt Disney] asked me what kind of job I wanted and the kind of job I wanted was his. But I got to know him and like him.

Jones worked at the Disney Studios from July 13, 1953, to November 13, 1953. He recounted that experience in his autobiography, *Chuck Amuck* (Farrar, Straus and Giroux, 1989). His stint with Disney began when Jack Warner, head of Warner Bros., decided to shut down his animation department. Warner believed the future of filmmaking would be 3D, and that it was too expensive to make 3D cartoons because the cost couldn't be recouped with rental fees. Jones had a contract with Warner Bros., but he didn't want to stay there after his team had been laid off and there was scant opportunity for future work.

Jones recalled:

> I called up Walt Disney and asked him if I could come over there for a while. He said, "Sure, come on over." I was there for four months. I worked on *Sleeping Beauty* and the beginning of the television show. But I couldn't adjust to waiting for Walt ... the Disney people were raised that way, and used to it. You'd finish a sequence, and then you'd wait, maybe for weeks. Five or six men, just sitting around waiting for Walt to come around. When he did come around, he'd already been there the night before when the plant was dark and looked at the boards, and everybody knew he'd seen the sequence, but they still had to show it to him as though he hadn't.

The culture and process at the Disney Studios were so different that Jones, with no regrets, leapt when the opportunity arose to return to Warner Bros. He explained:

> Eventually, I felt I just couldn't take it any more, so I went in and talked with Walt. He said, "Well, what do you want to do? We can work out something for you." I said, "Well, you have one job here that I want, and that's yours", because he was the only one there who could make a decision. He said, "I'm sorry, but I'm afraid it's filled." So we shook hands and I left. By that time, Warner's had decided to start up again, because 3D hadn't completely revolutionized the world. That was the only time I left Warner's until they closed it down again in 1962.

Eyvind Earle, the artistic designer for *Sleeping Beauty*, recalled the months when Chuck Jones worked at Disney:

> Way back when we did *Melody* and *Toot, Whistle, Plunk and Boom*, Walt had let Ward Kimball sort of take over and strive for a new look at Disney. He was put on *Sleeping Beauty* at the same time I was. I remember he had a special room up on the third floor, and with a newcomer to Disney's — the famous Chuck Jones, animator, director from some other studio — the two of them [Ward and

Chuck] sat upstairs in their private room, and talked and talked and talked, and for many months did absolutely nothing at all. I have never been able to figure it out. I asked Ward Kimball once, "Why aren't you doing anything?" And Ward Kimball answered me, "You don't know Walt Disney", whatever that was supposed to mean.

Years later, when Earle's comments were shared with Kimball, he responded:

I was just filling in between animation assignments. Walt had said, "Why don't you go up and work on that sequence about the fairies changing colors" and so forth. I was a fill-in. That happened a lot. I could leave the animation department and go and work on things of that sort, as a story man. All we [Chuck and I] did was sit around. I think every time Eyvind came up there, Joe Rinaldi, he and myself and Chuck Jones would get into these gabfests. Chuck had just discovered one-upsmanship, and he ran into his nemesis with Bill Peet, because Bill Peet wouldn't say much, but he was funny, and he could cut you to the quick. I started enjoying it, because I knew Chuck always wants to dominate the conversation, and Peet would cut his legs out from under him. Maybe that's one reason he didn't want to work there.

Disney producer Harry Tytle:

Chuck's brief stint with Disney in 1953 lasted only four months. During this short time, he earned no screen credits and, to the best of my recollection, made no significant contributions. Chuck has joked that the only job he wanted at Disney's was already filled by Walt. He and Walt were used to being the biggest fishes in their respective ponds. Chuck was a talented innovator but at Disneys', as far as Walt was concerned, he was the new kid on the block and had to prove himself. This must have been a new and confusing role for Chuck.

Fortunately, like Kimball, Tytle kept a detailed diary of his time at Disney. Thanks to those entries, a fuller insight exists into the brief Disney experience of Chuck Jones, co-creator (with writer Mike Maltese) of the Road Runner and Coyote, Pepe Le Pew, and many other classic Warner characters.

Relevant excerpts from Tytle's diary include:

June 10, 1953: This morning I was called into Walt's office. Chuck Jones at Warner Brothers had called Walt applying for a job. Walt asked my opinion of Jones. I said, to the best of my knowledge, he was a very nice fellow personally and considered to be one of the best directors on the outside. That he had done a lot of work for Warner Brothers across the years.

However, the first meeting with Chuck and Walt did not go as well as expected. Chuck did not understand that he was viewed as the "new kid on the block" and felt he could slide into the same position of authority that he had at Warners.

June 15, 1953: At 9 a.m. we met with Chuck Jones. Chuck explained how he had been working, stating he would like to work here. That he was not under contract anymore and could be available to us in a month, after winding up what he had to do at Warners and taking a vacation. Walt knew what Chuck's salary was. Peterson had gotten it for him and we had discussed it — so Walt pulled a cutie by saying he didn't know "what your salary is, Chuck, but whatever it is, you must be worth it to Warners, and I will pay you the same." Chuck, I believe, expected more because he mentioned something about working under scale. The one thing that I thought Chuck failed in was he made clear to those in the meeting that he dominated his unit, especially story, which is un-Disney.

While Chuck respected Walt, Jones was used to doing things his own way and at the Disney Studio there was only one way and it was Walt's way as many other talented and independent artists learned that hard lesson over the decades.

June 23, 1953: Chuck Jones knows he is definitely coming in on the 13th. Although I do not think we should bring it up, he will probably ask about contract and we have no decision or directive as to Walt's thinking. Incidentally, Chuck was in today and Hal told me he didn't make out so well in his meeting with Walt. He had a sheet of typewritten suggestions he tried to hold forth, and Walt was not interested. Chuck is going to have to learn to work with Walt. I presume that he feels he was called in for his creative thinking and ability. He will soon have to learn that Walt sets the direction, the pace, and even the topic of conversation. Hal stated that Walt made the remark to him later on that Chuck had a lot to learn.

Jones was placed with another independent and creative animator/director, Ward Kimball. This pairing seemed to stir up even more trouble as Kimball was well known for his ego and for prodding others into doing things.

September 15, 1953: I heard today, through Hal, that Chuck who was just put on *Sleeping Beauty*, and had never directed for Disney's, requests the same salary as the other feature directors. Hal is going to present this demand to Walt this morning. It will be very interesting to see the outcome.

September 16, 1953: [Walt] got into the Chuck Jones deal and asked me if I knew that Chuck has asked for an increase, which he indicated he would have no part of. I told him that I was very interested in what his reaction would be, that I for one, feel as Walt does, Chuck should prove himself here first. Walt got a little upset because I understand he feels maybe this increase was instigated by Ward [Kimball]. He made it clear again that nobody is indispensable, Ward included. It was the organization that counted.

Things quickly escalated to the point that Jones actively pursued other offers and eventually left the Disney Studio.

November 5, 1953: Chuck hit Walt the second time, through Hal, for an increase. Supposedly, he has an offer from Sutherland for $500 and an offer to return to Warner Brothers. Walt's remarks to Hal were "Have Chuck make up his mind as to what he wants to do. There is no increase until we find out Chuck's ability — he has shown nothing to date."

November 13, 1953: The Chuck Jones situation came to a head today. ... The story is that he left for New York this evening, starts work at Warner Brothers again the first of the year at a $40 increase, making the new salary $400. I had heard in the morning that he was telling people that "the place here worked at too slow a pace". ...

A letter from Chuck Jones to his daughter Linda, dated November 30, 1953, states in part:

At Disney's it was always necessary to be certain places at certain times. God knows why, nothing ever happened, so it was nearly impossible to work there without a timepiece. You could get along without talent, but not a watch. As you know I gave up time about a year before leaving here and I must say I never missed the damn stuff. ... I had not realized how much I missed the sweetness of my own solitude. At Disney's, aloneness or desire to be alone generates suspicion, you are always surrounded by people, drifting in and out, exchanging hackneyed pleasantries or just sitting, staring with baleful intensity at one's own navel. What a waste! What a waste of wonderful talent!

Despite his brief tenure at Disney not being satisfactory either for himself or for Walt, Jones still held the Disney Studios and Walt in the highest regard for the rest of his life:

Disney was not a good animator, he didn't draw well at all, but he was always a great idea man, and a good writer.

In a 1975 interview with Greg Ford and Richard Thompson, Jones stated:

Disney's was to animation what Griffith was to live action. Almost all the tools were discovered at Disney's. They were the only ones who had the money, and who could and did take the time to experiment.

It was obviously better for everyone that Jones returned to Warner Bros. to create more memorable cartoons and characters in his distinctive style. He later formed his own animation studio. When Jones was at Disney, however, Walt was cutting back on theatrical short cartoons, an area of strength for Jones, and concentrating less on animation and more on the creation of Disneyland ... and after all, at the Disney Studios, there could be only one Walt Disney, and Walt was doing that job pretty well himself.

Walt's Women:
Two Forgotten Influences

Despite Walt's joking complaints to reporters that he was surrounded by nothing but females in his life, he enjoyed women, not as objects of lust or as fodder for humiliating humor or as second-class citizens, but as interesting people — an uncommon attitude during that time period.

In *Walt Disney: An American Original*, Bob Thomas wrote:

> He [Walt Disney] lived surrounded by women. Besides Lilly and the two daughters and the cook, there was often a female relative living with the Disneys. Walt complained wryly that even the family pets were female. But his grumblings seemed half-hearted. He appreciated femininity.

There are countless examples of how Walt was cautious about his casual swearing around women, how he was always respectful, and how he expected the same from his employees, although that didn't always happen. He employed talented women in positions of authority and influence at the Disney Studios, an approach not often followed at the other studios.

Walt's daughter Diane Disney Miller remembered:

> It puzzles me why people think that dad was "shy", or "uncomfortable" with women. Quite the opposite. He was very easy around women, and liked and respected them, with the exception of those who were pretentious or domineering, and I am aware of a few of those sorts that he complained about … none family members! This should seem obvious, because of his well-documented close relationship with his sister, his mother, his Aunt Margaret, his sisters-in-law Louise and Edna, my mother's sister Hazel, her daughter

Marjorie, his secretaries Dolores Voght, Tommie Willke, and Lucille Martin who was not with him for too long before he died. The letters he received from old girlfriends, and his responses, and Ruth's interview with Dave Smith, are documentary proof of his genuine, natural, healthy appreciation of the women in his life.

In the interview that Diane mentions, Walt's younger sister, Ruth, told Disney Archivist Dave Smith that, when Walt wanted to take a Manual Arts class at McKinley High School, the only class available was a cooking class, so he took it. He was the only boy in the class. Ruth remembered:

> Oh, he was as happy as could be in there, because the girls were all making over him something terrible. The only boy! And he loved it. He used to come home and tell about it and all the fun he had there. He had a lot of friends everywhere and especially the girls. One time coming home from high school there in Chicago, my mother saw ... we had such big snow that there were big, about four or five foot, banks on each side of the side walk, and here, coming down there, was a boy with a girl on each arm. She was just casually looking at him wondering "you know, that boy was popular!" When he got closer, she saw it was Walt!

Two of the most interesting women in Walt's life saw him nearly every day of his life, but don't get enough recognition for the positive influence they had on Walt.

Thelma Howard was the Disney live-in housekeeper and cook for thirty years, beginning in 1951. Her nickname was Fou-Fou, (sometimes spelled Foo-Foo), the closest one of the Disney grandchildren could come to pronouncing Thelma. Walt just referred to her as "the real-life Mary Poppins".

Thelma has also been described as being more like the feisty maid in the Ted Key comic panel *Hazel* than like Mary Poppins, because she was gruffer than a spoonful of sweetness. Like Walt, she loved to smoke. She also loved to play gin rummy, and she was accepted as part of the Disney family.

Her friends described Thelma as a handsome, quick-witted woman who loved football and the color pink, and who baked a lovely boysenberry pie. She was a perfectionist in her work, making sure the Disneys were well cared for, down to the tiniest details, and she did not hesitate to give orders. Jack Shakely, president of the California Community Foundation, said:

> She was a combination of real loving and kind of crusty, a chain-smoking, no-nonsense type, but very loving, like TV's old Hazel character.

Thelma had her share of tragedy in her early life. She came from a poor family in Southwick, Idaho. Her mother died in childbirth when Thelma was just six years old, and her sister died in a fire in their kitchen years later.

After graduating from high school, Thelma attended business college in Spokane, Washington. She hoped to become a legal secretary, but ran out of money and had to drop out. She stayed briefly with relatives in northern California, and then in 1931, moved to Los Angeles, where she did office work and cleaned homes.

Before working for the Disneys, she was married briefly and had a son, Michael, who was constantly in trouble.

Thelma made sure that the fridge was filled with hot dogs, because when Walt came home from work, he liked to grab a few. He'd give one to his pet poodle, and then eat the other two himself, even though they were cold and uncooked.

Although he acknowledged that Thelma was a great cook, Walt would often try to get her to visit Biff's, a diner near the Disney Studios, to learn how to cook some of Walt's favorite items from their menu. Grudgingly, she would make the trip, and then back home attempt to duplicate Biff's pan-fried potatoes (actually hash browns) that Walt loved so much, or the silver dollar-sized pancakes.

On Thelma's days off, Walt and Lilly went out to eat, usually at the Tam O'Shanter or the Brown Derby.

Walt's grandchild Chris Miller said:

> My grandfather had an incredible rapport with her [Thelma]. They seemed to share everything, from a sense of humor to their notions about what was happening with the kids and what was best for them.

Walt felt comfortable teasing and joking with Thelma, but she was capable of giving back as good as she got.

Howard's niece Cheryl Wallace remembered visiting her aunt at the Disney home and staying in Thelma's quarters. When the Disneys were gone, they would spread themselves out, pretending the house was their own:

> We would sit at their big dining room table, and I remember she would act silly, like a schoolgirl. She would sit at one end, and I would sit at the other end, and we would shout like, "Could you pleeeeeeze pass the peas?"

"I guess there isn't any sucker bigger than the one who sounds off about the fair sex," moaned Walt when, during an interview, he was reprimanded for suggesting that women don't have a sense of humor. (What he said was that he no longer brought Disney films home to screen for his family because Lilly and Thelma didn't "laugh loudly enough" during them.)

When Thelma started as a housekeeper for the Disney family in 1951, at age thirty-eight, she'd get a few shares of Disney stock for Christmas as well as for her birthday and for special events. Walt advised her to hang on to the stock, because it might become valuable one day. She lived frugally throughout her life, apparently unaware that the rising value of the stock had made her a multi-millionaire by the time of her death.

Through numerous splits, her holdings had grown to 192,755 shares. Between 1980 and 1993, the stock increased in value tenfold, and her shares were valued at $8.39 million. Her property and savings pushed that total to over $9 million.

Thelma left nearly four-and-a-half-million dollars to poor and disabled children, and nearly the same amount to her son, Michael, the only child from her brief marriage. Michael was then in his mid-50s, living in a home for the developmentally disabled.

Jack Shakely, whose California Community Foundation assists the Thelma Pearl Foundation in dispensing the money, said:

> She was told to hang onto it, and she did. She never sold a share of it. I don't think she knew what it was worth. She had great faith in the Disneys and wouldn't part with it.

In 1981, Howard retired to a modest, two-bedroom bungalow in West L.A. Her health began to fail, and by 1991, she had been moved to a nursing home in Santa Monica, where she was not treated well, and where a man claiming to be her husband (with no proof) was trying to gain control of her estate.

Around that time, Diane Disney Miller became concerned because she hadn't received Thelma's usual Christmas cards, and she discovered her in the nursing home. Thelma had kept a framed, autographed photo of Walt and Lillian by her bedside, but recently it had been stolen. Diane gave her another that Thelma kept hidden.

Soon, Thelma was moved to a retirement home, with beautiful gardens, where she had a private room. Diane sent fresh flowers every Monday and visited often.

Thelma Howard died on June 10, 1994, just before her 80th birthday, and was buried in Forest Lawn in a pink coffin. Her grave overlooks the Disney Studios in Burbank, California. The foundation that bears her name has awarded over four million dollars in grants since 1995.

If Thelma Howard was like the fictional character Hazel, there was an actual Hazel in Walt's life: Hazel George, the nurse at the Disney Studios, whom he relied upon for Studio gossip and for keen story insight on proposed productions.

Walt's old polo injury caused him considerable pain. Sometimes, he wasn't even able to bend over to get into his car. In a room next to Walt's office, a room Walt called his "laughing place", Hazel applied hot packs and traction every evening, usually after 5:00 PM, to ease Walt's pain.

He spent this time to use Hazel as a sounding board for his plans, as well as to exchange gossip while he unwound from the pressures of the day. Often, Walt would get philosophical, but Hazel's sharp wit never let him get maudlin.

"After I die, I would hate to look down at this Studio and find everything in a mess," Walt moaned, as he was getting his nightly massage.

"What makes you think you won't be using a periscope?" she replied.

"Smart ass," Walt muttered under his breath as he lay there.

Once, after Hazel had deflated another of his stories, Walt said, "You know what my next project is going to be? An Audio-Animatronics nurse."

Hazel claimed in an interview that "Walt was more at ease with women than he was with men". He certainly was very much at ease with Hazel, and appreciated her honesty and outspokenness. He also appreciated her discretion, since during his sessions with her, Walt became vulnerable, and opened himself up in a way he didn't with others. Even after Walt's death, Hazel was discreet about what he shared in those sessions.

Born Hazel Gilman on February 21, 1904, in Bisbee, Cochise County, Arizona, she was the oldest of three children. Her father was a copper miner. Perhaps due to the labor uprisings against local copper miners when she was thirteen, Hazel ended up a ward of the juvenile court.

A brief marriage in 1928 resulted in a daughter and the quick disappearance of her husband, Mr. George. By 1930, Hazel was living with her divorced mother and younger brother in Los Angeles. She eventually graduated from a nursing college, and was later hired by the Disney Studios during the infamous strike of 1941.

In an interview shortly before her death, Hazel said:

> I felt that Walt's greatest talent was recognizing the potential in others He really sought to bring out the best in people, whether they were artists, story people or accountants. He personally went through every day's work at the Studio. He didn't just ask someone how things were going. He found out himself. He was a very hard worker and a wonderful man. He encouraged me to get into writing lyrics for music at the Studio, as he knew that I wasn't really using my college degree in literature as a nurse. So I did, and he loved my writing. Walt was a special man, even today, I have a lot to thank him for.

Under the pseudonym Gil George, Hazel co-wrote over ninety songs for Disney. Her work included songs for films like *The Light in the Forest*, *Perri*, *Tonka*, *Westward Ho, the Wagons!*, and *Old Yeller*. She was a frequent song contributor to the television shows, including *Zorro* and *The Mickey Mouse Club*, for which she wrote songs for Talent Roundup, the Corky and White Shadow serial, and several of the Jimmie Dodd "Doddisms", among her other contributions.

In addition, Hazel was a lyricist, collaborating mainly with her long-time companion, Disney Studio composer Paul Smith, but she also worked with George Bruns and Jimmie Dodd to write songs for *The Mickey Mouse Club*.

Incredibly, her contributions to the musical heritage of Disney are often overlooked in the various books and articles devoted to Disney music. Her influence in the creation of Disneyland has also never been fully explored.

Hazel was the one who suggested that Walt attend the Chicago Railroad Fair with Ward Kimball to help him relax. That trip helped Walt formulate his plans for Disneyland.

When Walt was considering how to build his "Mickey Mouse Park", Hazel became the head of the Disneyland Boosters and Backers Club to raise contributions from Studio employees for the project, an act that helped convince Roy O. Disney to lend his support to Walt's dream of a theme park.

Hazel's songwriting career seems to have ended when Paul Smith retired from the Disney Studios in the early 1960s. As a nurse, however, she continued treating Walt right up until he went into St. Joseph's Hospital.

Hazel passed away on March 12, 1996 (roughly ten years after the death of Paul Smith, whom she lived with and cared for in his final years). Fortunately, several oral interviews with her survive, although they remain unpublished.

In one of those unpublished interviews, Hazel recalled:

> One thing that I learned from my long-time friendship with Walt was that in most cases, he was strongly motivated by love. He loved his family very much, and would tell me about his daughters' exploits, and about his wife Lilly. He really loved them dearly, and enjoyed telling me all the wonderful stories of what they were doing. He also loved kids in general and animals, especially his own little dog. He would often tell me stories about that wonderful little poodle. He never got tired of talking about animals.

Bob Thomas, author of the biographical *Walt Disney: An American Original*, acknowledged that Hazel provided him with the key to understanding Walt's personality.

Unfortunately, Hazel suffered from the effects of prolonged alcoholism (as did Paul Smith). In her later years, her memories were not always reliable, and there are some outrageous observations credited to her.

Diane Disney Miller, who didn't meet Hazel until years after her father Walt's death, said:

> She was a good friend to my dad and somewhat his confidante. My mother had the same sort of relationship, as some women do, with her hairdresser. I sent Hazel flowers every month until she was gone.

The Man Who Shot Walt Disney

Renie Bardeau is the man who shot Walt Disney — multiple times. As the official photographer for Disneyland, he was responsible for many of the most famous and beloved photos of Walt Disney.

Born in 1934, Bardeau was raised in Tucson, Arizona, where he attended college at the University of Arizona. When the Korean War broke out, he enlisted in the Navy, serving as a Petty Officer with a specialty as aviation photographer's mate. It was in the Navy that Bardeau's photography career began.

After the war, he returned to the University of Arizona to finish his degree in marketing. He also married, fathered two children, and today has three grandchildren.

Bardeau's high school photography teacher knew the chief photographer at the *Los Angeles Herald-Examiner* newspaper, and in 1959 arranged an interview for his twenty-five-year-old former student for a summer job. When Bardeau arrived in Los Angeles, he found the position had just been filled.

However, the *Herald-Examiner* photographer sent Bardeau to see Charlie Nichols, then Disneyland's chief photographer. Bardeau had never heard of Disneyland and knew nothing about the place, but he needed a job.

After a one-minute interview, Nichols hired him.

During his first summer at Disneyland, Bardeau worked mostly in the darkroom, since publicity photos were then processed right there in the park. Bardeau recalled:

For many years, my fingernails were brown from the chemicals. When newspapers switched to color photos, it was no longer cost-effective to process photographs at the park and so outside labs were used.

One day, Bardeau went to Frontierland to take pictures of the mule ride. It was there that he first met Walt Disney, who shook his hand and welcomed him to the park. "Walt had a firm grip and a twinkle in his eye," Bardeau remembered.

Bardeau's first big assignment was to take publicity photos of the opening of the new Tomorrowland attractions, especially the dedication of the Monorail, with Walt Disney and Vice President Richard Nixon and his family doing the honors. "To this day," Bardeau said, "that picture is still being used."

In those early days, Bardeau took black-and-white photos using four-by-five Press cameras with film holders. During an interview in 2005, he explained the process to me:

> You had to reach into a big bag with your film, stick the holder in [the camera], pull out the slide, shoot your picture, stick the slide back in, change the flash bulb, turn the slide around, put it back in — fast. You had to do it fast or the moment of the picture would be gone.

Bardeau stayed through the summer, then returned to Arizona for another year of college, often working winters in Tucson as a photographer. His summer job at Disneyland continued until his graduation from college in 1963. He assumed he would work at the park while he looked for a job in the advertising.

"One year became five and five became ten, then ten became twenty and so on," Bardeau said. It was a familiar story for many of the people (like Disneyland Band Leader Vessey Walker and Golden Horseshoe star Wally Boag) who began working at Disneyland when Walt was still alive.

As the years passed, Bardeau spent less time in the darkroom and more time in the park. He would receive three or four assignments each day to photograph celebrities or new attractions or firework displays.

United States presidents, politicians, award-winning performers, famous athletes, royalty, and a host of foreign dignitaries have visited Disneyland, and Bardeau was there snapping pictures for press packets, Disney photo archives, and in-house newsletters. Bardeau claims that he found athletes to be the friendliest and most down-to-earth.

When he did not have an official assignment, Bardeau roamed Disneyland, shooting guests, workers, parades, and attractions, capturing all those moments that were presented in newspapers, magazines, souvenir guides, and advertising.

Bardeau has ridden every ride at Disneyland since 1959, many of them while sitting backwards to get specific angles for photos used as publicity shots.

In 1968, Charlie Nichols retired, and Bardeau replaced him as chief photographer.

Before digital photography and its creative uses, Bardeau at times had to create his own magic. He said:

> Many mornings the "June Gloom" was with us and we had gray skies. Nowadays, you can supplement the picture — take out the sky and put in a beautiful blue sky. But that's not true journalism. That's cheating — it's not what was there.

But with a twinkle in his eye and a slight smile, he did confess that he often had to resort to some of his own ingenuity.

The one time he felt that he cheated was when he needed a shot of Tinker Bell over Sleeping Beauty Castle with the fireworks exploding behind her. In those days, for safety reasons, Tinker Bell took her flight before the fireworks were set off. So, Bardeau took a picture of Tinker Bell in a studio, against a black background. Then, in the darkroom, he reduced the size of the image. "A little glue ... and pfttt ... Tinker Bell and the fireworks in the same shot," he laughed.

Other shots didn't require trickery so much as cleverness. Fireworks light up the sky behind Sleeping Beauty Castle in dozens of his photos, but only because he exposed the same frame several times, capturing one burst after another. For the picture to be effective, he needed several bursts.

First, he took a picture of the castle. Then, he would cover the lens and uncover it to re-expose the film when a burst went off. He repeated the process several times. The layers gave him the effect he wanted.

That beautifully timed shot of the monorail soaring over a submarine in the lagoon was also rigged. Each vehicle stopped as Bardeau took one photo after another. Later, Bardeau had fun with one of his young employees who stood patiently by the lagoon to capture the same shot, with Bardeau swearing that the two vehicles would eventually line up.

Of course, Bardeau took shots of the celebrities who visited Disneyland, and has hundreds of funny stories. When he was shooting photos of Egyptian President Anwar Sadat enjoying the Golden Horseshoe Revue, he recalled how Sadat asked to see the six-shooter pistol that Wally Boag used during the show. He was fascinated with it. Always happy to oblige, Wally pulled it out of its holster and "about fourteen Secret Service agent bodyguards snapped into action", Bardeau said with a laugh. After a few tense moments, things calmed down and everyone had a good laugh.

Bardeau's favorite celebrity story is when, after taking some photos of James Garner, the actor insisted that Bardeau join him and his family for lunch in the park. Politely, Bardeau declined, but Garner was persistent, asking who he had to call to clear things so Bardeau could join them. Bardeau had to confess that he was the boss, and he accepted the invitation.

However, working at the Happiest Place on Earth wasn't always happy for the photographer. Whenever there were accidents or deaths at the park, one of Bardeau's responsibilities was to record the incident for Disney's legal files.

Bardeau was responsible for one of the most beloved and iconic photos of Walt at Disneyland, now entitled Footsteps. It was what Bardeau referred to as a "grab shot", a photographer's term to describe an unplanned event that leaves only seconds for the photographer to react and capture it on film.

On an early Saturday morning in 1964, before Disneyland opened to the public, Bardeau and Charlie Nichols were wandering the empty park with cameras slung around their necks. They were returning from an early morning photo shoot.

At the same time, they spotted Walt inspecting the premises, as he often did. He was walking through the arched gateway of Sleeping Beauty Castle. Hands shoved in pockets, Walt was in mid-stride, head turned to his right, dwarfed by the castle looming over him. Bardeau and Nichols each "grabbed" for the shot, but it was Bardeau who got it, and it has become the famous image that Disney fans treasure today.

Another grab shot presented itself during the debut of a Disneyland Christmas parade. Bardeau saw Walt and Lillian sitting at the top of the bleachers (Walt's favorite place, according to Bardeau), and when he spotted them waving to the crowd, he snapped the shot. He sent a copy of the picture to Walt, who returned it with the inscription, "To Renie, lots of luck, Walt Disney."

Bardeau was also responsible for the final professional photo taken of Walt Disney in Disneyland. As Bardeau recalled, it was at the end of August 1966 (Walt died a little more than three months later), and Walt had been shooting a commercial for Kodak. Walt was in front of Sleeping Beauty Castle, sitting in the front seat of the Disneyland Fire Department "Engine No. 1" vehicle, along with a costumed Mickey Mouse. Diminutive former ice skater Paul Castle was portraying the mouse.

Near the end of the shoot, Bardeau and Nichols were called to take some photos. Nichols shot in black-and-white, Bardeau in color. What happened next is one of Bardeau's favorite stories, which he told many times over the years:

> There is a little story of when I was shooting that particular picture. It was shot on a Rolleiflex [camera], and there are twelve pictures on a roll. I had shot eleven pictures of Walt at different angles ... watching for his smile, watching to make sure Mickey was looking the right way, making sure the spires weren't hanging out of Mickey's ears. Anyway, I had shot eleven pictures, and I had said, "Thank you, Walt, that's it."
>
> He asks me if I was sure, and I told him I was. He then told me that at the Studio we treat film like paper clips. You shoot, shoot, shoot all the film you need, because if it's not in the can, you will never have it. So he asked me to shoot one more ...
>
> So, I shot one more, and he said, "That's fine, thank you, Renie," and he walked away.

Those multiple shots also explain why there are occasional variations, especially in the position of Mickey's upraised hand. A blow-up of that photo is at the entrance lobby to the One Man's Dream attraction at Disney's Hollywood Studios in Orlando. Bardeau's wife, Marlene, arranged to have the photo emblazoned on blinds in her husband's den.

One of Bardeau's favorite Walt stories took place on a Saturday morning at Disneyland about thirty minutes before opening. To start his day, Bardeau often went to the Hills Brothers Coffee shop on Main Street to read the morning newspaper and have a cup of coffee. Because the park wasn't open, the place was empty, but he still picked a table toward the rear so that the other tables would be neat and clean for the incoming guests.

As he was reading his newspaper, Walt came in, looked around, and asked Bardeau if he could join him. Bardeau invited Walt to sit down. A waitress appeared and was so nervous to see Walt that she was physically shaking. She asked "Mr. Disney" what he wanted.

Walt reminded her that he was just "Walt". According to Bardeau, Walt said to the waitress:

> There are only two misters in Disneyland. Mr. Lincoln and Mr. Toad. Call me Walt.

She returned with a cup of coffee for Walt, but was still shaking. Walt talked to Bardeau about the weather, the expected attendance, and the park itself, asking for Bardeau's opinion on several things. Just before the park opened, Walt excused himself and slipped backstage. Walt was usually mobbed when guests spotted him in the park.

Bardeau said:

> He was a genius. He was very easy to talk to. He loved Disneyland and loved to talk to you about the Park, asking you what you thought of it.

Divorced from his first wife, Bardeau reunited with his high school sweetheart, Marlene, and they were married. After Bardeau retired in 1998 (after thirty-nine years, six months, and two weeks, although he always said "forty years"), Bardeau returned to Arizona, but soon relocated to Glendale, California.

He was active in the University of Arizona Hispanic Alumni Association, which raises funds to award deserving high school students with scholarships to the University of Arizona.

At his retirement party, Bardeau's friends at Disneyland put together a special thick, heavy photo album edged in silver and containing many of the memorable shots he had taken over the years, including a shot of Vice President Richard Nixon in the front cabin of the monorail with Walt standing nearby, and a shot of Robert F. Kennedy riding the Matterhorn Bobsleds just days before his assassination.

In March 1999, Bardeau received a window on Disneyland's Main Street above the photography store, inscribed "Kingdom Photo Services — Renie Bardeau Photographer, Archivist".

The reason for the archivist designation is because Walt told Bardeau that the top priority for his photos was not park publicity but rather for the historical record of Disneyland.

Even though he snapped more than one million published photos, ranging from Bob Hope golfing with the Disney characters to Elizabeth Taylor's star-studded 1992 birthday bash in the park to famous foreign heads of state like Emperor Hirohito of Japan and Prince Rainier of Monaco enjoying the magic of Disney, Bardeau is virtually unknown, even to Disney fans, because his name does not appear on any of the iconic photos that were sent to the media. It was Disneyland's policy that photographs be credited to Disneyland (or later just to Disney).

Bardeau said:

> This job is really an art and taxes your creative juices. How many ways can you photograph the Matterhorn and make it interesting? There is a way. I'm always looking for a different angle.

Bardeau understood and appreciated Disney magic as he documented attractions and people coming and going over nearly four decades, with great skill and affection. He remains an inspiration to all who take photos at Disney theme parks.

Song of the South: Frequently Asked Questions

My newest book, *Who's Afraid of the Song of the South? And Other Forbidden Disney Stories*, is now available from Theme Park Press in print and digital editions. For the first time, the complete history of the infamous Disney feature film, *Song of the South* (1946), is documented, from Walt Disney's initial interest in making the film mere months after the successful release of *Snow White and the Seven Dwarfs* (1937) to the controversy still surrounding the film today.

The book features the true, untold stories behind the politics and struggle over the screenplay and the animation, along with little-known facts about the live-action performers, how misunderstandings developed about the final film, the lavish premiere in Atlanta, Georgia, and so much more.

Disney Legend Floyd Norman, Disney's first black animator and storyman, provides a lengthy foreword in which he reveals his affection for the film and his belief, based on personal observation, that neither Walt nor others who worked on the film held racist beliefs.

In addition to the secrets of *Song of the South*, the book includes seventeen extra stories about such forbidden topics as:

- **Sex**: How Disney created one of the most popular and effective sexual education films ever made, plus the story of the most notorious blacklight poster featuring Disney characters in pornographic poses.

- **Secrets**: Little-known episodes in Walt's life, such as the urban myth about his final words, and why he thought it would be funny for Mickey Mouse to commit suicide.

- **Flubbed Films**: Why the serious film *Kingdom of the Sun* became the buddy comedy *The Emperor's New Groove*, and how Tim Burton became depressed working for Disney.

As a brief preview of the book, here are answers to the most commonly asked questions about *Song of the South*:

WHAT IS SONG OF THE SOUTH?

Song of the South is a feature-length film released by the Disney Studios on November 12, 1946. It combines live action and animation, and was last shown theatrically in the United States in 1986.

WHAT IS THE STORY IN THE FILM?

The live-action story is about a young boy taken by his estranged parents to live on his grandmother's plantation in Georgia shortly after the Civil War. The boy has difficulty adapting to his new home. He encounters an old black storyteller named Uncle Remus, who tells him tales of Brer Rabbit, Brer Fox, and Brer Bear. These stories help the boy learn some important lessons about life, and are told in animation scenes created by six of Disney's iconic Nine Old Men.

DID JOEL CHANDLER HARRIS WRITE SONG OF THE SOUTH?

No. Joel Chandler Harris was a newspaper reporter for the *Atlanta Constitution* in the late 1800s. He wrote a column about a black storyteller named Uncle Remus who told tales of Brer Rabbit and the other animals.

These stories were based on tales he had heard as a young boy from a dozen different storytellers at the Southern plantation Turnwold. The newspaper columns were later collected into nine books.

The character of Uncle Remus and the three stories in the film were inspired by Harris' work, but the screenplay was original and primarily the work of author Dalton Reymond, who had a reputation as an expert on the Old South and had worked as a technical consultant on several Hollywood films. This was his only screenplay, and it includes contributions from writers Maurice Rapf and Morton Grant. The behind-the-scenes intrigue in the creation of the screenplay is fully covered in the book.

The animated stories were storyboarded by Disney Legend Bill Peet, using the Uncle Remus tales as a foundation.

IS SONG OF THE SOUTH BANNED?

No. Because of concerns about its depiction of black characters and the heavy use of dialect, the Disney Company feels that the film may be offensive to modern audiences. In 1986, Disney voluntarily pulled it from distribution in the United States.

Song of the South is still released commercially in several countries, including the United Kingdom, France, Italy, Germany, the Netherlands, Japan, Argentina, and Brazil. It has been shown several times on the BBC2 television channel in England. Viewers in those countries have not complained.

WILL DISNEY RELEASE THE FILM AS A BLU-RAY SPECIAL EDITION?

Disney President and CEO Robert Iger has been adamant for years that *Song of the South* would not be re-released in any form in the United States. At the 2011 Disney Shareholders Meeting, he stated that, even considering the context and the time period in which the movie was made:

> ... there are elements in the film ... it's a relatively good film ... that would not necessarily fit right or feel right to a number of people today.

The film has many vocal supporters, and petitions have been sent to the Disney Company urging its re-release. Until then, the only way that a person in the United States can see the entire film is by purchasing or downloading an illegal copy, or by obtaining a foreign release and converting it to a U.S. format.

DOES SONG OF THE SOUTH DEPICT SLAVERY?

No. The film takes place after the Civil War, and depicts black sharecroppers (not slaves) at work in the fields of an old plantation. At one point, an upset Uncle Remus packs his bags and decides to leave. If he were a slave, he would be the property of the plantation owner and confined to its grounds.

The film does include elements similar to those in films like *Gone with the Wind* (1939) set during the slave era, such as blacks in threadbare clothes working in the fields and singing spirituals, and this may have led to some audience confusion.

But *Song of the South* was never intended to be an accurate historical documentary of a troubled time in America's past. It was meant to be light, fantasy entertainment, similar to other films produced during the 1930s and 1940s.

Actress Shirley Temple was partnered with talented black performer Bill "Bojangles" Robinson in films like *The Little Colonel* (1935) and *The Littlest Rebel* (1935), both meant to be seen by family audiences with young children, but which present an even more fanciful and inaccurate (as well as potentially more offensive) representation of the same time period depicted in *Song of the South*. Yet these films, and others like them, are readily available everywhere.

IS SONG OF THE SOUTH A RACIST FILM?

All the black characters in the film are warm, friendly, and clever. Uncle Remus helps a troubled young white boy, Johnny, whose parents ignore and misunderstood him. Johnny plays freely with Toby, a young black boy of about the same age.

In 1947, African-American reporter Herman Hill reviewed the film in the *Pittsburgh Courier*, a black newspaper.

He stated:

> The truly sympathetic handling of the entire production from a racial standpoint is calculated to prove of estimable good in the furthering of interracial relations.

However, also in 1947, Walter White, executive secretary of The National Association for the Advancement of Colored People (NAACP), released this statement to the newspapers:

> The National Association for the Advancement of Colored People recognizes in *Song of the South* remarkable artistic merit in the music and in the combination of living actors and the cartoon technique. It regrets, however, that in an effort neither to offend audiences in the North or South, the production helps to perpetuate a dangerously glorified picture of slavery. Making use of the beautiful Uncle Remus folklore, *Song of the South* unfortunately gives the impression of an idyllic master-slave relationship which is a distortion of the facts.

Some reviewers were confused, thinking the story focused on slaves at a plantation before or during the Civil War, the common setting for many other Hollywood films of this type, rather than during Reconstruction. To be fair, neither the film itself nor its publicity material clarified the time period.

When *Song of the South* was released, the NAACP was acting as a legislative and legal advocate, pushing unsuccessfully for a federal anti-lynching law and for an end to state-mandated segregation. It was an emotionally charged time.

Perception was much stronger than facts. Since *Song of the South* was based on the controversial works of Joel Chandler Harris, the film was used as a rallying point to focus attention on how blacks were portrayed in all Hollywood films.

In the 1940s, black performers often were given only comic roles as characters who were lazy, slow-witted, illiterate, easily scared or flustered, subservient, and worse. That image was what the American public then saw and accepted as the norm for African Americans.

Actor James Baskett, who played Uncle Remus, was given an honorary Academy Award on March 20, 1948, for "his able and heartwarming characterization of Uncle Remus, friend and storyteller to the children of the world" by actress Ingrid Bergman. He was the first black male to ever receive an Oscar.

In 1947, Baskett commented

> I believe that certain groups are doing my race more harm in seeking to create dissension than can ever possibly come out of the *Song of the South*.

WAS WALT DISNEY RACIST?

No. There is no evidence that Walt was racist. For a man of his time, he was remarkable in embracing different races, religions, and cultures into his organization from the very beginning of the Disney Studios. Unlike other animation studio heads, he also hired or promoted women to fill key positions.

In the foreword to *Who's Afraid of the Song of the South*, Disney Legend Floyd Norman wrote:

> I survived three different managements at the Disney Company, beginning in the Fifties when I worked as Disney's first black animator and later as a storyman. My unexpected move upstairs to Walt's story department was something I never anticipated. Not only was I privy to the Old Maestro's story meetings, I had the unique opportunity to observe the boss in action. This included his management style and his treatment of subordinates. Not once did I observe a hint of the racist behavior Walt Disney was often accused of long after his death. His treatment of people, and by this, I mean all people, can only be called exemplary.

WAS SONG OF THE SOUTH SHOT IN ATLANTA, GEORGIA?

No. The Disney Studios claimed that, because of "technical difficulties", the film had to be shot outdoors on specially made sets in Phoenix, Arizona, with some interior shots done at the Samuel Goldwyn Studio in Hollywood, California.

ISN'T SPLASH MOUNTAIN BASED ON THIS FILM?

Yes. In the mid-1980s, Imagineer Tony Baxter was stuck in traffic on the Santa Ana Freeway in southern California. He began thinking about Disneyland's America Sings attraction, soon to close, and how Dick Nunis (then Chairman of the Disney Theme Parks) wanted a water flume ride for the park. America Sings had dozens of singing Audio-Animatronics animals designed by Disney Legend Marc Davis, who was one of the main animators on *Song of the South*. Rather than store or destroy Davis' creations, Baxter suggested re-adapting them for an attraction based on the film.

Splash Mountain officially opened at Disneyland on July 17, 1989. It was designed by John D. Stone, working closely with Bruce Gordon (show producer who wrote new lyrics for the songs used in the attraction) and Tony Baxter (executive producer). CEO Michael Eisner insisted that the character of Uncle Remus not be included, so Brer Frog, a friend of Remus in the film, became the narrator.

In the storyline, Brer Rabbit runs away from home and is caught by Brer Fox and Brer Bear. The tricky hare convinces the villains to toss him into the Briar Patch, a watery drop of almost fifty feet, down which guests plummet at the end of their slow ride in a hollowed-out log past scenes from Brer Rabbit's adventures.

Splash Mountain was so popular that another one was built at the Magic Kingdom in Walt Disney World, opening officially on October 2, 1992.

WHY DID WALT DISNEY MAKE SONG OF THE SOUTH?

"It was a film he really wanted to do," recalled Walt's daughter Diane Disney Miller. "My dad quoted so much from Uncle Remus's logic and philosophy."

When the film premiered in 1947, Walt Disney recalled:

> I was familiar with the Uncle Remus tales since boyhood. From the time I began making animated features, I have had them definitely in my production plans. It is their timeless and living appeal; their magnificent pictorial quality; their rich and tolerant humor; their homely philosophy and cheerfulness, which made the Remus legends the top choice for our first production with flesh-and-blood players.

In addition, as Walt remarked in a 1956 interview, he knew that he had to diversify from just making animated films if his studio was to survive and grow:

> I wanted to go beyond the cartoon. Because the cartoon had narrowed itself down. I could make them either seven or eight minutes long or eighty minutes long. I tried package things, where I put five or six together to make an eighty-minute feature. Now I needed to diversify further and that meant live action.

Walt's film distribution contract with RKO stipulated the delivery of animated features. However, the contract also stated that the films could be a mixture of live action and animation, since Disney releases like *Saludos Amigos* (1942) and *The Three Caballeros* (1944) included live-action segments that helped keep down production costs.

Walt felt that combining a live-action storyteller with short animated stories would be a perfect balance, both creatively and financially. In fact, if *Song of the South* had been the success that Walt expected, he had plans to make several sequels using the same format.

WHAT IS ZIP-A-DEE-DOO-DAH?

It is an expression of happiness and joy reportedly suggested by

Walt Disney himself, who was fond of nonsense words like Bibbidi-Bobbidi-Boo to Supercalifragilisticexpialidocious. The song "Zip-a-Dee-Doo-Dah", written by Allie Wrubel and Ray Gilbert, won an Oscar for Best Song. It has been recorded by many singers, including Johnny Mercer, the Dave Clark Five, Doris Day, Louis Armstrong, and Miley Cyrus.

WHAT ARE SOME OF THE UNUSUAL THINGS THAT CAN BE FOUND IN WHO'S AFRAID OF THE SONG OF THE SOUTH?

Clarence Nash, the longtime voice of Donald Duck, was well-known for his bird calls. He supplied the chirps for Mr. Bluebird on Uncle Remus's shoulder.

In 1956, to earn some extra money while in high school, Luana Patten (who portrayed the young girl Ginny in *Song of the South*) was working nights in the box office at the Lakewood Theatre in Long Beach, California, when the movie house was robbed. The film playing at the time was the first theatrical re-release of *Song of the South*.

Brer Rabbit's laughter during the Laughing Place sequence in the movie is reused in *The Jungle Book* (1967) for the scene where Baloo tickles King Louie. That laugh was voiced by actor James "Uncle Remus" Baskett, filling in for Johnny Lee, the voice of Brer Rabbit, who at the time of the recording was on a USO tour and unable to do it.

Actor Bobby Driscoll didn't know how to skip, so many people on location, including legendary animator and director Hamilton Luske, had to physically skip around to show him how it was done.

All of these stories and many more about *Song of the South*, plus seventeen previously censored tales about sex, Walt, and flubbed films, are featured in *Who's Afraid of the Song of the South*, available now in print and digital formats.

For more information, visit www.ThemeParkPress.com.

Acknowledgements

I would like to take this opportunity to acknowledge not only those people who directly helped me with this book but those who have inspired or supported me over the years and deserve to see their name printed prominently in a Disney-related book.

This book and this author have been greatly enriched by the generosity and enthusiasm of Diane Disney Miller, whose many kindnesses truly honor the memory of her parents.

Many thanks to my good friend Didier Ghez, whose passionate love of Disney history and his editing and publishing of the book series *Walt's People* is a constant inspiration.

Thanks to my brothers, Michael and Chris, and their families, including their children Amber, Keith, Autumn and Story, who never really understood what their uncle does or why he does it. Uncle Jim loves you all very much. Please don't throw away Uncle Jim's Disney collection after he is gone.

Thanks to Bob McLain of Theme Park Press for making this revised edition a reality.

Many thanks to Lou Mongello, Jim Hill, Werner Weiss, Mark Goldhaber, Adrienne Vincent-Phoenix, Shoshana Lewin, Jim Fanning, Greg Ehrbar, Michael Lyons, John Canemaker, Mark Kausler, Michael Barrier, Paul Anderson, Dave Smith, Kim Eggink, Brad Anderson, Wade Sampson, John Cawley, Kaye Bundey.

Marion and Sarah Quarmby, Tom and Marina Stern, Jerry and Liz Edwards, Kendra Trahan, Marie Schilly, Tommy Byerly, Nancy Stadler, Lonnie Hicks, Michael "Shawn" and Laurel Slater, Tom Heckel, Kirk Bowman, Jeff Kurtti, Amber Walls, Ryan N. March, Michelle, Randy and Belinda Swiat, Phil Debord, Todd James Pierce, Greg Dorf, Betty Bjerrum, Jeff Pepper, Jerry Beck, Amid Amidi, Michael Sporn, Leonard Maltin, Robin Cadwallender, John Culhane, Scott Wolf, Pete Martin, Bill Cotter, J.B. Kaufman.

Bob Miller, David Koenig, Kevin Yee, John Frost, Dave Mruz, Rich Cullen, Mark Matheis, Danni Mikler, Tracy M. Barnes, Sarah Pate, Tamysen Hall, Evlyn Gould, Tom Heintjes, Bruce Gordon, David Mumford, Randy Bright, Jack and Leon Janzen, Mickey Boyd, Chad Emerson, Jennifer Solt, Malcolm and Mary Joseph (and their children Melissa, Megan, Rachel, Nicole, Richard).

Keith Seckel, Larry Lauria, Paul Naas, Mark Jones, Rachel Nacion, Danielle Wallace, Tom Nabbe, Tim Foster, Arlen Miller, Floyd Norman, Lock Wolverton, David Lesjak, Phil Ferretti, Anne Smith, Jim Ryan, Howard Kalov, Jennifer Bacon, Dana Gabbard, Dave Bennett, Margaret Kerry, Wanda Perkins, Howard Green,

Micki Thompson, Bob Thomas, Alex Maher, Melanie Skinner, Kathy Luck, Brian Blackmore, Kaye Malins, Heather Sweeney.

And sadly some people that I have foolishly forgotten for the moment. Their kindness and generosity, like that of the people listed here, have lightened my journey through life and made this book possible. I hope all of you, both acknowledged and temporarily missing, live happily ever after. I also hope that each one of you buys at least a dozen copies of this book because your name appears in it.

About the Author

Jim Korkis is an internationally respected Disney Historian who has written hundreds of articles about all things Disney for over three decades. He is also an award-winning teacher, professional actor and magician, and author of several books.

Jim grew up in Glendale, California, right next to Burbank, the home of the Disney Studios. His third-grade teacher at Thomas Edison Elementary School was Mrs. Margaret Disney, the wife of Walt Disney's brother Herbert.

As a teenager, Jim wrote down the names he saw on the credits of Disney animated cartoons, went to the Glendale-Burbank phone book, and cold-called some of them. Many were gracious enough to ask him to visit them, with the resulting articles sometimes appearing in the local newspapers or in various fanzines and magazines. Over the decades, Jim pursued a teaching career as well as a performing career, but was still active in writing about Disney for various magazines.

In 1995, he relocated to Orlando, Florida, to take care of his ailing parents. He got a job doing magic and making balloon animals for guests at Pleasure Island. Within a month, he was moved to the Magic Kingdom, where he "assisted in the portrayal of" Prospector Pat in Frontierland as well as Merlin the magician in Fantasyland for the Sword in the Stone ceremony.

In 1996, he became a full-time salaried animation instructor at the Disney Institute, where he taught every animation class, including several that only he taught. He also instructed classes on animation history and improvisational acting techniques for the interns at Disney Feature Animation Florida. As the Disney Institute re-organized, Jim joined Disney Adult Discoveries, the group that researched, wrote and facilitated backstage tours and programs for Disney guests and Disneyana conventions.

Eventually, Jim moved to Epcot, where he was a Coordinator with College and International Programs, and then a Coordinator for the Epcot Disney Learning Center. During his time at Epcot, Jim researched, wrote, and facilitated over two hundred different presentations on Disney history for Disney Cast Members and for Disney's corporate clients, including Feld Entertainment, Kodak, Blue Cross, Toys "R" Us, Military Sales, and others.

Jim was the off-camera announcer for the syndicated television series *Secrets of the Animal Kingdom*, wrote articles for such Disney publications as *Disney Adventures*, *Disney Files* (DVC), *Sketches*, *Disney Insider*, and others. He worked on special projects like writing text for WDW trading cards, as an on-camera host for the 100 Years of Magic Vacation Planning Video, and as a facilitator with the Disney Crew puppet show. His countless other credits include assisting Disney Cruise Line, WDW Travel Company, Imagineering, and Disney Design Group with Disney historical material. As a result, Jim was the recipient of the prestigious Disney award, Partners in Excellence, in 2004. Jim is not currently employed by the Disney Company.

To read more stories by Jim Korkis about Disney history, please purchase a copy of his newest book, *Who's Afraid of the Song of the South*, also available from Theme Park Press. And make sure to visit the following websites which feature archives of Jim's many other stories about Disney history:

- www.MousePlanet.com
- www.AllEars.net
- www.Yesterland.com
- www.WDWRadio.com

Made in the USA
Middletown, DE
10 May 2021

39395880R00149